MODERNISING PROBATION AND

Modernising Probation and Criminal Justice

Getting the Measure of Cultural Change

Philip Whitehead

Shaw & Sons

Shaw's
Since 1750

Published by
Shaw & Sons Limited
Shaway House
21 Bourne Park
Bourne Road
Crayford
Kent DA1 4BZ

www.shaws.co.uk

© Shaw & Sons Limited 2007

Published November 2007

ISBN 978 0 7219 1730 6

A CIP catalogue record for this book is available
from the British Library

Printed in Great Britain by
Antony Rowe Limited, Chippenham

CONTENTS

ACKNOWLEDGEMENTS

I would like to express my gratitude to all those probation officers, including trainees and other members of staff, who have been willing to talk to me over a number of years (since the 1980s) about their experiences of probation work within a changing culture. Where this book is concerned, I am indebted to Roger Statham for reading and commenting on the text, and to all the 31 solicitors who allowed me to interview them. Marie Mallon found the time to read Chapter 5, and Audrey Gill transcribed the tapes expeditiously and with her customary humour. Furthermore, I want to thank the University of Teesside for a grant that enabled me to complete the research component of the book more quickly than would have been possible otherwise. Professor Jill Radford was generous with her assistance during the early stages of the project. As always, Carolyn assisted in the preparation of the book and Alex lent a hand with the tables.

Finally, the discussion on targets in Chapter 2, here amended slightly, first appeared in the *British Journal of Community Justice*, Volume 5, Issue 2, Summer 2007.

PW

ABOUT THE AUTHOR

After working as a volunteer attached to the Lancaster probation office during the mid-1970s, followed by a year in a hostel, Philip Whitehead qualified as a probation officer at Lancaster University between 1979 and 1981. The Cleveland Probation Service – which he had never heard of – was the first to offer him employment and he has remained there ever since. He has published several books and articles on the subject of probation, community supervision of offenders, temporary release schemes, and management. In 2001, he was appointed to work with trainee probation officers. This culminated in a textbook for trainees and practice development assessors, *Knowledge and the Probation Service* (2004). More recently, he co-authored *The History of Probation* (2006).

Philip Whitehead continues his involvement with trainees, students and aspects of probation practice in what is a rapidly changing organisation within the National Offender Management Service. He remains both interested in, and concerned to forge a synthesis out of, the dissonance that currently prevails between the concerns of some practitioners when working with people with problems and the increasing demands of politicians and managers for accountability in terms of quantifiable targets. As this book affirms, he wants to keep alive the probation ideal, including the importance of social work values and relationships, in an organisation which should be people-based but has increasingly become bureaucratic. Philip Whitehead works as a part-time probation officer and part-time lecturer at the University of Teesside, where he continues to research the implications of modernisation and cultural transformation in probation and the wider criminal justice system.

LIST OF TABLES AND FIGURE

Chapter 1

INTRODUCTION: THINKING ABOUT PROBATION AND CRIMINAL JUSTICE

'The Probation Service is now confirmed in its role as a public protection agency, directly accountable to the Home Secretary, with 'protection of the public', the 'reduction of re-offending' and the 'proper punishment of offenders' all statutory duties given by the Criminal Justice and Court Services Act 2000 ... While the Probation Service has a long history of reinvention in the face of policy change, the prospects of further reinvention should public protection and effective practice fail are bleak.' (Kemshall 2003 p102)

Preamble

The origins of this book can be traced to the confluence of numerous tributaries, one of which runs within a few pages written towards the end of *The History of Probation* (Whitehead and Statham 2006 pp261-264). At this point in the concluding analysis, attention was drawn to the concept of bureaucratic managerialism, an image brought into focus to expose the tension between political and practice-based agendas within what is currently referred to as the modernised probation service. On the one hand are the lineaments of a politically constructed organisation associated with New Public Management, which emphasises quantification and measurable targets as the exemplars of performance and accountability when working with people with problems, more usually known as offenders. This political vision is complemented by a body of terms that resonates with developments since the 1980s: nationalisation, centralisation, standardisation, tighter regulation, more penetrating power and control. These are the marker posts staking out the parameters of, and setting the tone for, what has become a modernising agenda within the probation and criminal justice system. In fact, this is a description of the new frontier of the business audit in a politically and bureaucratically reconstructed public sector (Power 1997; Rose 1999). On the other hand, and representing a significantly different pre-1980s culture, counter-culture or even sub-culture, are the vestigial remains of a professional agenda characterised by more qualitative and ineffable features. Some examples are: autonomy, discretion, and making qualitative judgments

1

about individual offenders with numerous difficulties. These features are now deemed to be politically passé if not naïve, exemplifying modes of thinking, being, and doing that are pre-modern, thus belonging to a primitive stage of historical development; or to use an Italian criminological image, organisationally atavistic.

These contrasting views of the probation world, amounting to acute ideological conflicts between political (electoral) priorities and professional culture, are currently expressed in almost Manichean terms as the final battle between good and bad, light and dark, truth and error, reformed and unreconstructed organisational dynamics, electable New Labour and unelectable Old Labour. This book takes up, with a view to developing but also refining it, the theme of bureaucratic managerialism within a broader context of modernisation, which enables a discussion to take place on some of the dimensions and implications of changing cultural codes. In fact, probation itself can be selected as a pertinent case study of New Labour's modernisation programme within the criminal justice domain; of the implications of cultural change in one public sector organisation over recent years.

New Labour has been modernising the probation service, which is an integral component of the criminal justice system, since 1997. Some examples of change are listed below.

- 1997 – Prisons-Probation Review announced only two months after the general election in May (but at this stage the proposals were shelved). Also at this time the What Works/Accredited Programmes were introduced.

- 1998 – New training arrangements in the form of the Diploma in Probation Studies (Dip.PS).

- 1999 – The beginning of a review of the criminal courts by Lord Justice Auld.

- 1999–2000 – Creation of Youth Offending Teams.

- 2000 – The Halliday review of sentencing began, culminating in the Criminal Justice Act 2003. The Criminal Justice and Court Services Act established the National Probation Service which began on 1st April 2001. Another important piece of legislation was the Powers of Criminal Courts (Sentencing) Act.

- 2001 – *A New Choreography for the New National Probation Service* was published outlining the main objectives to be pursued.

- 2002 – Patrick Carter was asked to review correctional services that created the National Offender Management Service (NOMS) at the beginning of 2006. Therefore the Prisons-Probation Review was revived.

- 2006 – Four significant documents were published:

  1) A Five Year Strategy for Protecting the Public and Reducing Re-offending (February)

  2) Re-balancing the Criminal Justice System in Favour of the Law-abiding Majority (July)

  3) Improving Prison and Probation Services: Public Value Partnerships (August)

  4) The Home Secretary's speech at Wormwood Scrubs on 7th November: 'Checks against Delivery'.

Some would say that the developments of the last decade are positive steps in the right direction (unquestionably morally right and neo-Thatcherite), the tangible manifestation of much needed and long overdue reform of outmoded ideas and working practices. In fact, to put it rather more colourfully, the haemorrhaging hearts and misplaced humanitarian social consciences of radicals and liberals, those with recalcitrant ideological inclinations, operating with a misguided social work philosophy out of step with the modernising and reformist zeitgeist, had to be brought into line as the new political brush swept clean all before it. Consequently, the profession of probation work had to be purged of all manifestations of undesirability by a process of political, managerial and bureaucratic modernisation. This could only be achieved by a controlling centre exercising its will over out of control local area services.

An alternative perspective is that we have witnessed the de-professionalisation and fragmentation of what was once a respected, albeit imperfect, public sector profession, resulting in the removal of trust from many staff deemed worthy of such trust. This transition has been lamented by questioning journalists (Jenkins 1995 and 2006b), as well as respected academics (O'Neill 2002).

This volume is a further attempt to refine some earlier work on probation related issues, to reflect again upon a set of concerns that were previously not terribly well understood. This is another tributary running into the book, irrigating its perspectives.

In the early 1990s, a significant stage in the history of probation, some of us got together to think about and produce some papers on management issues, while at the same time sounding a note of caution about what appeared to be happening (Statham and Whitehead 1992). One of the authors of this collection of papers (Whitehead 1992) argued that, notwithstanding the emergence of quantitative management information systems, such systems could not adequately capture the full range of probation work. He drew attention to a German theologian, Hans Kung, who made a Weberian point about efficiency posing a serious threat to man's humanity and people becoming lost in anonymous mechanisms and technologies associated with the modern world. In fact, Kung stated that human life is 'thoroughly organised, fully regulated, bureaucratised and rapidly becoming computerised from morning to night' (1976 p585). At this point, probation was a few years away from being mesmerised by bureaucracy and computers. The historian Lawrence Stone said that modern man walks a knife edge between the rational and the emotional. He went on to say that the rational is associated with:

> 'a technetronic society, smooth, impersonal, rational, and scientific, a kind of universal IBM company ruled over by the computer. While it can be supremely efficient, it is also drab and sterile, leaving no place either for the emotions, including the finer ones of love and compassion, or for the sense of aesthetic mystery and wonder which is at the root of all great literatures, art, and music' (1987 p198).

The dual warnings of Kung in the 1970s and Stone in the 1980s, expressed in these two brief passages, reverberate throughout this book, particularly the reference to the computer age and the impact of technology on the historic culture of probation as a people orientated profession. Contemporary concerns with modernisation in probation and criminal justice have their portents in battles fought and lost in previous decades.

Let me expand further upon the collection of managerial papers alluded to above. At a time of uncertainty brought about by rapid change within probation at the beginning of the 1990s – facilitated by a Conservative party emboldened by its third successive election victory in 1987, swelling centralisation that increasingly intruded into many aspects of social and economic life, and tensions between ideas personalism, radicalism, and burgeoning managerialism that vied for dominance (McWilliams 1987) – some kind of response was demanded from within the probation world itself. There was at this time a good deal of pressure to accept the new political situation in the public sector, premised upon the expectation of apparently more effective management in the private sector, which had been evolving since 1979. This posed enormous problems for a number of staff because, although the discomfort associated with such developments generated not a little resistance, not to accept the new reality would have been tantamount to organisational suicide. A pragmatic counter-strategy was to acknowledge that there was little choice but to accept imposed change, as the lesser of two evils, and therefore to accept the new developments, while working to make them more palatable (better to change things from the inside than not to be on the inside at all, thesis). In this way it would perhaps be possible to preserve the best elements of what probation stood for while accommodating change.

Probation indubitably found itself in a hostile climate, particularly after 1993, and the question of its survival was a real concern. It was reasoned that all-out resistance was not an option, although perhaps it should have been: because the organisation lacked political clout, some accommodation to radical change was deemed to be politically and managerially astute (or was this appeasement in the face of the inevitable?). Just what was the correct strategy if the service was to make it to its centenary in 2007? Perhaps if we had known then what we have come to know and experience since 1997, some of us would have resisted more than we did and marshalled more cogent arguments at the time. It seems much easier to say what we should have done with the benefit of historical perspective, than it did at the time while events were rapidly taking shape and carrying staff towards an unknown destination. It can also be suggested that probation was always one step behind a political agenda being driven forcefully forward: responding to events rather than being able to control them. From 1993 to 1997, the service just about managed to survive when the forces of conservatism developed an approach to crime that became incrementally more punitive, a combination of punishment in the community and punishment in prison that suddenly 'worked' (that is in political rather than penological terms). Credibility, when responding to crime related issues, was premised upon tougher and harsher attitudes. Therefore probation was forced to make far reaching re-adjustments to ensure its survival.

Some of us thought the general election in May 1997 would result in a return to pre-1979 political thinking about criminal justice matters, rather than another manifestation of neo-Thatcherism and neo-Majorism/ Howardism. We hoped for a return, naïvely as it transpired, to Old Labour's notion of probation rather than New Labour's reconstructed version, to a more positive climate for the re-growth of the probation ideal. This was misplaced optimism, as this book will show. It should be stated that this volume, which complements the earlier and more comprehensive history book (Whitehead and Statham 2006), is a further attempt to draw critical attention to aspects of probation as it reaches its centenary – in 2007.

It is acknowledged that probation is a complex and rapidly changing social institution (Garland 1990) which at one level has had its own historical determinants over many decades, its own internal *modus operandi*, and is one of many public institutions with a distinctive role to perform within the criminal justice system and on behalf of the state. At another level it has been, and continues to be, affected by wider political and social events, in addition to being implicated by rapidly changing media headlines that create the latest folk devils and moral panics, normally from the ranks of the poor (Cohen 1973). It is therefore affected by the political electoral cycle, battles between parties for credibility in law and order, and emotive media images which are translated into the clamour for quick fix policies and further legislation, with additional powers to punish more deeply and enforce orders made by the courts more onerously.

It is also a climate more suited to focusing on the neo-classical perspective of *what* people are doing (and accompanying themes of personal responsibility and gradations of punishment), rather than thinking hard about *why* they are doing it; the more difficult task of attaching possible meanings to behaviours. Consequently, probation is a site of acute tension between the political controllers and re-shapers at the centre, and those who continue to work with offenders in a confused, uncertain, fragmented organisation, which remains in the grip of a permanent revolution (although no one appears to have a clear vision of its final destination). Change as an end in itself rather than a means to a clear destination; instability rather than stability; bureaucratic processes rather than professional accountability; central dominance rather than responsible localism flexibly responding to the needs of local communities and courts; these factors will come to be seen as the new modernising realities during the decade 1997–2007.

When I began to prepare this book I thought of creating a reader on probation and criminal justice matters that I hoped would appeal to a wide readership. I particularly wanted to write in a serious and critical manner for practitioners who take their work seriously; in fact, for all those who want to engage thoughtfully but also questioningly with what have been difficult matters for many years. Accordingly, the book offers several journeys into different facets of probation – philosophical, political and cultural, criminological, and the theme of understanding which is of central importance to practitioners when working with various repertoires of behaviour. I also wanted to undertake some innovative research into cultural change to support, or not as the case may be, the more theoretical sections on the rapidly changing cultural scene. However, I am afraid my publisher was less than impressed with the rather bland word "reader", which is why it does not appear in the final title. Furthermore, the book does not necessarily provide the reader with a chronologically continuous narrative thread. Each chapter has not been written to begin at the point at which the previous one concluded. From a chronological standpoint, therefore, there is a measure of discontinuity. On the other hand, there is an underlying unity, a degree of coherence, provided by the book's themes and ideas: the probation domain at the heart of this book that is approached from different angles to build a composite picture of its contemporary and ever changing reality. In an ideal world, the reader should begin with Chapter 2 and proceed logically, that is sequentially. However, it is also possible to adopt the Oscar Wildean method and start in the middle or wherever your thematic inclinations lead you. So the reader can choose; authors are only too glad to have their work read at all, and in any order or none as the case may be. Therefore, with this preamble in mind, I will provide a brief summary of each chapter.

The next five chapters

Chapter 2 embarks upon the first of three journeys into cultural change by analysing the shift from probation's association with what can be described as people work, to the emergence of bureaucratic positivism. The view is advanced that probation work has been profoundly transformed since the 1980s by a process of modernisation, and that the computer has become the dominant symbol of cultural change. In other words, probation has been placed in a different cultural context typified by the rise to prominence of machines, the emphasis upon quantification, the use of measurement tools to undertake risk assessments, and of course the achievement of measurable targets.

A brief historical survey of probation developments during the 20th century differentiates the nature of people work from what used to be a minimal supporting bureaucracy by producing two vignettes contrasting old and new cultural forms. The steps from old to new cultures are plotted; targets and risk are isolated as two significant dimensions of cultural change. In fact, this chapter is a critique of the modernised cash-linked target-driven culture which currently prevails within probation, and which should not go unchallenged.

Chapter 3 begins with an exploration of some of the major criminological theories put forward since eighteenth century classicism was associated with the European post-Enlightenment period. This chapter considers a number of explanatory theories for both understanding and constructing offending behaviour, which will be of particular relevance to practitioners working in the field of criminal justice. One of these theories, the positivist rather than classicist tradition, is associated with measuring behaviour to establish causes, patterns, and ultimately to separate the law-abiding from the law-breaking. This theoretical tradition is in marked contrast to, for example, Weberian *verstehen* (*understanding* the *meanings* people attach to their behaviours); the Chicagoan *'feel'* for hobos, taxi drivers and prostitutes; and Matzean *appreciation* (Matza 1969).

This chapter develops into a discussion of a number of interrelated factors (currently neglected features) necessary, it is suggested, for the development of a framework of understanding when thinking about and working with offenders. My main concern here is an exploration of those ingredients conducive to understanding and appreciating individuals who resort to offending, within an increasingly bureaucratic organisation. I draw attention to the following elements: the importance of the probation officer's self-understanding; understanding other people; avoiding negative labelling; not losing sight of the social dimension within which to locate behaviour; and the probation officer as artist when writing court reports that contribute to sentencing decisions. Finally, a brief note on the future implications of probation training is included. In other words, I want to establish a framework of understanding within the widest possible parameters, thus helping to define the probation task in circumstances where this approach has been under threat for some time. There is much to think about, in fact that the practitioner is forced to think about, when working with people who offend, although the prevailing political and managerial injunction appears to be 'just get on and do the job' within a neo-classical and more punitive political context. However, unless probation staff take the trouble to think for themselves, engage in critical reflection, and learn to pose the right questions, how will they know what to do?

I unreservedly admit, and it is helpful to get this confession out of the way as soon as possible, that Chapter 4 could be described as a little unusual. Those colleagues prevailed upon to read and then comment on this chapter had certain difficulties with it, as they cogently pointed out. Its approach is at times dense, discursive, certainly allusive, and perhaps sometimes ambiguous. Nevertheless, its central proposition is intended to be very simple: you cannot reduce work with people to the blunt instruments of quantification or measurement. The objects of natural science cannot and should not be approached in the same way as people within the social sciences. While assembling the materials for this philosophically grounded chapter, I read the following insightful comment by Bertrand Russell, whom we shall have cause to meet as the chapter proceeds. He said that:

> 'Philosophy is to be studied, not for the sake of any definite answers to its questions, since no definite answers can, as a rule, be known to be true, but rather for the sake of the questions themselves; because these questions enlarge our conception of what is possible, enrich our intellectual imagination, and diminish the dogmatic assurances which close the mind against speculation' (1967 p93).

It is within this spirit that this chapter is composed, because it challenges prevailing orthodoxies.

The main purpose of Chapter 4 is to build a loose philosophical framework from Plato to the logical positivists of the Vienna Circle in the twentieth century. This framework of philosophical ideas allows questions to be posed of an ontological (what is real), epistemological (how do we know what is real), and axiological (about ethics and values) nature, that have resonance for probation and other organisations in which people/staff work with people/offenders. Specifically from the period of the Renaissance and inchoate empirical approach of Francis Bacon (1561–1626), through later British empiricists and even later nineteenth century positivists, culminating in the logical positivism of the twentieth century, there is a discernible route to knowledge and understanding of what purports to be objectively and certainly real. This is the paradigm which proceeds on the basis of empirical observation, discoverable 'facts', and induction, with a view to establishing the causal, predictive and invariant laws of the natural *and* later social worlds. A central place within this paradigm is afforded to mathesis and measuring things.

This philosophical framework is established to advance the view, which of course is pertinent to developments within probation since the 1980s which have gathered pace since 1997, that we cannot measure everything when working with people with problems. In other words, people in the social world are different to material objects in the natural world. Consequently, one must acknowledge qualitative and ineffable dimensions, as well as the quantitatively and numerically measurable, that the heuristic device of *otherness* is designed to illustrate. This chapter suggests that within probation work, as within teaching, nursing, social services and youth work, there are layers of reality and knowledge; significant dimensions of meaning, worth, inestimable value of an ineffable and qualitative nature which exist outside a politically and bureaucratically reconfigured organisation and its current preoccupation with number, weight and measure. Neither people, nor organisations that have emerged to work with people, can be reduced to, and therefore adequately represented by, the disclosures of even the most sophisticated statistical tabulations. Quantification may well elicit questions about practice that demand an answer, but numbers can never provide all the answers. Therefore the journey into philosophy functions as an analogy – it loosely resembles what has happened within probation with all its potentially reductionist and distorting effects. Probation work, it can be argued, should be more concerned with understanding behaviour by exploring possible meanings, than measuring it; providing insightful judgments based upon a body of knowledge and skill rather than encasing individuals within a statistical table or locating them on a measurement scale.

Chapter 5 is an empirically grounded piece of work on cultural change in probation and the criminal justice system. It is perhaps helpful to clarify at this point that I have been associated with probation work since working as a volunteer in 1977, on the inside looking in. Since then I have been observing and experiencing, trying to think and reflect on, while unavoidably caught up in, those political and organisational changes analysed elsewhere (Whitehead and Statham 2006). I have periodically spoken to numerous staff about their experience of probation matters and the impact of change. It therefore occurred to me that talking to probation staff was the most obvious way to research cultural change within probation. However, I abandoned this approach quite early on, not on the grounds that it was not valid, but rather because it would have been difficult to be dispassionate about a subject so close to me. That is why

I changed my mind and chose instead to approach and interview, during 2006, a group of independent-minded professionals who work closely with probation staff at the Northtown Magistrates' Court. I theorised that a group of solicitors would be well placed to talk to me about their experiences, perceptions, understandings, and awareness of cultural change within probation and the criminal justice system over the last few years. This chapter contains some of the findings of the first phase of an ongoing research project; the second phase should include the views of magistrates, clerks, and district judges, as well as barristers and judges, and will create a more multi-faceted picture. It should be acknowledged that little research on this subject has been carried out with solicitors.

Chapter 6 concludes the book with further reflections on modernisation and cultural change. Attention is drawn to refining the essence of the probation ideal; the probation service as a social work profession rather than computerised bureaucracy; an organisation with objectives rather than targets; and a central role for probation information within the criminal justice system.

This introductory chapter provides a clue to the material which underpins the substantive title of the book on modernising probation and criminal justice. The subtitle – Getting the Measure of Cultural Change – is suggestive of the increasingly important role played by the theme of numbers and measurement, specifically in Chapters 2, 3 and 4. It is as though the point has been reached when numbers provide even people-based organisations with much needed comfort and reassurance (or not as the case may be) through the computerised production of hard data. This is manifested in the way outputs demonstrate measurable activity; enable individual members of staff to be compared with each other in terms of their performance; and facilitate the production of league tables that enable comparisons to be made between the 42 probation areas, resulting in either positive or negative consequences. In other words, numerical calculations are used to punish area probation services financially if cash-linked targets are not met. But there are alternative perspectives, different ways of understanding the world, other ideas about performance and accountability of a more qualitative nature that this book will consider as it embarks on a series of interconnected journeys. As it does so, it cuts across the grain of modernising inclinations; it builds a temporary dam against the incoming tides, incrementally rising since the 1960s, which have been eroding a set of values associated with the probation ideal. It is an attempt to describe and analyse the place where probation finds itself in its centenary year of 2007.

Chapter 2

FROM PEOPLE WORK TO BUREAUCRATIC POSITIVISM: A PROBATION JOURNEY INTO CULTURAL CHANGE

'The early nineteenth-century Warwickshire countryside with its farms and fields, canals and coach-roads in which George Eliot grew up, and which she wrote about with such clarity, seems like an image of steadfast British solidarity. In fact it was already entering an era of fluidity and change, and by the time she came to write *Felix Holt* in 1865, she looked back to it as to a vanished world. The pace of life had accelerated, the railway had pierced provincial seclusion, the traditional political patterns had vanished with the 1832 Reform Act, and the old economic base of farms and market towns was crumbling with the development of the mines and rise of the factory system, which was already throwing local hand-loom weavers out of work when she was a girl.'
(Jenny Uglow 1987 p13)

'Throughout the public sector, all those on whom targets were imposed have gradually found themselves working in systems that largely reduce them to impotent cogs in machines. Millions who once took great pride in their work no longer have much autonomy in how they do it. That makes them sullen or enraged, because they know how the restrictions on them are distorting the jobs they should be doing'
(Jenni Russell quoted in *NAPO News*, July/August 2006)

Introduction

This chapter explores how what was once a people orientated enterprise, predominantly based upon (or most certainly with the potential for) human relationships between probation officer and client, has been transformed into a politically dominated, centrally controlled, machine driven system for bureaucratically managing, containing and controlling both staff and various categories of offenders. The current emphasis is on systems, procedures and processes, the accoutrements of quantification, targets, and measurement scales (for managing gradations of risk), rather

13

than on spending sufficient time working with people in a process of understanding and positive change. Probation now exists within a different cultural context which has been taking shape since the 1980s. This chapter considers how various interconnected features of cultural change have attenuated dimensions of meaning and value that are arguably fundamental categories for people orientated organisations – person focused, working with individuals within the context of human relationships, ethics of personalism (McWilliams 1987), including the 'how' distinguished from the 'what' of practice (Whitehead and Thompson 2004). It is suggested that the events of recent years have in fact distorted probation's reality by attenuating qualitative and ineffable features, thus undermining the concept of *otherness* which will be considered in a subsequent chapter. To account for this process, the chapter begins with an overview of probation's early decades to contrast the differences between what can be described as old and new cultures.

Police Court Mission from 1876

During the early years of the organisation of that which evolved into the probation system after 1907, there was an emphasis upon religious mission and the promotion of temperance (Home Office 1936 p35; Young and Ashton 1956; the McWilliams quartet of 1983, 1985, 1986 and 1987; Oldfield 2002). It is also of interest to consider the offender conceptualised as a person within a theistic and personalist framework (Weston 2006).[1] Moreover the reader is invited to consider a brief reference in Abrams to the training of police court missionaries (1968 p110) by alluding to the *Sociological Review* journal of 1910. In this journal, the creation of the probation system of 1907, indebted to the American system, is understood in terms of reforming the Victorian punitive system which, it is said, could be capable of yielding excellent results (probation, that is, not prison). However, this depends on two conditions being satisfied: those appointed as probation officers must be suitable; and magistrates must be prepared to entrust them with suitable cases. The missionaries were qualified to undertake work which had a religious and temperance orientation, but the qualifications of the new probation officers had to include knowledge of social organisations which provided the means by which children who offended were brought under positive influences (Urwick 1910 p68). Therefore, the beginnings of the system can be characterised in terms of people work, religious mission and dealing with human problems with a view to the moral reform of individual offenders.

Interestingly, the Probation of Offenders Act 1907 does not make any reference to the bureaucratic accoutrements of record keeping, or even the collection of statistics. At section 4 the legislation emphasises the role of the probation officer in the language of 'advise, assist and befriend' the probationer. The 1909 Departmental Committee (Home Office 1909) states that the success and efficiency of the new probation system primarily depends upon the person and character of the probation officer. Paragraph 28 makes it clear that

> 'It is a system in which rules are comparatively unimportant, and personality is everything. The probation officer must be a picked man or woman, endowed not only with intelligence and zeal, but, in a high degree, with sympathy and tact and firmness. On his or her individuality the success or failure of the system depends. Probation is what the officer makes it.'

At this early stage, the duties of the probation officer included the provision of information to the courts prior to arriving at a sentencing decision, in addition to court attendance and progress reports on probationers to magistrates. Paragraph 39 goes on to say that 'The probation officer should keep for reference a book containing a record of all his cases, with entries of the visits paid and other particulars'. This is one of the earliest duties alluded to in the 1909 report.

The 1918–1923 Police Court Mission Diary

In my judgment, the Police Court Mission report book or diary, to which I was given access to complete an earlier project (Whitehead and Statham 2006), is a good example of the reference book containing the record of cases envisaged by paragraph 39 of the 1909 Departmental Committee. The diary provides an account of the day-to-day work undertaken by two unnamed officers based in Sunderland under nine variables. By way of illustration, the entry for the month of September 1922 can be reproduced as follows:

Table 2.1 September 1922

Date	New Arrivals	Remands	Men	Women	Boys	Girls	Protestant	Catholic
Fri 1	2		2				1	1
Sat 2	4		4				2	2
Mon 4	7		6	1			4	3
Tue 5	3		1	2			1	2
Wed 6	2		1	1			1	1
Thur 7	3		3				3	
Fri 8	4		4				2	2
Sat 9	2	1	2				1	1
Sun 10								
Mon 11	4	2	4				3	1
Tue 12	4	1	4				3	1
Wed 13	2	1	2				1	1
Thur 14	5	1	4	1			2	3
Fri 15	7	2	6	1			4	3
Sat 16	4	2	4				1	3
Sun 17								
Mon 18	9	2	5	4			5	4
Tue 19	2	1	2				1	1
Wed 20	2	2	1	1			1	1
Thur 21	7		6	1			4	3
Fri 22	1		1				1	
Sat 23	6		6				5	1
Sun 24								
Mon 25	10	2	8	2			6	4
Tue 26	2	1	1	1			2	
Wed 27	2		2				1	1
Thur 28	6		5	1			3	3
Fri 29	4	1	3	1			2	2
Sat 30	6		5	1			4	2
Totals	110	19	92	18			64	46

In addition to the daily tabulation under these nine variables, we encounter a summary of work undertaken for the same month:

Table 2.2 Probation officer tasks

Visits to cells, remand homes, adults and juvenile	31
Prisoners in cells, seen and conversed with	110
Remand cases, which have been seen in cells, day by day	19
Persons conversed with at the Boro and County Courts	130
Juveniles conversed with at the Boro and County Juvenile Courts	17
Discharged prisoners met with, who have been in prison	4
Visits made to cases, at their homes	44
Visits from cases, seeking advice and help	30
Visits from cases on probation, or bound over	70
Visits to lodging houses, or boarding houses	2
Attendance at courts, adult and juvenile	32
Letters written to cases, or on behalf of cases	18
Persons who have signed the Temperance pledge	2
Men or youths assisted with food, clothing or lodging	6
Females or youths assisted with food, clothing or lodging	4
Young people, visited by request of parents	4
Married couples conversed with, to try to settle their differences	12
Visited parent of the girl, Conroy, who is at Borstal Institution and sent particulars to London who is to be discharged on the 8th October	1
Boys sent to industrial schools	—
Boys sent to reformatory schools	—
Youth sent to sea	1

Finally, in addition to the statistical digest contained in Table 2.1 and the summary of tasks undertaken in Table 2.2, the final contribution from the diary is a section of text. The following extract is the valedictory entry made by a probation officer/police court missionary:

'I have finished my course and now sit down having run the race, September 30, 1922.

'As I am completing my services as the Police Court and Probation Officer for the Borough of Sunderland, I may say that it has been a pleasure to work in the Borough. I have received every help and consideration from the justices and officials connected with the court. But also I have received every kindness from the people with whom I have worked and I have made many friends. Even amongst the poorest who showed me courtesy and sympathy. Though I could not always persuade them to a better way of living, they nevertheless treated me very kindly. I never received an unkind word but always a welcome to their homes and listened to what I had to say. I have many friends even amongst the erring ones. I am sorry at parting with the familiar faces, but I shall remember them who put no hindrances in my way of dealing with them.'

At the risk of being charged with eisegesis (reading *into* the text) rather than engaging accurately in exegesis (taking *out of*), the point I am disposed to extrapolate from a careful reading of these diary entries is that the probation officer, only 14 years into the probation system, spent the greater proportion of his time and energies engaged in the work he describes above. However, it would not have taken long to draw together the record of 'visits and other particulars' envisaged by the 1909 Committee.

1920s to 1960s

It is of interest to note that the next Departmental Committee Report (Home Office 1922) does not include any reference to records or diaries. Rather, it reinforces the position expressed a few years earlier that the probation system depends upon the influence of the probation officer in a beneficial relationship with the probationer, with a view to effecting moral reform and the restoration of citizenship. The officer is described as a friend, not an official or civil servant, and 'it is essential to the success of probation that the Probation Officer should be able to devote sufficient time and attention to each case' (p12). The qualities required are sympathy, tact, common sense, firmness and a keen missionary spirit. The religious influence which permeated the early years of the system (in fact from 1876) can be keenly felt when reading this document, which is not surprising, given that many probation officers were drawn from the ranks of religious organisations, particularly the Police Court Mission of the Church of England Temperance Society (Young and Ashton 1956). In fact, the 1922 Committee considered that religious conviction conducive to the probation enterprise.

The Probation Rules of 1926, paragraphs 48–58, deal with the subject of probation records. It is stated at paragraph 48 that: 'The Probation Officer shall keep a record of each case placed under his supervision in the form and manner prescribed by these Rules'. Furthermore:

'The particulars forming the record of each case shall be entered by the Probation Officer on a 'leaf' and one or more 'followers' which shall be kept in a cardboard envelope bearing on the outside the probationer's full name, with the surname written first, and the date of the expiry of the probation order' (paragraph 51).

Entries had to be completed expeditiously for each case (paragraph 54) and

'The Probation Officer shall have free access to the records of his cases at all reasonable times. He shall keep notes of the recorded particulars and reports relating to his current cases for use in the performance of his duties away from the Court or when the records are not accessible' (paragraph 55).

It is worth pointing out an important difference between the Police Court Missionary Report Book for 1918–1923 (see reference above) and the new specification contained in the Probation Rules of 1926. In the former there is a paucity of data on individual cases. While the diary refers to a number of individuals by name, it does not contain one record for each probationer. However, by 1926 it had become necessary to have one record for each individual. It may also be suggested that this method was more conducive to the collection of statistics on the success or otherwise of the probation system. Again, only a relatively small proportion of the officers' time would have been occupied by record keeping. It was an activity which supported and facilitated the main task of working and engaging with individual probationers.

In 1935, Le Mesurier published her book on probation, Chapter 4 of which examines the work of the probation officer, including record keeping. To summarise, the probation officer had to provide reports to the Probation Committee on the progress of probationers, pay attention to correspondence, filing and card-indexing, as well as maintaining proper records and 'complete case histories' to serve as an *aide memoire*. Additionally, the probation officer is enjoined to keep a note book which should not be used during interviews because it is a distraction and would create the wrong impression.

'But the moment the officer is alone he should jot down facts and impressions in his note-book as quickly as possible, before memory fades or the next case obliterates them. From his notes and recollections he can write up his records later in the office with desirable fullness' (1935 p57).

Le Mesurier also clarified that records are required to facilitate the collection of statistics. By the third Departmental Committee Report (Home Office 1936), the importance of the personality and character of the probation officer who is primarily involved in court-based social work is confirmed. The objective of probation is clarified as the 'ultimate re-establishment of the probationer in the community and the probation officer must accordingly take a long view' (p58). Furthermore, records have become essential in probation work for supervisory purposes and the benefit derived from having a complete history of what has happened during probation is acknowledged. 'We have received evidence that too often records are not kept or are kept inefficiently' (paragraph 87).

Prior to moving into the 1950s, it is helpful to pause to allude to a booklet produced and circulated by the Home Office in 1938: *The Probation Service – Its Objects and its Organisation*. This slim publication was prepared for circulation to the Justices of the Peace and was commended and signed by the Home Secretary, Samuel Hoare. It relied heavily upon the findings of the 1936 Committee and was written to promote a better understanding of probation, including the diverse work of its officers and its developing organisational structures. As in the Departmental Committee report of 1922 there is no reference to record keeping, although this booklet includes statistics on the success of the system and brief information on organisational matters. It reinforces the point that the relatively new system of probation is an alternative to punishment and prison; probation requires the consent of offenders; and the principle to 'advise, assist and befriend' is central. Moreover, probation is based on co-operation rather than compulsion and there is some evidence that courts appreciated the range of social work tasks being undertaken by their officers. Significantly, 'No amount of organisation can be a substitute for the spirit in which the work is undertaken and this will largely depend on the character and personality of the men and women who are employed' (Home Office 1938 p36).

By the 1950s, E.R. Glover (1956), in her text on *Probation and Re-Education*, was included an appendix on records in which the salient points were expanded as follows. First, she clarified the three-fold function of records as a) aide memoire and for assessment purposes; b) assisting the Probation Committee to manage cases if something happens to the officer; c) providing information to test theories of crime 'because there has been comparatively little scientific research into crime in this country' (p279). Secondly, she referred to the four-fold nature of records:

- Face sheets – factual information the courts may need on an offender.

- Narrative records – comprise a chronological account of contacts in addition to a periodic (quarterly) summary that should include a plan of work. The summary 'should in short be a frank and thoughtful analysis of the whole business' (p280).

- Special reports – are those provided by GPs, psychologists, or social agencies.

- Correspondence – letters.

Finally, probation officers are enjoined to keep a card index of all clients, filed alphabetically.

In the early 1960s, paragraphs 62–63 of the *Morison Report* (Home Office 1962), address the subject of probation recording. In the summary of the report it is pointedly stated that 'The keeping of full records of supervision is an integral part of casework. Officers should not spend disproportionate time on written work: but this can be avoided by providing adequate clerical help and equipment' (p149). The point being reinforced is that records, within the developing yet by this stage well-established organisation, should be kept to a minimum because the primary task remains engagement with offenders within a casework relationship for the delivery of treatment. The people-focused nature of probation work remains intact.

Against this background, my next task is to paint two pictures, one circa the early 1980s and the second circa 2005/06. I do this to begin to illustrate profound cultural and ideological shifts in probation practice on the basis of the above discussion. Before doing so, it is helpful to summarise what has been said so far.

Reprise

The position established at the end of this first section is that, from the missionary period of late Victorian times until several decades after 1907, probation work took place through personal contact between the probation officer and probationer. Probation work can be constructed in terms of a person-orientated vocation. Change and development occurred at different levels over a number of decades: ideologically, from religious and moral reform to a more 'scientific' and secular form of treatment associated with casework; organisationally, from a horizontal to a vertical and hierarchical structure; the supervisory role of the Home Office was formalised with the creation of the inspectorate during the 1930s; the evolution of local areas at different rates reflected the vagaries of local conditions. Nevertheless, the one constant factor was the professional relationship and supervisory contact between the parties involved in supervision (Biestek 1961; Monger 1964). In fact, Lowson confirmed that probation was not a science but an art-form (1975 p76). This was a person orientated enterprise to control and reduce crime on behalf of the state (see the Marxist analysis of Walker and Beaumont 1981) and some of the salient features and mixed motives can be summarised as follows: the influence of religion, promotion of temperance, moral reform, effecting change towards normalisation through personal influence, the promotion of citizenship, material help, social work assistance, care and supervision, surveillance, discipline and control (Foucault 1977).

Furthermore, the personality and character of the probation officer were of central significance in the enterprise. To emphasise this point, during the 1970s Jarvis stated that the

> 'quality looked for in potential probation officers, *in addition to a wish to work with people* (emphasis added), is above all else a resilient personality. Good intelligence, a good general education, some varied life experience, some experience of other forms of social work; all these are valuable too, together with flexibility of mind and a capacity for listening to and understanding others. People with these attributes are well suited to go forward to acquire in training the specific knowledge and skills required of a probation officer' (1974 p268).[2]

This was not inconsistent with the tone of the Morison report of 1962, which was the last departmental committee to undertake a major review of the service. As late as the fourth edition of *Jarvis's Probation Officers Manual* (Weston 1987), the fundamental aims of probation work were clarified as upholding the law and the protection of society. Importantly, these aims were to be achieved by the probation officer working with offenders through the provision of skilled help held in common with all social workers; advise, assist and befriend were reinforced, as in 1907. Moreover, the 'success of supervision turns on the ability of the individual probation officer first to gain the offender's confidence and then work with him to overcome some of the problems which may have given rise to the offence' (1987 p28). In this process, bureaucracy was rudimentary and record keeping could be kept to a minimum. There is a clear view that the aims of the service include upholding the rule of law and public protection and that these aims will be achieved by attracting the right person to the job and by training that will equip the officer with a range of social work skills conducive to the task. Therefore the point can be established that, even as late as the mid-1980s, elements of probation work were continuous with previous decades. By contrast, what began to emerge, particularly during the 1990s and beyond, was increasingly discontinuous with the nature of probation work as it has been traditionally understood.

It should be acknowledged that, to some degree, there are elements of the 'ideal type' construction of Max Weber in this summary, elucidated by Ritzer and Goodman as follows:

> 'At its most basic level, an *ideal type* is a concept constructed by a social scientist, on the basis of his or her interests and theoretical orientation, to capture the essential features of some social phenomena...Although ideal types are to be derived from the real world, they are not mirror images of that world. Rather they are to be one-sided exaggerations... of the essence of what goes on in the real world' (1997 p204-205).

This functions as a heuristic device to facilitate understanding but also to compare what was ostensibly a people focused enterprise with a contemporary system marked by bureaucracy, expanding records and files, quantification, measurement, statistical tables and computers. Consequently, the next step in this chapter is to introduce two vignettes, created from my own probation experiences since 1979, and complemented by conversations with other probation officers, which draw attention to certain features of cultural change within the probation service and allow certain contrasts to be drawn. This will push the story along from the 1980s and then into the present framework occupied by the National Offender Management Service (NOMS).

Picture 1 – elements of the old culture

This probation officer's initial training was undertaken at Lancaster University between 1979 and 1981, and significant parts of these two years were spent on placement at two probation offices in Preston and Morecambe. This was my initiation into the post-Morison probation culture represented by the Lancashire probation service. Upon qualification, the trip was made over the Pennines to work for a service in the north-east.

The snapshot presented in this chapter, developed long ago but recently rescued from the mental archive to produce this vignette, brings into focus an organisation not burdened with records, statistical demands, numbers, managerial bureaucracy, or computers (Weston 1987 p262f). One of the reasons for this was the direction given to the service at its last major review (Home Office 1962) to keep the accoutrements of bureaucracy, specifically record keeping, to a minimum. In fact this probation officer recalls his first senior probation officer, on several occasions, referring to the Departmental Committee Report of 1962 in what remained a service operating in the shadow of Morison. Of course there were numerous administrative tasks to undertake associated with organisational life: letters to compose to lads in Borstal and men in prisons; letters of appointment to those on probation; correspondence with other organisations in pursuit of money, jobs and accommodation; files to maintain in a semblance of order and preferably up to date (some staff operated the card index system alluded to earlier). But there was no sense of being overly troubled by these functions; little sense that administration or bureaucracy imposed onerous demands. On the contrary, these minor encumbrances could be completed with alacrity. The pressures, when they did surface, emerged from the demands of clients in a person centred organisation, often manifested by having too many reports to write for criminal and civil courts, about too many people from deprived communities. These were people-generated and problem-focused pressures rather than bureaucratic demands.

During the early 1980s, the probation record system comprised a series of related documents known as the Part 'A', which contained the personal particulars of the client including accommodation, family and other relevant details. The Part 'B' was a quarterly summary of work completed and contained plans for the next quarter. The Part 'C' was a contact log containing a running commentary of work being undertaken on a weekly or often more regular basis. If there was any contact at all with a client (home or office visit, letters, telephone calls, court appearances, new offences, breach, etc.) a record would be kept by annotating the Part 'C'. These documents, including letters and copies of orders or licences, were secreted in a manila envelope kept secure in a filing cabinet in the probation officer's office. After being granted access to examples of probation records from the 1940s and 1960s, it is clear that the record system of the early 1980s had links with the 'Record of Supervision Facts Sheet', 'Follower' and 'Continuation Sheets' from the 1940s. Moreover (and this was a considerable perk), it was possible to dictate record entries and get clerical staff to produce a typed version, particularly of the Part

'B' quarterly summaries. Therefore, although the content of the record was not always captivating in its Freudian casework insights, at least the records looked presentable and could easily be deciphered by the senior officer for record check purposes, and even one of the periodic Home Office inspections.

It should also be added that this administrative tour would be incomplete without pointing out that at the end of each month the probation officer had to complete what were known as Form 20s and 30s. This was the statistical component of the job and the two forms were used to account for caseload changes, for example new probation orders and terminations, and breaches, also how many criminal and civil reports had been completed during the month. When completed, the forms were submitted to the senior probation officer who checked them before sending them off to the designated (good with numbers) member of staff in HQ who, in turn, forwarded them to the Home Office to enable probation statistics to be compiled on an annual basis. This was the extent of the probation record system and its statistical demands: not terribly exciting or demanding, yet necessary in support of offender-focused casework.

The sound advice of Morison during the early 1960s that probation officers should not spend too much time on written work (get the clericals to do it) was indubitably the kind of advice to which probation officers could assiduously adhere and they did not need to be told twice. The primary reason underpinning Morison's judgment was an acknowledgement that the rationale of probation practice was working with people usually called clients, sometimes offenders, who required case-working either at the probation office or their home located on the officer's patch, and sometimes both, to help with personal problems and prevent re-offending. This benefited the individual offender, his or her family and, of course, the local community. The job also entailed regular attendance at court because probation officers remained officers and social workers within the court setting, thus maintaining those links with magistrates established in 1907. Most of us in those days seemed to have joined the service because it was a person-orientated organisation; in addition to earning a living we wanted to make a difference to how other people lived their lives. We understood the job entailed the completion of service records to demonstrate accountability, some administration, and a rudimentary bureaucracy that played a supportive yet relatively minor role. The service was just that; a service to others that over recent decades had resorted to the language of rehabilitation and casework (Whitehead 1990). The job was more a vocation than an opportunity to 'get rich quick', imbued with humane ideals, values, and personalist philosophy. In other words, the job could, and you felt was expected to be, undertaken within an ethical context so that supporting, influencing and caring for people was *de rigueur*. This was not an organisational culture dominated by targets, quantification or measurement, or even machines (unsophisticated typewriters were the preserve of clerical staff, not probation officers). It could still be described as a social work organisation with a social work ethos. Notwithstanding future changes being adumbrated by the Home Office in the Statement of National Objectives and Priorities – SNOP (Home Office 1984), its culture was still being influenced by post-Morison rehabilitation, treatment and one-to-one relationships with clients, more than the inexorable pull of the new politics of right wing Conservatism and all that would mean over subsequent years. In other words, there was a degree of continuity with features of probation articulated in the four Departmental Committee Reports (Home Office 1909, 1922, 1936, 1962).

Of course, some of us had concerns and our professional lives were not idyllic by any means, certainly not in the post-industrial north-east. While there could be a cogently argued ideological commitment towards a combination of personalism (social work with individuals) and radicalism (social change), we were always mindful of being employed as part of a state machine for managing, containing, controlling and correcting predominantly working class people so that they would play by the rules (Walker and Beaumont 1981).   There was, at times, an acute tension between the motivation to advise, assist, befriend and help the deprived and disadvantaged who lived on various housing estates not far from the city centre and the uncomfortable expectation that probation officers were also expected to effect change, correct and straighten dysfunctional individuals and families, when the 'real' problem was being part of an unjust socio-economic system that created winners and losers exacerbated by the economic dislocations of the 1970s. Probation staff invariably worked with those labelled as 'losers', who were themselves victims of circumstances not of their own choosing, and arguments could have been advanced for social rather than individual change. Yet we had ways of reconciling this conflict by vociferously arguing with anyone who would listen that probation officers were sorely needed within the criminal justice system to mitigate its worst punitive and exclusionary excesses by, for example, providing *social* information to magistrates and judges through what were then *social* enquiry reports. Moreover, probation remained ideologically committed to eschewing custody wherever possible because of the damage such a sentence could inflict upon people already damaged by their experiences of life. In this way, we hoped to redress the balance. Yet it was this approach that led those of a more right wing persuasion during the 1980s to conclude that we were more on the side of offenders than of victims of crime. In other words, when it was thought we resorted to professional skills to facilitate an understanding of people, it was sometimes suggested that we were excusing rather than explaining certain forms of delinquent behaviour.

Within the probation culture of the early 1980s, it is important to acknowledge that file/record checks were undertaken periodically by the senior officer within the team. There was a serious side to this because the probation officer could be taken through a process of capability/discipline if the records were not in order. There was a professional duty to maintain the record system and gaps were plugged if it was considered deficient. Yet a critical point should be made here concerning the role of the senior probation officer. A supervision session between the probation officer and senior probation officer could allude to the most recent file check and remedial action agreed. However, staff supervision was not dominated by, or located within, a managerial or bureaucratic process that focused on record keeping and the achievement of service objectives and targets. There were no objectives or targets until well after 1984. Supervision consisted of the senior officer enhancing the knowledge and personal skills of the probation officer to work with clients; it was a supervisory process for the inculcation of insight, awareness and understanding of individuals with various problems. Certain clients who had committed the most serious offences would be discussed individually and regularly. There is little doubt that many officers derived enormous benefit from their senior officer handing down knowledge and experience of people with a view to reducing deficiencies in what was a process of cultural transmission. In fact at this stage (early 1980s) senior officers themselves continued to work with a handful of cases, thus maintaining a crucial link with the people-based nature of the job and maintaining those skills that could be handed on to the next generation of officers. The job was about people who had offended and all grades of staff worked with offenders. It was only when the job became more managerial, when the senior role changed from supervising to managing and later auditing, that this practice was stopped. Consequently, from the mid-1980s to the early years of the third millennium, probation was culturally transformed.

Picture 2 – elements of the new culture

If the tape is allowed to run on to 2006/07, a profoundly different picture begins to form, again drawn from first hand experience of probation work during this period. Dedicated members of staff, mostly young and all hard working, begin to arrive well before 9am at the open plan office that provides accommodation for a busy field team serving one of the most deprived localities in the north-east of England. The first task performed each working day, more by necessity than choice, is to switch on the computer which activates the logging-on routine. A machine is positioned on everyone's desk, from clerical staff and typists to all probation officer grades, and hardly anyone or anything can function without it. It has rapidly acquired a position of dominance in the office environment and exercises considerable control over staff as they pursue their daily routine. The reader has just stepped inside the modern world, not of the probation service of the post-Morison early 1980s, but the post-SNOP National Offender Management Service; a world no longer staffed by probation officers but redesignated offender managers; not social workers of the courts, but bureaucratic technicians and data entry operators predominantly within the office environment. The computer, facilitating and symbolising the new culture, is the conduit through which the increasingly number-dependent job flows. In this culture, the worker spends a disproportionate amount of time interacting with a machine rather than other members of staff or clients. In fact, within field-work offices, members of staff are more likely to be asked technical questions about resolving computer queries than people-related problems. This can be illustrated by listing some of the many computer-controlled tasks that staff must perform which did not exist until recently (that is, before 2002/03):

- Entering data into the computerised Offender Assessment System (OASys) under the following headings: offending; analysis of offences; accommodation; education, training and employability; finances; relationships; lifestyle; drugs; alcohol; emotional wellbeing; thinking and behaviour; attitudes (Mair et al 2006 for an interesting discussion on the merits and de-merits of OASys).

- Entering data into the risk of harm screens.

- Pre-sentence report outline plans.

- Offender self assessment data should also be entered.

- Sentence plan reviews every 16 weeks or earlier as required.

- Offender Group Reconviction Scale (OGRS) data to enter which calculates risk of re-offending.

- Additional (CRAMS) data on clients (no handwritten contact logs that were formerly Part 'Cs').

- Blank letter templates can be accessed so that officers can type their own correspondence.

- Enforcement templates when offenders are in breach of their court orders and licences.

- The daily routine of receiving and sending emails.

These developments have gathered pace over a relatively short period of time (since 2001), arguably without sufficient consultation and debate concerning the impact on probation services; the rationale of computers in a people orientated organisation; the impact upon staff and offenders; the implications for changing roles and working practices; the transformation from person focused to machine-based organisation and greater use of numbers (Rose 1999); costs (computers do not eliminate the need for paper or files); the disproportionate amount of time spent sitting in front of a machine rather than face-to-face contact with clients; the implications for values, professional status, acquisition and maintenance of professional knowledge and skills; and motivation. In fact it is rare to hear anyone ask what the implications are if members of staff spend between 70 and 80 per cent of each working week entering data into a computer rather than in face-to-face contact with offenders. This can be further illustrated by considering another critical change which has occurred in the process of writing court reports (Social Enquiry Report prior to 1991 when the document became Pre-Sentence Report) in the 1980s, and currently referred to as Standard Delivery Reports.

1980s	2006/07
SER allocated to officer	PSR allocated
Interview client	Offender manager interviews offender
Write report	OASys process – computer data entry
Typed by clerical staff	Consult NICH re: proposal/targets[3]
Submit to court	Write or type report
	Formatted by clerical staff
	Read, checked and altered by SPO/office manager
	Return to author for amendments
	Final checks then submit to court
	Reports can now be generated from OASys

Under the present system, the OASys data entry stage of the process can take longer than interviewing the offender and typing the report (sometimes it can take between two and three hours to complete OASys, particularly if the full risk of harm is required – Mair et al 2006). Furthermore, reports are currently written within a tightly controlled bureaucratic process. One of the features of this process is the diminution of the report writers' discretion and autonomy to make their own judgments, decisions and sentencing proposals. It is now possible that reports prepared by experienced staff with many years' service can be read, scrutinised and altered by managers: this is indicative of cultural and professional dislocation. Specifically within the context of writing reports for courts, this is a shift from professional accountability and responsibility to meeting the demands of bureaucratic and computer driven processes associated with target achievement.[4]

When reflecting upon the benefits and disadvantages of computer technology, it should be acknowledged that it is capable of producing and handling copious amounts of data. Yet probation officers functioned effectively and produced quality work in the BCC era (before computer culture), as evidenced by the staff appraisal system. However, the computer flatters to deceive, because it does not tell the skilled, experienced and knowledgeable officer anything not already known; nor does it save on the commodity of time. It should be clarified that the officer has already collected and evaluated the data before it is entered into the machine, so the machine can only disgorge what has already been fed into it. The machine is able to produce a graph or two, based upon data provided by the data entry technician. One of the critical changes is reflected in the fact that one used to hear the question: "What is your assessment and understanding of the client?" But now you are just as likely to hear: "What does the computer say and how do I perform this or that computer task – which key should be pressed?" The person-focused service contained in Picture 1 has become a machine-driven organisation in 2006/07. In fact, it may be suggested that the computer has become the defining symbol of the new modernised culture.

The essence of probation practice, facilitated by appropriate training, includes the acquisition of the knowledge, experience and skill to collect and use information gleaned from clients during interview; undertaking insightful assessments; weighing the relevance of information to make judgments and exercise discretion; arriving at decisions about need, public protection, risk and harm; communicating a professional understanding of people to sentencers that contributes to criminal and social justice (Whitehead and Thompson 2004; Whitehead and Statham 2006). This is fundamentally premised upon the ability to establish relationships, engage with people, and spend sufficient time with clients. However, the introduction of a complex, time consuming and burdensome computerised bureaucracy, with its plethora of data entry screens and accompanying policies, processes, procedures, and systems, has begun to erode the experience, knowledge and skills considered relevant only a few years ago – an impersonal 'it' is de-professionalising and de-humanising what was once a people orientated enterprise. To put the point simply, what was considered essential when many of us joined the service and reflected in Picture 1 – engagement with clients and building people skills over a period of time through which to achieve service objectives – is now considered much less important. This represents a profound professional, cultural, and also ethical, shift of direction.

It is of interest to digress at this point and recall how, from the late eighteenth century, the industrial revolution transformed society with the expansion of towns and cities, arrival of large factories, new class relations, and of course machines. Prior to this industrial transformation, the primary trade in the north was weaving and cropping wool and cotton, largely undertaken within the home. The new system of mass production economised labour at the expense of the livelihoods of those working in traditional crafts, and the machine replaced what craftsmen used to do by hand, for example finishing cloth. It was the unemployed domestic weavers in Yorkshire who responded by destroying the new machines in the Luddite riots of 1811 to 1816, because they were concerned about the impact of factory machines on their cottage industry craft skills (Luddites operated in the Midlands, Lancashire and Cheshire as well as Yorkshire). Computers within probation do not necessarily put people out of work; but they have transformed the culture of what was once a people based organisation by undermining professional (craft) skills. This type of cultural change is captured well in Jenny Uglow's book on *George Eliot* (1987 – see quotation at the beginning of this chapter). It is also of interest to refer to the criticisms of industrialism found in Blake, Coleridge, Carlyle, Dickens, Arnold, Ruskin, Morris and Lawrence and the nineteenth-century social problem novels of Dickens, Gaskell, Kingsley, Disraeli, and George Eliot.[5]

It can be argued that the rise to prominence of the computer is the acme of managerial, bureaucratic and centralising processes that have gathered pace and seized the organisation since the 1980s. The computer has transformed the culture in the direction of numbers, measurement scales, quantification and statistics. It reflects a politically-driven process which has indubitably created a more technically efficient and accountable service, but at the expense of qualitative features that are important, given the essential nature of the organisation. Consequently the probation service has lost its sense of *otherness*, those ineffable and multidimensional features which help to provide this book with its thematic structure and rationale. It is as though the organisation has gained the whole world (in the form of more data) at the expense of its soul; it has become more technologically competent, but increasingly at the expense of an insightful understanding of the people with whom it purports to work. In its headlong rush to produce copious amounts of numerical data to justify its existence and demonstrate accountability in an evidence based environment, the probation service has excluded important dimensions of reality from its field of vision and thus distorted professional practice.

So the computer casts its long shadow from the employee's desk, a silent, inanimate, yet demanding and controlling presence. Members of staff are observed by an impersonal 'it' that requires constant attention when switched on and even when turned off continues to gather data from various sources into its inexhaustible memory. In fact it can cope with a regular diet of data, regardless of the quantity received and entered. It is never satisfied and always wants and can handle more. If attempts are made to ignore it, its demands become much greater because of what staff must do to catch up. One is never really on top of it; there is always something else to do; the computer exercises far reaching control over the working day. In fact, because of the amount of work it handles the machine controls the working day of the officer, not the reverse. It creates a demand for instant responses, particularly via email, rather than pausing, reflecting, and thinking. The computer has profound implications for all grades of staff throughout the organisation, so much so that the new culture is qualitatively different from the old. The following points are worthy of consideration:

- The computer has facilitated the production of copious amounts of text and increasingly numbers, but has not reduced the amount of paper.

- The generation of more data is not necessarily tantamount to a deeper understanding of the person – now more concerned with prediction than diagnosis.

- The computer has facilitated more local managerial, bureaucratic, and central political control in relation to individual performance and service accountability.

- It is accompanied by a process of de-skilling the probation officer role because of the amount of time required to enter data, rather than allowing the necessary time to build people skills that should facilitate understanding and effectiveness.

- It promotes a Weberian-type bureaucratic structure rather than a professional culture.

- It does not make the job easier or faster because of the time consuming demands of data entry.

- It burdens and oppresses rather than liberates the working day.

- It does not add meaning or value to probation practice.

The cultural change within probation has been accurately captured by David Garland within the context of alluding to Max Weber. Garland explains that the

'move from traditional or affective practices to rationalised forms of action is seen by Weber (and Foucault) as a distinctively modernising development, in which social practices become better informed, more efficient, and more self-consciously adapted towards specific objectives. In the course of this development, 'science' comes to replace belief, calculation replaces commitment, and technical knowledges replace traditions and sentiments as the leading determinants of action. In consequence, social practices and institutions become more instrumentally effective, but at the same time they become less emotionally compelling or meaningful for their human agents' (1990 p179; also see MacRae 1974).

Although this comment was published in 1990, it remains just as pertinent in the first decade of the twenty-first century. This is because it captures the nature of cultural change within probation. How can we account for the transition from Picture 1 to Picture 2, from one distinctive culture to another? What are the salient features on which we need to touch? The following looks succinctly at some of the more significant steps in a sequential format (for a broader and more detailed historical analysis see the relevant chapters in Whitehead and Statham 2006; Oldfield 2002).

Plotting the steps from Picture 1 to 2, old to new cultures

Raine and Willson suggested that after 1979, under the Conservatives, a specific strategy emerged for the criminal justice system that had three main elements: cash limits; greater standardisation to reduce professional autonomy and discretion; and greater central control/local control and accountability through managerial developments, policies, objectives and targets. This was because the criminal justice system was deemed to be 'spendthrift, idiosyncratic and unaccountable' (1997 p82). Long before such thinking gathered pace, Keith Joseph described the Heath government from 1970 to 1974 as 'managerial' (somewhat pejoratively, I think) in the way Derek Rayner, then of Marks & Spencer, was brought into the Ministry of Defence to 'raise the efficiency of its purchasing methods' (Halcrow 1989 p46). Having said that, management was an important concept in the Department of Health and Social Security because continued expansion had made it a complex and unwieldy organisation, which required managing effectively and efficiently.

Christopher Hood (1991), Stewart and Walsh (1992), McLaughlin et al (2001), and Ryan (2003) provide further contextual information on how, from the late 1980s, the concept of New Public Management injected managerial practices drawn from the private into the public sector (see also Power 1997). Consequently, the new approach became identified with the following lexicography throughout public services: the application of market mechanisms; competition to secure contracts; markets that respond to consumer demand that in turn drives up standards and creates more efficiency; greater emphasis on the 3Es (economy, efficiency, effectiveness) and VfM (value for money); clear standards, targets, measurable performance, transparency, key performance indicators and auditable performance (evidence based). When this approach was applied to probation, it eventually narrowed the criteria by which effectiveness was understood and therefore evaluated. In fact, when reflecting on the post-1997 period, McLaughlin et al state that

> 'New Labour's long-term programme of public sector reform increasingly acknowledges that central features of the Conservative's managerial reform process of the late 1980s and early 1990s were necessary acts of modernisation that improved productivity, delivered better value for money and enhanced quality of service' (2001 p306).

Consequently some of the main steps that created this situation can be summarised as follows.

1982 saw the launch of the Financial Management Initiative (FMI) to promote managerial improvement in government by having clear objectives. Accordingly, one begins to encounter a number of emerging themes that draw attention to the 3Es and VfM: better use of resources; performance management; greater accountability; objectives, priorities and targets; and a corresponding requirement for information systems to manage the inevitable consequence of generating more numerical data (Whitehead 1992). By 1983/84 the *Statement of National Objectives and Priorities* (Home Office 1984) had become the document through which the principles of the FMI were promoted in probation. This development culminated in certain tensions in relation to the nature of the service between social work ideals associated with working with people, values, the importance of relationships (lineaments of the old culture); also centrally inspired objectives which threatened this ethos along with probation officer autonomy and discretion. It should be added that if the probation service had to contend with SNOP, the prison service had its Statement of Tasks which was adopted by the Prison Board also in 1984 (Morgan 2002 p1148). Then in 1985/86, local area services responded differently to SNOP (Lloyd 1986) and the Home Office continued to encourage services to create better information systems linked to measurable objectives.

By the second half of the 1980s, Grimsey (1987), in her review of Her Majesty's Inspectorate of Probation, contributed to the themes of economy, efficiency and effectiveness, and recommended establishing a working party on performance indicators. These were understood as quantitative rather than qualitative indicators of performance. Therefore the Grimsey report constituted a further impetus in the direction of numbers, statistics, quantification, measurement, and what was quickly becoming a target-driven rather than person-centred service. In fact, the year 1988 saw the beginning of centrally imposed national standards, which have passed through various manifestations, and which gave further impetus to the developments under discussion (Whitehead and Statham 2006). Furthermore, in 1989 the Audit Commission endorsed the language of objectives, targets, and quantitative measures of accountability and performance. Such developments were occurring throughout the public sector, not just probation (Hood 1991). Consequently, qualitative and ineffable features (the dimension of *otherness*) were being forced to the margins.

From 1992, the production of Home Office three-year plans continued to emphasise quantifiable objectives, measurement and targets. A further refinement to this process was the emergence of key performance indicators. Additional refinements to national standards and the introduction of cash limits were to culminate in cash linked targets in subsequent years. Then, in the autumn of 1998, new probation training arrangements were introduced through the Diploma in Probation Studies. The introduction of the national vocational qualification (NVQ) ensured that not even probation training could escape the new managerial culture in the way knowledge was codified and evidence of a quantitative nature was produced to demonstrate competent performance (Whitehead and Thompson 2004). In other words, there was much greater emphasis upon measuring performance in relation to performance criteria and range statements through the increasing bureaucracy of training arrangements.

The year 2001 witnessed the development of the Offender Assessment System (OASys) that made a significant contribution to the need for numerical data, as earlier discussed. In fact, the introduction of the computer enabled the production of data that was already being generated and collected in relation to targets to be handled more efficiently. By the period 2004/05 examples of national targets could be provided as follows:

- Offending Behaviour Programmes 15,000 completions.

- Enhanced Community Punishment 30,000 completions.

- There must be a clear proposal in 95 per cent of reports to courts on minority ethnic offenders.[6]

It is important to draw attention, albeit briefly, to some of the key chronological steps of recent years which have arguably led the service into a cul-de-sac of rigid codification, quantification, measurable targets and statistics, at the expense of more qualitative and ineffable, ethical, social work and human features. I do not wish to expand upon these events any further at this point because of the groundwork undertaken in previous work. Rather it is my intention in the next section to isolate two specific illustrations of cultural change by first expanding upon the emergence of *targets* in probation, prior to raising points of interest concerning this way of thinking and working in person focused organisations. Secondly, I will turn to the concept of *risk*.

However, before proceeding, the story recounted so far in this chapter can be summarised as follows. The first section tries to capture the people orientated nature of probation work which prevailed for most of the twentieth century. If you wanted to work with people, imbued with the motivation illustrated in the above quote from Jarvis ('wish to work with people') then probation was one option among many including social services, psychiatric social work and education welfare. Probation was part of the state's network of caring and controlling professions, supported by necessary but minimal bureaucracies for demonstrating professional accountability. Section two begins with a continuation of the theme established in the first section, this time with a view to contrasting two distinct cultural forms. The old culture was predominantly people-based; the new culture, which is with us now, is a computerised bureaucracy. Section three plots some of the salient steps which account for the cultural transformation from the 1980s to the present, with particular reference to the prevailing context of new public management. This signals a transformation from a *social* to *economic* style of reasoning (Garland 2001). With these three sections in mind, I turn to illustrations of cultural change by expanding on targets and risk.

Thinking about targets and risk

Throughout its long history, the probation service has been orientated more towards psychodynamic individualism than the Marxist social change agenda (Stewart et al 1994 p16). This orientation used to manifest itself, particularly in the 1950s and 1960s, in an attempt to understand the individual with a view to providing an insightful assessment of the person associated with an appreciation of his or her needs and problems. A repertoire of social work skills facilitated this approach and was linked to the medical model, 'scientific' treatment, rehabilitation and casework, delivered primarily on a one-to-one basis. Since the 1980s, a significant shift has occurred from the professional task of understanding the person as a basis for change (although more imagined than real at times), towards an approach that puts greater emphasis on managing, containing, controlling and categorising levels of risk and harm based more upon presenting than underlying problems. This is not to say that the notion of offenders having needs that should be addressed has been eliminated, or that probation staff should no longer try to understand, or that little heed should be given to the complex variables that comprise a person's unique biographical details. Although there have been cultural changes, a vestige of the old cultural features remains, but at the margins rather than at the cultural centre and defining its essence.

It can be discerned that a particular way of thinking, associated with social work and welfare (Picture 1 above), has been weakened, which helps to explain why some members of staff upon joining the modernised service are not, as a matter of course, inculcated in a repertoire of people-orientated skills, ideals and values. Instead the priority is currently the acquisition of computer skills, how to enter data correctly, and how to assess and manage the risk of re-offending and harm via the new technology. These are some of the critical shifts that have occurred:

- From rehabilitation to managing, containing and controlling categories of risk of re-offending and harm.

- From a panoply of social work people skills to computer skills.

- From clinical judgment to actuarialism.

- From engaging with and developing an understanding of people to managerial and bureaucratic processes and systems.

- From probation officer to offender manager.

- From clients to offenders.

- From offenders to victims.

- From social workers of the courts, qualitative and ineffable features, to quantification, measurement, targets, audits.

- From a professional probation service to a much more bureaucratic National Offender Management Service.

During this transition the service has, to some degree, detached 'what have you done' from an insightful understanding of 'why'. It is less concerned with understanding 'why' and more with managing the risk presented by the immediate 'what' within a neo-classical context (see Chapter 3). One significant point to extrapolate from this is the way information is considered, its nature, and how it is used. When organisations work with people within a culture oriented towards welfare, social work values, understanding and rehabilitation, a requirement for language-based information emerges from personal contact and communication. But when attention is turned to managing categories according to levels of risk and harm, in pursuit of objectives and targets, within a framework of quantification and measurement, then numbers are required as well as, if not more than, words. Different organisational cultures, reflecting different rationales, outlooks, ideologies and values, require different types of information (Rose 1999), and I have already traced the steps that explain this transition in probation. Nevertheless, it is necessary to say a little more about the rise of targets within an organisation that did not require them before the 1990s, in order to develop what has become a central theme.

Exploration and critique of targets

One line of enquiry to pursue when exploring the reliance on and increasing need for quantitative data and measurement, within a more bureaucratic organisational context, is to explore in more detail the creation of a target culture. The language of objectives and later targets began to surface during the 1980s with a view to giving a sharper focus to priorities, use of resources, accountability and performance. This is rooted within the framework established by New Public Management, already outlined above, and therefore indicative of a particular way of thinking about the rationale of organisational life. I do not suggest that such a development has been erroneous *per se*; but I would argue that it has altered the balance of the organisation by skewing its approach to an understanding and evaluation of its practices. The important point to consider here is how the grafting on of these quantitative features and the introduction of targets has had profound implications for what was once a more people and qualitative-based culture.

To have an objective is to have a goal or purpose which can be achieved by pursuing a particular course of action. For example, to reduce the number of custodial sentences being imposed by the courts (which has markedly increased since 1993) would be an objective for the criminal justice system to which probation could contribute. If the word target is introduced, then one is dealing with something much more precise. Reducing the number committed to custody in 2007/08 by 2 per cent compared with 2006/07 is a target that is measurable. Targets are at the heart of New Labour's approach to improvements across the whole public sector, as they are deemed critical to performance management and provide focussed direction for organisations (Jenkins 2006a and 2006b). The Audit Commission endorses the position that targets are essential for the promotion of change (2003), but with qualifications. After clarifying the new terminology, I want to explore and raise a number of concerns under the following seven headings.

1 Arbitrary nature of targets

Setting targets is not a prerequisite for organisational life. However, it can be argued that political concerns over public expenditure and taxation created fertile ground for their development. When considering using targets as a mechanism to control the money supply to the public sector, Simon Jenkins arrestingly commented that it 'was procrustean, chopping, hacking and sawing the public sector to fit it into a preordained shape' (2006b). Nevertheless, targets are not some unavoidable 'given' in probation, or any other public and private sector organisation, and for decades (from 1876 until the 1980s to be precise) the probation service managed without assuming that some essential ingredient was missing. So the phenomenon of targets is politically and organisationally constructed more than inherently necessary. With this in mind, I believe that targets are arbitrary, once it has been decided to weave them into organisational dynamics. Why should the target to reduce the proportionate use of custodial sentences be set at 2 per cent? Why not 2.7, 5 or even 10 per cent? Should there be 6, 8, 12, or 16 contacts with all offenders subject to a community order with a supervision requirement during the first few weeks? Should the target be 'x' or 'y' for accredited programmes or any other probation activity subject to the discipline of measurable targets?

The language of objectives and priorities clarifies the direction for the organisation; targets are more specific because they are measurable; but the process of target setting is arbitrary, a matter of opinion, subject to human judgment and therefore possibly unintended consequences, particularly within an organisation that purports to work with people.

2 Objectives or targets in a people-based organisation?

If targets are not, and do not need to be, an inevitable feature of organisational life, but are arbitrarily constructed by political and managerial processes, and therefore a manifestation of one possible methodology for thinking about performance and demonstrating accountability, it should be asked whether they are desirable within a people-focused organisation? It can be argued that in organisations that work with people, such as the probation service, it is legitimate to establish a culture in which professionally trained staff aspire to do the right thing, in pursuit of broad objectives, rather than aiming for targets. Doing the right thing would initially depend upon the organisation's primary task being clearly specified, including the inculcation of corresponding ideals and values among staff which, when translated into action, would mean doing what is appropriate with different individuals in different circumstances. What is right for one person in a probation officer's caseload may not be right for another. To proceed on this basis would require more imagination, discretion and professional judgment than currently allowed by a culture of standardisation and uniformity. This way of working is arguably as legitimate as pursuing targets, but reflects different political priorities, historical circumstances, organisational dynamics and cultural forms. This way of working is based on professional trust, insightful leadership and therapeutic imagination, underpinned by the moral dimension of social work values and an understanding of people as unique individuals. It believes in professionalism, enabling staff to be accountable and responsible for what they do with clients. The other way is much more bureaucratic, mechanised and subject to routine, and reflects a one-size-fits-all approach as the net of targets is cast over all areas' services. Both approaches are concerned to be effective in terms of working with offenders to reduce the likelihood of reconviction and protect the public, but the *modus operandi* is very different. It should be acknowledged that the imposition of a target culture on probation by central government constitutes a challenge to a public service once dominated by 'the traditions of administration, hierarchy and professionalism' (Stewart and Walsh 1992 p504).

Not for the first time, in the pages of the *Sunday Times*, Simon Jenkins applies his acute journalistic intelligence to targets and public service. He advances the view that civic life requires effective leadership within its public institutions which, for a number of years, has been stifled by a combination of centrally imposed targets and burgeoning bureaucracy. Jenkins accurately states that 'An edifice of internal prices, legal contracts and top-down targets now spreads into every corner of the public sector... targetry now wholly dictates the relationship between government and all public service institutions' (2006a p18; see also Jenkins 2006b). This neatly encapsulates developments within the public sector which have enveloped probation (Power 1997; Rose 1999).

3 We don't have total control over target achievement

Even if a case can be cogently established for the desirability of targets, the probation service does not have total control over target achievement. Some of the factors that could militate against target achievement can be expanded upon as follows. If the reduction of custodial sentences, to resort to an example already cited, is a specific target, it should be acknowledged that its achievement is at the mercy of the vagaries of a constantly changing political and criminal justice climate. During the 1980s, culminating in the Criminal Justice Act of 1991, the political climate under Douglas Hurd, John Patten and David Faulkner was conducive to taking seriously the notion of alternatives to custody (Windlesham 1993). This approach was undermined after 1993 when a new political climate reflected different political priorities for probation and the criminal justice system, associated with Michael Howard and John Major. Secondly, the reduction of re-offending by 5 per cent by 2008 and then 10 per cent by 2010 is not completely within the gift of probation officers. It could be said that the achievement of this target has not been assisted by the more stringent and onerous approach to the enforcement of orders since the Criminal Justice Act 2003; or by the inimical and discriminatory benefit sanction that persists in a handful of area services. These two factors could militate against the achievement of this target. The first because enforcement, accompanied by more onerous requirements, could culminate in more people being committed to prison for breach. The second could encourage offenders to re-offend in circumstances of financial hardship. Sometimes there is a lack of strategic 'fit' between imposed targets and political decision-making that affects the workings of the criminal justice system at different points. Finally, the target for the number of contacts that should be achieved during the first 16 weeks must allow for the problems experienced by many offenders who are subject to community orders (financial, addictions, accommodation). In other words, life's contingencies can obstruct regular weekly attendance and therefore the successful completion of court orders and additional requirements. Consequently, a range of intervening variables is often at play, conspiring against target achievement over which organisations have little control; changing political priorities, decisions in relation to enforcement and benefit sanctions, and the personal and social circumstances of offenders (Stewart et al 1994). This must be factored into any discussion on the viability of target achievement and allowances made for so-called failure.

4 Competing targets in the criminal justice system

Target achievement in one organisation could be affected by target priorities in another. The main organisations comprising the criminal justice system are the probation service, police, Crown Prosecution Service, courts and prisons, yet they do not share the same primary task. Of course there is some commonality between them because the aims of the criminal justice system, as a whole, are to reduce crime, reduce the impact of crime on people's lives, reduce the economic costs of crime, and dispense justice fairly and efficiently to promote confidence in the rule of law. Moreover, the objectives of the system are timely justice, meeting the needs of victims, respecting defendants' rights and treating people fairly. Nevertheless, the precise targets set for one organisation within the system could be adversely affected by the rationale of and decisions made by others. Target achievement within the different organisations of criminal justice can also be affected by a range of variables among individual members of staff: reason for joining, level of motivation and commitment, personal values, attitudes, approach to the job, ethics, level of understanding of offenders and philosophical approach, training and educational background, to name but a few.

5 Competing targets in probation

Another point for discussion is the possibility of a target culture generating unhealthy and needless competition between different components of the 'business' (various community based court disposals, Unpaid Work v Think First, for example). Can targets be divisive? Do they keep staff on their toes, or create the wrong climate and set a negative tone within people-based organisations? Does competition culminate in one service robbing another of some of its resources, and is this right when staff and offenders could suffer as a result? Do targets create unnecessary pressures for hard-pressed staff and local services doing a difficult job? Are they more negative than positive and do they carry within them the possibility of unintended consequences? Such questions help to develop the argument that within organisations that work with people, a stronger case can be made for being clear about aims and objectives, underpinned by aspirations, ideals and values, complemented by effective leadership endorsing notions of responsibility and accountability, than for 'hard' targets.

6 Threat of sanctions for target failure

At present there are in the region of 13 high priority targets within probation, in addition to a similar number of medium priority targets. Examples of the former are victim contacts, offending behaviour programmes completions, breach action, and the completion of computerised OASys risk management plans within tight timescales. Examples of the latter are ethnic representation in the workforce, staff wastage, and hostel occupancy. If certain high-priority targets are not met by individual members of staff and, in turn, the organisation as a whole, a regime of sanctions is activated. These are not "punitive" sanctions as such, but local services which fall short of their targets will fail to earn their performance bonus (which for one local area during 2005/06 was worth £112,000). Such punitive cash penalties, coupled with the linking of targets and performance-related pay for senior managers, could result in the probation service giving the courts advice on sentencing for questionable reasons. For example, section 148(2) of the Criminal Justice Act 2003 makes it clear that a community sentence must be the most suitable for the individual offender, not the most suitable for the achievement of centrally imposed targets and the preservation of area service budgets. A regime of measurable targets, some of which are cash-linked, could result in unintended consequences, as professional decision-making and the intentions of the 2003 Act are skewed by the politics of modernised probation.

7 Probation work is more than achieving measurable targets

The final point for exploration is, I think, persuasive. The language of objectives and targets which has become widespread since the 1980s, should be understood as one approach to the politics of organisational life associated with the 3Es, VfM, inputs and outputs, national standards, audits, and KPIs. Furthermore, these features are complemented by an approach to performance and accountability based upon the quantification and measurement of tasks. At this juncture within the history of probation services there is an obsession with measuring things, which constitutes a serious problem for the following reason. Within what I continue to refer to as people-based organisations – probation, social services, education, health service – it may be conceded that certain features of the job are amenable to setting targets and measuring the results, primarily to maintain focus, raise standards and provide value for taxpayers' money. However, there are other aspects of the job which cannot be measured. In fact it could be argued that those aspects that cannot be measured are the most essential in an organisation where the primary rationale is to work with other people to achieve certain desirable results: insight and awareness, a feel for other people's difficulties, understanding, knowing how to ask the right questions during interview, the ability to communicate, imagination and problem-solving skills, including the ability to listen actively, artistry through reflection (Schon 1987), and a passion for the job (Whitehead and Thompson 2004). Furthermore, it is the quality of the relationship between helper and helped, manifested by empathy, acceptance, and 'non-possessive warmth', which remains critical (Smith 2004 and 2006). These are the features that have an ineffable quality and belong to a different order of tasks to those which the service currently measures within its target culture. However, those aspects of the job I have just described that lie beyond (are *other* than) mathematical computation make a major contribution to the assessment process of offenders (what have you done, why have you done it, what can we do about it), which in turn makes an important contribution to risk assessment and public protection. It seems to me that ministers, civil servants and senior managers have lost sight of this in their pursuit of more bureaucratic forms of accountability. In other words, key elements of professionalism have been eclipsed by bureaucratic demands as the pursuit of targets becomes an end in itself.

This point can be taken to another analytical level by saying that those features that lie beyond targets and measurement sit more easily within a social work model of organisation than the principles associated with New Public Management, endorsed by Gilpin-Black during the 1980s (Whitehead and Statham 2006 p128), which applied private sector managerial and business solutions to the public sector. If a people-oriented organisation is reduced to a set of quantifiable and measurable targets to improve performance and accountability, much that can be considered of meaning and value will be omitted. One way forward is to acknowledge the case that can be made for a better balance between quantity and quality, outputs and outcomes, broad objectives and precise targets, the obvious and more ineffable features of organisational life. Neither staff nor offenders should be reduced to working within a positivist or economic paradigm that draws attention solely to quantity, number, weights and measures, targets and outputs, precisely because of what is left out. Probation work is about people working with people, 'how' to do the job as well as 'what' should be done, expression of values, and sometimes being with people rather than doing things with numbers. Unfortunately, targets are currently the scaffolding wrapped tightly around the organisation, trapping all those inside, thus impoverishing its cultural inheritance. If the development of objectives and targets in probation is a significant illustration of cultural change, at this point I want to consider a second dimension. This is the new penological context of risk.

The new penology and risk

Malcolm Feeley and Jonathan Simon identified the phenomenon of what they call the 'new penology' that surfaced in the early 1990s (1994; see Henry and Einstadter 1998 p451). Some of the features of the new penology can be summarised as the transition from rehabilitation and treatment to a language of probability and risk. Additionally, there is a move away from ideals and values associated with people, towards managerial, technocratic and bureaucratic procedures. From individual assessment to 'techniques to identify, classify, and manage groupings sorted by dangerousness (risk of re-offending and harm). The task is managerial, not transformative' and also regulative. This constitutes a critical shift from person centred and qualitative work to a system of risk assessment, creating statistical tables, and the language of aggregates, probabilities, quantification and actuarialism. Therefore

> 'The new penology is neither about punishing nor about rehabilitating individuals. It is about identifying and managing unruly groups. It is concerned with the rationality not of individual behaviour or even community organisation, but of managerial processes. Its goal is not to eliminate crime but to make it tolerable enough through systemic coordination' (Henry and Einstadter 1998 p455).

Feeley and Simon exaggerate the transformation they describe, and do not do justice to the ongoing penchant for punishment, but there is an element of truth in their analysis.

There is an echo of this position in the concluding chapter of David Garland's book on *Punishment and Welfare* in which he says that the penal-welfare system no longer reforms, remoulds, or improves the lives of clients. Nor does the criminal justice system successfully stop people from offending because it is the normative forms of socialisation and community integration that do that. Rather the penal-welfare strategy derives its 'success' from its 'ability to administer and manage criminality in an efficient and extensive manner, while portraying that process in terms which make it acceptable to the public and penal agents alike' (Garland 1985 p260). However, since this book was published criminality has been conflated with talk about risk, which is illustrative of the new culture of probation.

Risk

The political and criminal justice context, within which probation work is undertaken in the first decade of the third millennium, is characterised by a number of interrelated themes which can be reiterated as: seriousness, dangerousness, public protection; punishment in community and prison, onerous enforcement and benefit sanction (the latter in selected areas); central control and more bureaucratically managed area services; the legal context of the Criminal Justice Act 2003; risk of re-offending and gradations of harm. The current preoccupation with risk has grown in significance since the 1990s. This category is associated with the transition from the period of penal modernity (eighteenth-century Enlightenment to the 1970s) to a late or post-modern society (Giddens 1991; Beck 1992; Kumar 1995; Hudson 2003a; Mythen 2004). It can be suggested that the cultural changes of the 1960s, followed by the crisis of capitalism of the 1970s, have created a more economically insecure world, a more risky environment in which to live. Against this background can be situated a criminal justice system increasingly concerned with reducing the risk certain individuals pose in relation to self harm, property, and of course physical harm to other people through offending behaviour. This confirms that one of the major shifts in practice has been from working with individuals within a framework of social work and rehabilitation (understanding the past); to managing, containing and controlling categories of risk (managing the future); from working with what people have already done to what they *might* do.

Tools for assessing risk – OASys and OGRS

Since the creation of the National Probation Service in 2001, probation services have used OASys, initially the paper version prior to computerisation, which combines clinical and actuarial approaches to collect information, assess, and then make judgments about offender needs, risk of re-offending and harm. Kemshall informs us that actuarial risk tools are rooted in statistical computations of probability from as early as the eighteenth century (2003 p28). She proceeds to clarify that 'Actuarial risk, or the calculation of risk probabilities derived from statistical models based on aggregate populations, was extended to numerous areas of social and commercial life throughout the twentieth century' (p5). In probation, actuarial tools are used to compute statistically the probability of offending. They predict an 'individual's likely behaviour from the behaviour of others in similar circumstances, or predicting risk on the basis of an individual's similarity to others who have proved to be risky in the past' (p65). Hudson contributes to this discussion by saying that 'The calculation of probabilities of risks being realised, used in insurance, applied to forms of contemporary penology which use similar factorial calculations rather than individual diagnostic and assessment techniques' (2003b p193). In both theory and practice, clinical judgment and actuarial tools combine in OASys to allow an assessment which:

- Enables the worker to produce information on criminogenic needs and on the risk of re-offending and harm in relation to low, medium, high and very high categories.

- Draws attention to issues such as domestic violence, public protection, child protection, sex and violence, and Schedule 1 offenders which precipitate internal decisions on risk management (via multi-agency risk management meetings (MARMM) and multi-agency public protection arrangement procedures (MAPPA)).

- Indicates the most efficient use of resources.

- Allows targeted interventions.

- Enables allocation to accredited programmes.

- Helps tiering decisions – that is, which grade of staff supervises which offender category in relation to needs and risks.

Furthermore, the OASys instrument contains within it the Offender Group Reconviction Scale tool (OGRS) which uses previous convictions data to produce a likelihood of reconviction percentage score. A clear distinction must be drawn between an OGRS score generated by the computer and previously aggregated data used to compute the probability of reconviction for a specific individual. In practice this means that if the OGRS score allocated to an individual is, for illustrative purposes, 40 per cent, then 40 out of 100 conforming to a certain profile were reconvicted. The 40 per cent score does not unambiguously inform us whether the individual the probation officer is working with is in fact destined to re-offend, what the possibility of change might be or whether the individual has in fact decided to eschew offending in future. The figure deals in probabilities not certainties; we do not know how, why, when, or even if the individual will re-offend.

Consequently, there is a danger of investing actuarial tools with a form of knowledge they do not possess and ascribing a weight that should not be attached. It is therefore questionable whether OASys/OGRS tools are more accurate than previous clinical and professional judgments when the adage 'the best predictor of future offending is past behaviour' was the professional rule of thumb. While such tools draw attention in a more systematic and detailed manner to areas of need, in addition to indicators of risk of re-offending and harm, the status of the information provided to practitioners should be clarified. It should be emphasised that whatever tools are employed, regardless of their sophistication a) they do not provide certain, unambiguous, 'scientific' knowledge in the sense of establishing predictive and invariant laws of human behaviour and b) there is no substitute for the professional assessment and judgment of the officer based upon time spent in face to face contact with the client, in addition to the application of social work knowledge, skill and understanding. Applying the methods of natural science to the social world is problematic primarily because human beings, including those who offend, are unpredictable (Smith 2004).

When working with people in people-based organisations, the following points are self evident:

- Attention should be directed towards specific individuals rather than aggregates.

- The possibility of contingency, choice, unpredictability and surprise should be left open.

- The computer and generation of numbers should not be invested with an efficacy they do not and never can have.

- The possibility of individual change regardless of statistical prediction; the danger of over-prediction in the sense that the tool is somehow establishing a fixed law to which the person will conform.

- The inherent danger of using statistical data to label and fix the essence of a person based on a specific risk category.

As Oldfield helpfully comments:

'Welfarism's approach to social problems such as crime was retrospectively oriented, seeking to understand the circumstances and events from which such behaviour emerged – in contrast to contemporary concerns with prospective knowledge which seeks to identify groups whose future behaviour *may* pose some form of risk' (2002 p46).

This is illustrative of the cultural changes considered in this chapter, the implications of which should be handled with great care. At this stage I want to proceed deeper into the concept of risk.

Artefact and constructivist approaches to risk

The artefact approach to risk can be elucidated as follows (see Kemshall 2003 for detailed discussion; Mythen 2004 p97). Crime can be approached as an object or thing in the world, a naturally occurring phenomenon existing outside the mind of and independently from the observer, thus allowing theory-neutral and value-free judgments to be made. Similarly, one approach to risk is that it has an objective quality, is a thing or artefact out there in the world, with physical attributes, existing separately from and independently of the person making judgments about it. In other words, it is something about which we can produce certain knowledge within a scientific, positivist paradigm. On this basis, it is considered the probation officer is able to assess risk accurately, quantify and measure it, with a view to allocating the offender to a specific risk category – low, medium, high, very high. Within this artefact and positivist paradigm risk, like crime, is a quality that inherently belongs to the offender about which an objective assessment can be made. This is the objectivist and realist position explicated by Mythen (2004) and it encourages the view that it is possible to produce an unambiguous form of scientifically derived knowledge.

When we turn to the constructivist approach, rather than crime and risk being approached as an objective thing *out there* in the world, they are understood instead as socially constructed phenomena (not so much object as product). Within a post-Kantian orientated epistemological perspective it is considered that the mind of the observer (in this case the probation officer) is involved in constructing reality, rather than objectively providing an unmediated description of phenomena. This is the relativist approach of Mythen (2004), which means that political processes, media manipulation, cultural features, and the vagaries of subjective individual interpretation, all have a bearing on how one thinks about, constructs, and makes judgements about risk. Mythen says that this perspective articulates the position that risk is not an artefact that can be 'meaningfully objectivised' (p97). In other words, we are dealing with a complex phenomenon riddled with uncertainty, ambiguity, and subjective interpretations, compared with the objectivist claims made by the positivist operating within a 'scientific' paradigm.

Therefore the constructivist approach (to knowledge and reality) injects a note of caution into our thinking, assessments, judgments, decisions, and claims to provide factual knowledge of crime and risk; to describe accurately phenomena that are considered to be un-problematically 'outside' of and separate from us. It draws attention to the social construction of certain categories labelled with a view, it could be reasoned, to serving political, bureaucratic, and managerial ends. It continues to situate crime and risk within the person. The political and organisational implications of this approach; the manipulation of reality for political purposes, and the attendant problem of over prediction and establishing invariant laws risk inflation, because the probation officer does not want to take any risk with risks in the current political climate.

Locating risk in the individual

We also need to be aware of the danger of regarding risk as something that should be primarily located within the person, as something for which the individual is personally responsible. Within this conceptualisation, crime is basically a problem for the criminal, in the same way as poverty is the problem of the poor, and risks the problem for the risky individual. In other words, the phenomena of crime, poverty and risk are ontologically rooted and fixed in the person, belonging to the essence of the individual, rather than located within a wider social, economic and cultural context that creates the framework for a discussion on risk. While it is possible to advance the view that people make themselves, that they are responsible for their own lives, it should be stated with equal force that they do not do this in circumstances of their own choosing (Marxist perspective). Probation officers working within the more deprived areas of the country should be able to provide ample anecdotal evidence to support this view.

The circumstances within which the probation service operates during the first decade of the third millennium are discernibly different to only a few years ago, as illustrated by two contrasting pictures and the prominence given to targets and risk as dimensions of profound cultural shifts. Against the background of the decline of the rehabilitative ideal during the 1970s, the policy of alternatives to custody in the 1980s; and transition from 'an alternative to punishment to an alternative form of punishment' (Hudson 2003b p154) that gathered pace in the 1990s, one of the current preoccupations is with risk assessment and the management of risk of re-offending and harm. Hudson comments that individual offenders have become data constructs and 'collections of items of statistical data, occupants of statistical categories, rather than unique human beings' (2003b p159). Profound cultural change indeed.

Summary and conclusion
From the legislative beginnings of the system in 1907 until the early 1980s, the primary basis of the probation system was the relationship between officers and probationers (Home Office 1909; Home Office 1938; Home Office 1962; Whitehead 1990). The ideology of probation work may have changed from dominant religious influences to a more secular and 'scientific' form of treatment to achieve rehabilitation, but the *modus operandi* remained constant – personal one-to-one contact between officer and client at court, office and home. These human contacts afforded an opportunity for the officers to use their personal influence, mediated as the system developed through a professional relationship, encapsulated in the ethics of advise, assist and befriend. Over many decades the evolving organisation kept the accoutrements of bureaucracy, record keeping and statistics (actuarialism) to a minimum, primarily because of the person focused nature of its mission to prevent re-offending and protect the public on behalf of the state. People skills are fundamentally important in organisations that work with people. This is stating the obvious but nevertheless is sometimes worth stating because probation, in its politicised, modernised, and bureaucratised manifestation, has noticeably strayed from this ideal. Most people who join the organisation want to

spend as much time as possible with offenders. This is the job to which they are committed and there is a basic assumption – which can hardly be contested – that you cannot help, support and engage with people in a process of change, sitting in front of a machine. Unfortunately current political priorities (developing rapidly since 1997), quantitative notions of accountability, and organisational structures do not support a people orientated *modus operandi* or ideology. Against the background of the slow decline of the rehabilitative ideal from the 1970s, the emergence of alternatives to the custody agenda in the 1980s, and the rise of punishment in the community in the 1990s, the service has become more target-driven and risk focused, thus presaging the transformation of a people-focused culture into something profoundly different.

Kemshall (2003 p143) draws attention to the following features of the contemporary criminal justice system which help to locate probation within a wider context of change:

- Managing offenders through risk tools.

- Greater accountability through central political control and local area bureaucratic systems.

- More emphasis on offender personal responsibility than understanding (the difference between welfare and neo-liberalism paradigms) (Oldfield 2002).

- Detachment from social theorising yet the system continues to talk about need.

- Contestability within NOMS and mixed economy provision.

- Context of insecurity, risk, anxiety and danger.

- Harsher penal climate, punishment, prison, exclusion, enforcement and benefit sanction.

- De-professionalisation through lack of trust in staff (O'Neill 2002) and people skills being eroded.

- More concerned with the efficient functioning of bureaucratic systems than working with and understanding people.

Within this modernised criminal justice framework, the following shifts of emphasis are pertinent indicators of significant cultural transformations:

From	*To*
People	Computers
Language	Numbers
Profession	Business
Qualitative	Quantitative
Social features	Economics
Supervision	Audits
Old Public Management	New Public Management
Why and how	What
Underlying issues	Presenting problems
Understanding	Management
Problems rooted in past	Predict and control future risks

Consequently, the ideological and ethical transformation of probation is well under way within a modernised culture encapsulated by the term *bureaucratic positivism*, as opposed to a social work service to the courts. It is bureaucratic in the way the service under the National Offender Management Service relies increasingly upon systems, procedures, processes, mechanisation, technology, rules and regulations, including centrally determined standards in a business orientated organisation infused with New Public Management (NPM) principles. Positivism, a term which encapsulates a greater reliance upon numbers, statistical calculation, and mathematical categorisation (tiering of offenders according to risk and harm), denotes measurable targets within a more 'scientific' and routinised working environment.

Numbers have been employed to create a more 'scientific', quantifiable and measurable organisation, by reducing the role played by qualitative and ineffable features associated with people work. Numbers have been used to establish a more predictable and certain world, a greater sense of order and control, based upon a different and attenuated approach to accountability. Additionally, when applied to people organisations, numbers associated with measurable targets create a different rationality; they change the culture of an organisation by introducing different ways of thinking about the job, i.e. from people to business mentality. Rose makes the point when exploring the function of numbers that

'Quantification standardises the object, but it also standardises the subject of measurement: the act of exchange is no longer dependent on the personalities or statuses of those involved...The officials who use these statistical and calculative methods are themselves constrained by the calculative apparatus they use' (1999 p207).

This statement resonates deeply with the nature of modernised probation work in its centenary year.

Furthermore, the differences between the two pictures contrasted above can be articulated in terms of different frames of reference, conceptual grids and linguistic formats, the wearing of different lenses, by and through which staff make sense of and interpret the probation world. This is an echo of the philosophical position, to be explored in Chapter 4, that all of us are subjectively involved in constructing the world, shaping reality, as opposed to responding to and describing what is deemed to be objectively 'there' outside ourselves. It can be argued that, since 1876, the client/ offender has been constructed in different ways during different periods, and that until the late 1980s the probation officer, as social worker of the courts, constructed clients through a social work orientated lens. This lens comprised numerous layers and coatings – values, personalism, ethics – which I would argue were conducive to building an understanding of the individual. However the lens has been politically re-ground and new coatings added, with more opaque tints; frames of reference reshaped; the conceptual grid reconfigured and new nomenclature introduced. The result for the foreseeable future is that clients are being constructed in a way less conducive to the notion of working with and understanding the person. Probation practices constructed according to politically reordered priorities, new organisational structures, cultural impacts on the back of computerisation, regime of targets and risk categorisation, have implications for offenders as well as staff.

NOTES

[1] As one of the authors of *The History of Probation* (Whitehead and Statham 2006), it is fitting that I should acknowledge the thorough critique produced by Bill Weston during the summer of 2006. I am particularly grateful for his comments on and interpretation of the religious roots of the probation system. Weston confirms the influence of religion, the temperance movement, and humane values. I do not accept every point made in the critique, but his comments have been assimilated.

[2] Fred Jarvis OBE was for many years the Chief Probation Officer of the Leicestershire probation service. He is the author of Jarvis' Probation Officer's Manual which was an authoritative guide to probation practice for many years. The last edition of the manual was produced under the editorship of Bill Weston in 1987.

[3] NICH is an acronym for Northtown Interventions Clearing House (changed slightly from the original out of respect for colleagues). Against the background of the introduction of central government targets, specifically cash-linked targets, it is perhaps understandable that organisational exigencies required a mechanism for ensuring their achievement. Therefore what this means for day-to-day practice in one specific probation area is that probation officers, when writing court reports and arriving at a sentencing proposal, must contact the NICH unit to mediate the most appropriate proposal for inclusion in the conclusion of the report. It should be acknowledged that this development raises important professional issues in that it arguably undermines the autonomy, discretion, responsibility, and professional judgment of the probation officer. I am led to understand that such a unit is not located in every probation service throughout the country.

[4] I want to include an explanatory note on the way in which part of this chapter has had recourse on numerous occasions to the personal pronoun 'I'. There are those colleagues who would argue that in a book of this nature the pronoun 'I' should not appear, on the grounds that it detracts from ensuring academic respectability. In other words it makes it too personal and therefore not sufficiently academically dispassionate. I accept the principle but do not always apply it, particularly when trying to articulate my own experiences of probation work I have been involved in since the 1970s. I have no wish to offend the sensibilities of colleagues and so hope this explanation will suffice. I acknowledge that my experiences of probation work and conclusions extrapolated in this book may not be shared by all readers.

[5] A moment's reflection on different historical periods, resonant with our theme, can be included here. In the sixteenth century it can be argued

that the dissolution of the monasteries constituted a religious, artistic and cultural disaster, as assets were stripped and used for other purposes. A culture which had taken over 500 years to assemble was practically wiped out between 1538 and 1541. Next, in the eighteenth century, as I explain in the main text, the industrial revolution transformed society as the new system of capitalist production, associated with the arrival of the machine age, replaced the traditional skills and crafts of hand loom weavers. Resistance was located in the Luddites. The last two decades of the twentieth century have witnessed many changes in the probation service. Furthermore, and significantly, the culture has been transformed from a people orientated mission to a machine-based, number dependent and computerised bureaucracy, not within a generation but in less than five years.

6   The modernised target culture of probation has various manifestations: nationally determined high priority and medium priority targets; national targets are then translated into local area service targets; regional offender management (ROM) targets; also local criminal justice board targets and priorities. Each of the area probation services produces its own business plan which sets out in detail the targets which must be achieved.

Chapter 3

CRIMINOLOGICAL EXPLANATIONS: A PRACTITIONER JOURNEY TOWARDS UNDERSTANDING PEOPLE WHO OFFEND

'The idea that there could be any one all-encompassing theoretical explanation of crime has been shown to be absurd. Delinquent activities are too varied and too widespread in society for it to be sensible to even contemplate a single explanation. One might just as well attempt to provide a single mechanism for running, for unhappiness or for poverty.' (Rutter and Giller 1983 p266)

'Theorising about the nature of crime and criminal behaviour and its connections with changing social structures, institutions and cultures should always be regarded as fundamental to the development of our subject.' (Sir Leon Radzinowicz 1999 p457)

'But if you're asking me to arrest this fellow, it might help to have a clue to his motive. Anson disliked this sort of question, which in his view was nowadays asked far too frequently in police work. There was a passion for delving into the mind of the criminal. What you did was catch a fellow, arrest him, charge him, and get him sent away for a few years, the more the merrier. It was of little interest to probe the mental functionings of a malefactor as he discharged his pistol or smashed in your window.' (Julian Barnes 2005 p90)

Introduction

This chapter explores a number of issues that have a criminological theme and broadens the context within which offending behaviour should be addressed and understood. Consequently, there are points of interest, particularly for practitioners, to consider. The structure of this chapter is as follows:

a) A summary of the central tenets of criminological theories with a view to clarifying some of the better known explanatory frameworks that are available for probation staff when working with offenders.

It should be made clear that in this section I am dealing with broad themes and if some are given less attention than others it does not mean they are insignificant.

b) A preliminary sketch containing a number of elements which arguably combine to establish a framework of understanding for practitioners undertaking probation work.

c) A brief summary of factors currently militating against promoting a context of understanding, which have implications for the nature of probation practice.

Criminological theory – an overview

Since 1907, the probation system has drawn on a number of disciplines which have attempted to facilitate an explanation and therefore understanding of human behaviour. These disciplines have their roots in the emerging social sciences of the nineteenth century, namely psychology, sociology, and of course criminology. Where the latter is concerned Ferri, according to Radzinowicz, said it was a 'barbaric term joining a Latin word to a Greek one' (1999 p440; Garland 1985 on how criminology was a response, amongst others, to the crisis towards the end of the nineteenth century). It may be recalled that Comte advanced the view that human knowledge had passed through various stages of development – theological, metaphysical, then positive – and that, during the nineteenth century, positive science was seen as the paradigm of valid knowledge, thus holding out the prospect of solutions to human and social problems (Giddens 1974; Bryant 1985). Giddens says that, within the emerging discipline of sociology, positivism was premised upon 'the assertion that the concepts and methods employed in natural sciences can be applied to form a 'science of man', or a 'natural science of society' (1974 p3). The social realm was considered to have a reality independent of the individual observer; the collection of 'facts' was based upon empirical observation (induction) as the basis for establishing predictive laws; sociology and criminology proceeded on a theory-neutral and value-free basis. Therefore it is possible to draw an empirical and positivist line of development in the social sciences, primarily within sociology, through Montesquieu, Condorcet, Comte and Durkheim (beginning with Francis Bacon in the sixteenth and seventeenth centuries. See Chapter 4 for further information). Subsequently we encounter Lombroso, Ferri, and Garofalo within the discipline of positivist criminology which challenged the earlier classical paradigm of the eighteenth and early nineteenth centuries.

When turning our attention to the subject matter of criminology, it is interesting to speculate on the degree to which probation practitioners are influenced in their work with individual offenders by the rich body of criminological theories, particularly in light of all the cultural changes since the 1980s. Are practitioners conscious of bringing to their work, and then directly applying, a specific theoretical paradigm? This question matters because an attachment to one perspective rather than another affects one's view of the offender, whether the label 'offender' should in fact be applied to certain forms of behaviour and how behaviour is responded to and dealt with in the criminal justice system. In other words, the selection and application of either a classical, neo-classical, or positivist paradigm has profound implications for the type of questions that will be posed and of course the answers generated (White and Haines 2004 p11), as well as how information is collected and assessed, then used and shaped to formulate judgments and make decisions about an individual's behaviour. This has practical implications and not a little importance for the provision of information contained in fast delivery and standard delivery reports for magistrates and judges, and the relationship between the presentation of information and one's understanding of criminal and social justice. Jock Young (1999 p32) explains that the two central paradigms within the discipline of criminology, classicism and positivism, are the legacy of the eighteenth century Enlightenment and the positivist-scientific developments associated with the nineteenth century.

Within the probation services, the perspective which provides the working ideology of the practitioner is of more than academic interest because, on the one hand, it provides a range of concepts clustered around the offender as rational calculator, imbued with freedom and neo-liberal responsibility, rationally calculating the costs and benefits of certain forms of action according to some utilitarian calculus within conditions of freedom. On the other hand, a very different set of ideas associated with the later nineteenth and most of the twentieth century advocated the born criminal, determined behaviour, aetiology, intervention and correctionalism. This was the context more conducive to the development of probation. With these general comments in mind, this chapter turns to address in more detail the classical and positivist perspectives, prior to looking at some of the major criminological theories that have dominated the twentieth century. This task is not undertaken from the standpoint of the detached theoretical observer, but rather because of the practical implications for probation staff, and possibly other organisations, within the NOMS contestability framework, in their interpretation of the lives of, and work with, individual offenders during the next few years.

Classicism from the eighteenth-century Enlightenment

Against the background of demonic, religious, spiritualist, and therefore what may now be deemed to be unenlightened, accounts of behaviours categorised as criminal during the Middle Ages, a different approach to crime and criminal justice emerged during the eighteenth century. This more rational approach is known as classicism, associated with Cesare Beccaria (1738–1794; see Bellamy 1995), Carrara, and Jeremy Bentham (1748–1832: see Garland 1997; Lilly, Cullen and Ball 2002; White and Haines 2004). Classicism is associated with the emergence of a more enlightened and secular age during the eighteenth century (the Age of Reason) which brought about the creation of the 'modern' world that spanned the 1700s to the 1970s. This notion of the modern is a construction formulated in response to a previously religious as opposed to emerging secular and scientific world view, which included the dominant influence of the church over people's lives, too much respect for authority, deference, tradition, revealed truths and metaphysical explanations. By contrast, from the eighteenth century we see the development of an alternative set of ideas associated with reason, science, progress, secularism, liberalism, individualism and man's coming of age as a rational being manifested in a more self-directed than God-controlled life. In fact, Morrison comments in his expansive criminological text that 'Modernity is a complex structure with interacting processes which have different effects creating a range of conflicts, implications and legacies' (1995 p27; see also Porter 2001). Moreover, the divine right of kings was challenged; the legitimacy of the exercise of political power and authority was premised more on consent; and punishment and criminal justice were considered badly in need of reform.

Within this context, the classical school is recognised by its adherence to a number of propositions which have enjoyed a renaissance since the 1980s. The central tenets of these are:

- Human beings are endowed with free will, rationality and reason, which enables them to choose how they will behave.

- A focus on the crime committed rather than the motivation or inner dispositions of the person committing it.

- Human beings rationally calculate the costs and benefits of their actions.

- Punishment should deter and outweigh the benefits derived from crime.

In fact these were the views expressed by Beccaria in *On Crimes and Punishment* which articulated his new model for a reformed criminal justice system. Furthermore it is important to refer to the wider political context of social contract theory and utilitarianism within which the tenets of classical criminology can be located (Garland 1985).

When individuals come together to form society, the theory is that they have to trade a measure of individual liberty/rights to create conditions conducive to a peaceful, harmonious and consensual existence. This is what makes civilisation a possibility. Against the background of the divine rule of kings, which had been challenged by the civil war in England, the consent of the people was required for legitimate rule. In such circumstances the state is endowed with the responsibility to ensure harmony and security through a system of laws and punishments, without which the social realm could not function.[1] To establish and maintain society, individuals are bound to keep the laws, which permit certain forms of behaviour while proscribing others. All people are equal under the law and, as rational beings, give their consent freely to abide by it. However, for those who make a rational decision to break the law at the heart of the social contract, a system of punishments exists to deal with infractions through the operation of the criminal justice system. As White and Haines clarify: 'The criminal law reflects a social contract between individuals and the state, a contract that is based upon a rational exchange of rights and obligations' (2004 p29). According to Beccaria, punishment should not be orientated towards retribution or vengeance, but rather utilitarianism which means it should promote and increase the sum total of human happiness in society. Therefore there are elements of reform, incapacitation and general deterrence to control and prevent crime.[2]

It is possible to be more expansive by introducing the work of George Sabine, who explains that it was the spirit of the American and French revolutions in 1776 and 1789 respectively which embodied ideals that found expression in the nineteenth century, for example civil liberties and the freedom to think for oneself. Sabine says that the middle classes were in the vanguard of nineteenth-century liberal reforms, such as the modernisation of administration, improvements in legal procedure, the reorganisation of the courts and factory inspections. What is more, 'its philosophy tended to become utilitarian instead of revolutionary' (1951 p563). When elucidating the doctrine of utilitarianism, Sabine (p566) says that the social philosophy of the Philosophical Radicals was a programme of legal, economic and political reforms premised upon the principle of the greatest happiness of the greatest number (see also Copleston 2003 Volume 8 on utilitarianism). In other words, the measure of what is right and wrong is determined by whether an action promotes happiness or pain. It was Jeremy Bentham (within a tradition including Joseph Priestley, Helvetius, Beccaria and Hume) who believed that the individual rationally calculated the amount of pleasure and pain that would follow a particular action. This is the individual constructed as rational actor (Hopkins Burke 2005), involved in computing whether or not to engage in criminal activities. So pleasure and pain provide 'not only the standard of value needed for a 'censorial' jurisprudence but also the causes of human behaviour by which the skilful legislator can control and direct it' (Sabine 1951 p569). Consequently, the system of criminal law found in Bentham is characterised by:

- The principle of utility as a method of arriving at a rational theory of punishment designed to control human behaviour.

- However, punishment is always evil because it inflicts pain.

- Punishment can only be justified if it prevents a greater future evil (deterrence) or repairs evil already committed.

- Crimes must be classified in terms of injuries caused and the punishment must fit the crime.

- The pain occasioned by punishment must exceed the profit gained by the offence, but it must exceed as little as possible so as not to cause unnecessary suffering (Sabine 1951 p572).

Radzinowicz makes it clear that it was Beccaria, prior to Bentham, who wanted to establish a system of law that eradicated the many abuses associated with the *ancien regime*. In fact, Beccaria's 'unique achievement was to express, in the most coherent and concentrated form, that whole new conception of criminal justice emerging from the ideas of the Enlightenment and the growing force of liberalism' (Radzinowicz 1966 p8). Radzinowicz then proceeds to enumerate and explain the 12 tenets of the liberal doctrine of law.[3] It was Bentham who later applied Beccaria's ideas to the British situation (Morrison 1995 p74). Both Beccaria and Bentham wanted to eliminate the savage and arbitrary punishments of the pre-Enlightenment period, but Bob Roshier (1989) clarifies that Beccaria was more humanitarian than Bentham, who was more concerned about the rational efficiency of the criminal justice system. Moreover,

Carrara (Radzinowicz 1999) eschewed moral, psychological, and social investigations of offenders because of the primacy of the rule of law. It is law, under which it is considered that all human beings are equal, that defines criminal behaviour. If crimes are committed then punishment will follow and expiation, deterrence (including retribution – see Note 2 at the end of this chapter), could all be the by-products of the criminal justice system.

Roshier helps to bridge the transition from classicism through neo-classicism to positivism as he provides the following summary that contrasts the two positions in their explanations of offending:

a) classicism is marked by freedom, rationality and manipulability; positivism by determinism, differentiation and pathology. According to positivism, behaviour is determined and caused by biological, psychological and social factors. There is something quantifiably and measurably different about offenders compared with non-offenders because there is something identifiably wrong with the former (specific characteristics).

b) Classical thinking reflects the political, social and economic context of the eighteenth century age of reason, social contract, rationality and utilitarian thinking. Nineteenth century positivism reflects a different political, social and economic context, the culmination of change at different levels within society during the 1880s and 1890s (Garland 1985). This includes developments in social science and positivism.

c) Both classicism and positivism want to control and correct, one by an approach grounded in law, punishment and deterrence 'by appeals or threats made to free, rational, choice-making individuals' (Roshier 1989 p50); the other by reform, rehabilitation, treatment and welfare, that involves addressing underlying factors deemed to cause crime (same outcomes by different routes). When concluding this section, Radzinowicz states that the classical perspectives of Bentham, Beccaria and Carrara provided an incomplete platform for criminological theorising. Subsequently, classicism was modified by positivism when the notion of crime as a 'juridical entity', equality under the law and equal punishments, admitted the possibility of a range of individual and social factors influencing human behaviour (1999 p10).

Positivism from the nineteenth century

Towards the end of the nineteenth century, the tenets of classicism were challenged by Cesare Lombroso (1835–1909), Raffaele Garofalo (1852–1934) and Enrico Ferri (1856–1929: see Radzinowicz 1999 first chapter). These are the three thinkers of the Italian school who spearheaded a very different perspective to the one just considered. Positivism constitutes a more scientific approach to crime and operates with a set of ideas very different to those of classicism. It is interesting to observe that positivist criminology was considered to be a response (one of many) to the political, social and penal crisis of the 1880s which focused on the political priority to manage, contain and control working class offenders more legitimately than the previous paradigm, and included concerns over the Victorian prison (Garland 1985). In broad terms the main tenets are: application of scientific methods (induction) to create knowledge of the offender; empirical rather than deductive methods; determinism – people not responsible for their actions; concern with aetiology (from what has happened to why it has happened); the search for the criminal man/type; focus not on the offence and its consequences but the characteristics of the offender. This resulted in an approach more orientated towards reform, rehabilitation, treatment and correction, than punishment. According to the proponents of the Italian school, the notion of criminal responsibility and therefore punishment should be eliminated (Radzinowicz 1999 p10). Furthermore, the 'emphasis of positivism is on the scientist as neutral observer with the task of uncovering natural laws that regulate human behaviour, including criminal offending' (White and Haines 2004 p55). The influence of the founding fathers of the positivist school of criminology, and those who continued to work in this tradition in the twentieth century, means that it is helpful to provide the following vignettes.

Lombroso

'His general theory suggested that criminals are distinguished from non-criminals by the manifestation of multiple physical anomalies which are of atavistic or degenerative origin', says Wolfgang in his instructive essay on Lombroso (in Mannheim 1972 p246–247). Lombroso was indebted to a number of precursors who anticipated the relationship between the offender's behaviour and physical and mental features (Horn 2003). When summarising the many influences at work on Lombroso, Wolfgang draws attention to German materialism and the search for objective facts, Comtean positivism and emphasis on social facts and Darwinian biological evolutionary theory, extended to the social evolution of Herbert Spencer. In *L'Uomo Delinquente* (criminal man), first published in 1876 – also the year of the first police court missionary – Lombroso explained the sequence of events that led him to express an interest in crime. The sequence was the observation of tattooed soldiers when he worked as a physician in the Italian army; the application of physical measurement in his work; the extension of physical and physiological techniques to criminals; and the study of criminals compared to 'normal' individuals and the insane. Although Lombroso focused on atavism (the criminal as a reversion to a primitive or subhuman type, a subspecies different to the law-abiding), hence the concentration on biological positivism, he did not neglect the influence of the social environment. Subsequently, it was the Lombrosian framework of biological positivism that influenced Henry Maudsley (1835–1918); Goring (1913; also Mannheim 1972) and the way criminal behaviour is inherited, manifested as less intelligence and less stature; E. A. Hooton (1939) in that crime is associated with constitutional factors and inferior biological organisms; W. Sheldon (1949) and the link between crime and body type – the mesomorph delinquent (Mannheim 1972); Glueck and Glueck (1950) supported Sheldon. Within the tradition of biological positivism we can also refer to genetic abnormalities as in faulty chromosomes XYY, low intelligence, and biochemical factors (Pond 1999). It was Garofalo who rejected the classical position of moral responsibility, free will and associated deterrence. Crime was something organic and innate.

Ferri

Ferri studied with Lombroso in Turin in 1880 and coined the term 'born criminal'. He was committed, as a positivist, to the experimental and inductive method – the empirical and 'objectivist' route to knowledge. Ferri operated with the following five-fold classification: the born criminal; insane; passional (emotion); occasional and product of family and social milieu; habitual. The scientific method melded with the primacy of social defence against the criminal, but it should be acknowledged that for Ferri crime was the result of a combination of individual, physical and social factors. For the Italian School, including Ferri, 'The classification of criminals into certain empirically proved categories and according to their state of danger, also empirically assessed, were the two basic elements which formed the core of the positivist criminal policy' (Radzinowicz 1999 p15).

In addition to the tradition of biological positivism, it is important to consider psychological positivism associated with Eysenck's personality traits (1970); psychoanalytic theory and Freud's association of crime with inner disturbances, mental illness and a weak super-ego (conscience) that results in the acting out of unconscious intra-psychic factors; Healy and Bronner (1936); the Cambridge study of delinquency with West and Farrington (West 1982); Bowlby and maternal deprivation (1971 and 1975); and the importance of early childhood experiences associated with a lack of adequate socialisation in shaping future conduct. Consequently, if biological positivism locates crime in the body, psychological positivism draws attention to the mind and faulty personality development. It should be emphasised that an individual rather than social paradigm was at work, although not exclusively so, for much of the nineteenth century. This is explained well from the standpoint of the Victorian social-problem novel when Josephine Guy argues that, within the context of the classical political economy, the concept of the social was derived from autonomous and self interested individuals. In other words 'It was the 'laws' or 'principles' of human nature which permitted an understanding of the social, rather than the other way round' (Guy 1996 p80).

It is also interesting to acknowledge the existence of a more sociological orientation (in fact before the emergence of the Italian School) during the nineteenth and into the twentieth century at a time of rapid social change (Lilly, Cullen and Ball 2002 p31). This marks the shift from the individual as the unit of analysis, with the emphasis on individual pathology, to crime as a social product. This is the tradition that articulates the view that the locus of crime has its origins in the social and is therefore generated in conditions that have an independent existence from the individual (the social as a distinct reality). We encounter this sociological orientation in the work of Marx, and also the sociological positivism associated with Durkheim. Guerry and Quetelet suggest that crime was a regular activity within certain social arrangements. At the end of the nineteenth century Booth in London and Rowntree in York demonstrated that poverty was structural as opposed to caused by dysfunctional individuals (Abrams 1968). The Chicago School resumed the social, rather than individual, approach to understanding offending behaviour.

The social
It was in the city of Chicago during the 1920s and 1930s that attention was drawn to crime as a social rather than individual phenomenon. Conditions

within a particular area of the city, the zone of transition, were conducive to criminality and pathology. Notwithstanding changing populations, something distinctive within this zone, such as lack of integration and moral relativism, produced crime, according to Burgess, Shaw and McKay (Smith 1988). Consequently, social factors and social organisation became explanatory principles which led Henry and Einstadter to ask 'How could individual explanations account for some neighbourhoods having high rates and others not or how could some areas remain crime-prone despite population changes?' (1998 p130; see Bottoms and Wiles 2002 on environmental criminology and work in Sheffield).

While an analysis of the city drew attention to social factors rather than individual abnormality as the unit of analysis, it was Robert Merton in the 1930s who directed attention towards the criminogenic nature of American society itself. There was a disjuncture between the aspiration to material (financial) success to achieve the American dream, and differential access to opportunity structures – school and work – to realise success in these precise terms. Consequently some people responded to pressure and strain in a deviant manner (the disjuncture between the culturally defined goals of success, while not having the legitimate/structural means to achieve them).

It is instructive at this point to include a reference to Durkheim's understanding of anomie. Anthony Giddens helps us by saying that

> 'economic reorganisation also will exacerbate rather than resolve the crisis facing the modern world, since this is a crisis which is moral rather than economic. The increasing dominance of economic relationships, consequent upon the destruction of the traditional religious institutions which were the moral background of previous societal forms, is precisely the main source of anomie in contemporary society' (1971 p99).

In other words, against the background of the eighteenth-century Enlightenment, industrial revolution and rapid social change and the division and greater specialisation of economic functions (Giddens 1971 p74), moral regulation has not kept pace with these wide ranging socio-economic changes. However, after briefly alluding to features of Durkheim's sociology, Downes and Rock clarify that 'the source of anomie for Merton was not the asymmetry between talent and reward; it lay rather in the lack of symmetry between the culture and the social structure' (1988 p120). There are five possible reactions for those in such anomic circumstances according to Merton's typology:

a) Conform – accept the normative values and legitimate routes to success even if they do not succeed.

b) Innovate – accept normative values yet resort to illegal means to succeed.

c) Ritualism – just keep on conforming.

d) Retreat – abandon normative values associated with materialism and drop out.

e) Rebel – reject the values of the dominant culture and substitute new ones (White and Haines 2004 p67).

It should be acknowledged that not all those who find themselves the victims of anomie are destined to offend, yet some will. But is it possible to predict those who will succumb to delinquent activities?

Albert Cohen questioned Merton's analysis because delinquents were not in pursuit of the cultural goal of material success. In fact they were more likely to be engaged in behaviour that was 'non-utilitarian, malicious and negativistic' (1955 p25). The status problems of lower class compared with middle class youths are resolved by the creation of a subculture which allows them to succeed on their own terms. Middle class standards are inverted, rejected and replaced (see elements of Cohen's theory articulated in Box 1981 p101) by the 'D streams' revenge' (Downes and Rock 1988 p143). As White and Haines comment:

'Whereas Merton's typology spoke of the disappointed individual, Cohen saw crime and delinquency in terms of collective behaviour associated with the different aspirations, expectations, and lived experiences of two different class groupings. For Cohen the school was the point at which lower-class youth understood their choices were constrained by society' (2004 p69).

Richard Cloward and Lloyd Ohlin (1960) reconciled Merton's anomie and Sutherland's differential association with a labelling perspective (Box 1981 p102–103). They restate that individuals are disposed to be law abiding, yet this is attenuated in circumstances of anomie/strain. Although different classes may have the same cultural goals of economic success and security, it is clear that not everyone can achieve the culturally determined goals of success, particularly the disadvantaged working class. One response to such circumstances is delinquency. Therefore, for Merton, anomie/strain was engendered by problems encountered in the educational and employment opportunity structure. For Cohen, a status problem was created in circumstances where the adolescent could not live up to middle class standards. For Cloward and Ohlin, deprivation created alienation that culminated in the withdrawal of support for normative structures in conventional society orientated to economic success. Therefore a subcultural solution is sought in response to the problems created by a dominant culture that pursues success in terms of economic achievement. (The subculture manifests a set of values, behaviours, and norms that are different to those found within the dominant culture. The delinquents of Downes (1966) in East End London in early 1960s opted out.)

By contrast, David Matza in *Delinquency and Drift* (1964) takes issue with subcultural solution theories, which imply a rejection of the conventional moral order and the creation of an alternative. In other words, offenders conform, most of the time anyway, to conventional mores and grow out of their offending as they mature. Matza argued that teenage males are disposed to drift into delinquency because of anxieties associated with masculinity, status, and peer acceptance, and then resort to techniques of neutralisation to justify their episodic behaviour. Therefore there is a temporary suspension of commitment to society rather than wholesale rejection and solution through a sub-cultural response. Steven Box put the position neatly when he said that 'whereas Cohen argues adolescents *exile* conventional values to the cold wastes of their unconscious, and Cloward and Ohlin argue that adolescents *extinguish* conventional values, Matza merely argues that they *extend* conventional values' (1981 p112). In his view of delinquency, the free will of the offender is maintained in opposition to a positivist/determinist position. In other words, there is a soft positivism at work in Matza.

A brief comment on Sutherland's differential association theory (mentioned above) can be added at this point. Within the Chicago School tradition it was acknowledged that American society was comprised of various subcultures that manifested different norms and values. Consequently, it is likely that some subcultures were more disposed to expressions of illegality than others. Delinquency is therefore a result of associating with those who are in possession of delinquent norms and delinquency is learned from being in close association with offenders. As law abiding behaviour is learned from others who are disposed to play by the rules, delinquent behaviour is learned by the same process, but as a consequence of different formative influences. After this reflection on the traditions of biological, psychological and sociological positivism, other perspectives can be introduced at this point.

Control

Perhaps the most obvious question posed by professionals working within the criminal justice system when thinking about crime is: why do people offend? Box explains that according to theorists prior to Hirschi in the 1960s (1981 p122), delinquency was a consequence of, or response to, *something*: relative deprivation, strain within the social structure, anomie, status frustration, alienation, socialisation into a subculture, neutralisation. Travis Hirschi (1969) approaches the phenomenon from the other end by saying that people are disposed to break the law, but will not do so if the right conditions prevail. Therefore it can be said that delinquency is a naturally occurring phenomenon that does not require any special motivation. So do not ask the obvious question: why do people offend? Rather turn it on its head and ask: why do people not offend? (Roshier 1989; Pond 1999 p49 for some of the reasons why people do not offend, expanding on Hirschi). Hirschi answers this inverted but significant question by saying that it is because people have something to lose and also because of adequate socialisation into the norms and values of society which provides the mechanisms of control. The important factor, according to control theory, is the level of attachment and commitment to, and belief in, the conventional moral order – family, school, peers, work place – the four key elements of the social bond are attachment, commitment, involvement and belief (White and Haines 2004 p147; also Hirschi's original formulation 1969). One of the important policy implications of Hirschi's approach is to strengthen bonds in relation to the normative structures of society, rather than respond by negative punishment, deterrence and exclusion, which could in fact weaken attachments. This could be developed as an argument for a social policy rather than a penal solution to criminal behaviour. The response of society as a whole, and criminal justice system personnel in particular, to crime is extremely important, as the next theoretical perspective underlines.

Labelling theory

This approach draws attention away from deviant actions (the primary focus on what offenders do within the positivist tradition) towards social processes and the reaction of the criminal justice system after a 'crime' has been committed. Within the positivist paradigm crime is approached as an 'objective thing' out there in the world, an artefact, a phenomenon obvious to all of us within a society characterised by shared norms and values – so it is obvious what it is, is it not? The labelling perspective questions these assumptions and advances the view that crime is more a product of political and social processes; it is not inherent in behaviour but a quality ascribed by the powerful, or agents of the criminal justice system. This approach surfaced in the 1960s and 1970s (Becker 1963) and made one think about the way identities are shaped through interaction with others. It is stating the obvious that the actions of offenders, along with the impact on victims, must be taken seriously; equally, it is important to consider the reaction of officials in positions of power and the 'harm' labels inflict by conferring a deviant identity on another person, sometimes inadvertently and unwittingly.

This perspective can be illustrated by referring to an occasion when a probation officer was sitting in court waiting for a bench of three magistrates to pronounce sentence on an offender, during May 2006. Appearing before the bench was a 20-year-old male who had pleaded guilty to Section 39 Assault, Criminal Damage, and Possess Offensive Weapon x 2. Relevant background information, presented to the court in a pre-sentence report, included reference to a father who had spent time in prison when the defendant was relatively young, and a mother who had left the family home when he was only nine. His eldest brother had been killed when the defendant was 15; he was currently in the grip of problems associated with alcohol and drugs; unemployed; and previously known to probation. There was also an additional matter pending before the Crown Court – stabbing his brother. He was therefore a young man with considerable personal problems, connected to previous experiences of an adverse nature, in addition to which his behaviour was of deep concern to other people. The comment of the chair of the bench at the point sentence was pronounced was as follows: 'You have the makings of a violent and dangerous criminal…part of a dysfunctional family, but this does not excuse you…Five months' custody'. Given the nature of these offences, it is possible to argue that this sentence is justified on the grounds of public protection. However, the words accompanying the sentence can be deemed to illustrate the labelling perspective in operation.

Criminologists point out that the labelling perspective yields important insights into, and diverts attention towards, reactions within the criminal justice system and the consequences of these reactions. It thus takes issue with the positivist/scientific paradigm. In other words, do not think about crime as an objective, naturally occurring, uncomplicated phenomenon. We would do well to consider rather how certain behaviours are in fact being constructed and criminalised by the powerful, thus making 'criminal' a status that is conferred by someone as part of a complex political and social process. Therefore reject positivism and correctionalism in favour of an appreciation of diverse forms of behaviour. Reflecting on those who have the power to impose labels on others takes one into conflict theory. One of the important features of this approach is that no form of human behaviour is considered to be inherently criminal, which leads to a discussion on who has the power to impose labels on others. For as Giddens says:

> 'By and large, the rules in terms of which deviance is defined, and the contexts in which they are applied, are framed by the wealthy for the poor, by men for women, by older people for younger people and by ethnic majorities for minority groups' (1989 p129).

Similarly, within the conflict perspective it is possible to locate the sociology of law, which explores how law reflects the interests of those in power (Carson 1974). Therefore thinking about crime and criminal justice should take cognisance of existing power relations within society.

Marxist and conflict theory/radical criminology[4]

By way of introduction to conflict theory, it is important first to look at the work of Durkheim, Weber and Marx in relation to the transition from the feudal and agricultural society of the Middle Ages to the emergence of the modern world from the eighteenth century onwards. The latter is characterised by the industrial revolution, urbanisation, capitalism, secularism and individualism, which weakened the bonds of social solidarity (Giddens 1971). Durkheim was preoccupied with the moral implications of rapid social change and the way in which social solidarity in the modern world was achieved through the integration and regulation of the new division of labour (from mechanical to organic). In other words, a new moral regulation would be based upon the differentiation and specialisation of economic tasks and a proper fit between talent and reward: unity and moral regulation through difference not sameness, as had been the case under mechanical solidarity. The modern world presents itself as a moral problem. For Marx, capitalism produced alienation and exploitation, class division, inequality, conflict and power differentials. He analysed the causes of conflict in society accordingly, as we saw earlier in this chapter, the category of the social, not the individual, is important. Crime is one of the consequences of conflict and Bonger (1916) understood crime associated with poverty under capitalism. Additionally, Lilly *et al* (2002) allude to the conflict perspective in the work of Sutherland and Sellin, Vold, Turk, Chambliss, and Quinney.

Lilly *et al* (2002 p153) say that by the 1960s, to some degree at least, attention had been diverted away from aetiology. For example, control theory forced theoreticians to think about the mechanisms of conformity rather than deviance; labelling drew attention to the reactions of the criminal justice system and crime as a socially constructed phenomenon. Also 'Turk, Chambliss and Quinney explored the criminalisation process with a focus on factors that might explain *the behaviour of the authorities* rather than that of offenders' (p153), even though they did not completely abandon the aetiological question. The point should be made that, during the 1960s and early 1970s, conflict theory located the cause of crime in the criminalisation of certain forms of behaviour by the powerful.

The new criminology in the early 1970s

In 1973 *The New Criminology* of Ian Taylor, Paul Walton and Jock Young, stood outside what can be referred to as official Home Office criminology, with its predominantly individualistic explanation of crime. However, this perspective should be complemented with the social democratic and social deprivation thesis that advanced the view that a combination of the post-war welfare state, improvement in material conditions and abolition of poverty with a criminal justice system in pursuit of treatment and rehabilitation, including probation casework, would reduce crime. In fact, a combination of improving social conditions and individual attention would solve the problem. But crime continued to rise. It was the new criminology that took issue with consensus and functionalist perspectives, positivism, determinism and individual explanations. There was a renewed focus on the politics of crime; crime cannot be divorced from political, social and economic structures; capitalism itself is criminogenic. The system of law, criminal justice and penal policy must be explained in relation to the mode of production and the class-based nature of society, and the power of one group to exercise its will over another. Such an approach calls for a programme of political, socio-economic reform rather than individual change. In the radical political context of the 1970s, the new criminology broke with conventional, orthodox and traditional criminology associated with quantification, measurement, prediction and control/correctionalism divorced from an understanding of the wider political, social and economic context. Consequently Taylor, Walton and Young (1973) argue for a 'fully Marxist model of deviance and control' after offering a critique of other theoretical perspectives. In fact:

> 'To do otherwise than to work for the demise of capitalism, and the transformation of society to one of socialist diversity, is to implicate oneself in correctionalism, i.e. the coercive use of the criminal sanction to 'correct' behaviour on a personal basis when its roots lie in social structural inequalities of wealth and power' (Downes and Rock 1988 p247).

New-right conservative backlash from 1979

The neo-Conservative, new right and neo-Liberal context of the 1980s, both in the USA under Reagan and the United Kingdom under Thatcher, relocated crime within the individual in two main ways: the neo-classical tradition in which the individual is fully responsible for rationally chosen actions; and neo-positivism in which crime is a result of organic, psychological defects. This backlash emerged within a new political, social and economic situation characterised by conservative attitudes, less commitment to welfare, the decline of the rehabilitative ideal, greater emphasis on law, order and punishment, the need for discipline and authority, and of course personal responsibility. Lilly *et al* comment that:

> 'In the end, there are two hallmarks of conservative theorising. First, crime is attributed to individual choice or failings and not to the structural arrangements – or 'root causes' of society…second, in solving the crime problem, the focus is on placing more restraints or controls on individuals…There is a belief that threat of harsh punishment is the linchpin of effective social control' (2002 p192).

In other words, crime is firmly located in the individual's will, mind, and body; Roshier's point (1989) is that both major criminological traditions are concerned with control, correction and crime reduction. White and Haines proceed to say that the 'fundamental ideas of New Right criminology are based on two themes: placing responsibility for crime squarely on the individual, and reasserting the importance of punishment in responding to crime' (2004 p137). It is possible to group together conservative theories under the generic term of right realism which can be adumbrated as follows (Walklate 2003 Chapter 3):

- *Socio-biological* – during the nineteenth century we have already encountered the biological theorising of Lombroso and Darwin and the view that crime manifests inferiority or unfitness (atavism), a theoretical tradition continued by Hooton (1939) and Sheldon (1949), before declining during the 1960s. However, a biological resurgence occurred in the 1970s (E.O. Wilson 1975), associated with the view that crime is caused by biological, genetic, constitutional defects. Biosocial theories suggest neurological and biochemical variations between offenders. Therefore

  'Fishbein (1990) noted a number of biochemical differences between controls and individuals with psychopathy, antisocial personality, violent behaviour, or conduct disorder including levels of certain hormones, neurotransmitters, peptides, toxins, and metabolic processes as well as psychophysiological correlates of psychopathy such as electroencephalogram (EEG) differences, cardiovascular differences, and electrodermal variations' (Lilly *et al* 2002 p205).

And Wilson and Herrnstein's *Crime and Human Nature* (1985) is described by Lilly *et al* as the 'best publicised example of the return of individualistic explanations of crime' (2002 p210).

- *Rational choice* – where individuals in the tradition of Bentham's theorising make a rational decision about the expected utility of a particular course of action in terms of profit and loss, costs and benefits.

- *Routine activity* – reduces the opportunities people have to commit crime. This approach is linked to rational choice. Clarke and Felson (1993) say that offenders are just like us, non-offenders, because crime is embedded in the very architecture of everyday life. Therefore crime does not require any special explanation at the level of pathology or deprivation. There is no need to focus on aetiology. Both rational choice and routine activity are the new criminologies of everyday life in the post-rehabilitative and correctionalist era (Garland 2001 p127).

- *Administrative criminology* has been associated with the Home Office since the 1980s: this is the view that no one is really sure why people commit crime or knows with certainty what to do to stop it occurring, therefore it is something that must be managed rather than explained. As Jock Young explains, administrative criminology operates with a consensus view of society; that crime is an individual rather than social problem; that attention must be paid to dysfunctional families who constitute a blight on society.

> 'But above all the wider social structure of inequality and injustice is left out of the picture. It thus reverses causality: crime causes problems for society rather than society causes the problem of crime. Thus, just as left idealism attempts to disconnect the criminal justice system from crime, establishment criminology attempts to disconnect crime from the wider society' (1997 p479–480).

From right realism to left realism

The emergence of right realism precipitated the response of left realism, which is the heir of the new criminology from the early 1970s (Lea and Young 1984). Downes and Rock describe the left realism of the 1980s (the chronological sequence is left idealism of the late 1960s/early 1970s; then right realism from 1979; followed by the reaction of left realism in 1984) as a 'new form of pragmatism which is not very different at points from the older, conventional criminology that was deserted in the early 1970s' (1988 p267). However, left realism straddles: a) right wing law and order politics and b) left idealism and a 'romantic' view of crime. It draws attention to gender, the real impact of crime in communities, victims and the intra rather than inter-class nature of crime that affects working class communities. Left realism is captured by Downes and Rock as 'a practical administrative criminology of the left' (1988 p272).

Of course there were dangers inherent in the Marxist oriented left idealism (romanticising crime and perception of its inter-class nature), and Jock Young stated that:

> 'The springboard for the emergence of realist criminology was the injunction to 'take crime seriously' (1997 p474), an urgent recognition that crime was a real problem for a large section of the population. Therefore left realism as opposed to left idealism does take crime seriously by emphasising offenders, victims, reaction of the criminal

justice system, and reactions of the public. Furthermore the central explanatory variable employed by left realism is relative deprivation' (Walklate 2003 p50) (that is individuals who perceive themselves deprived in relation to others).

Finally, White and Haines summarise by saying that 'Left Realism can be seen as a left-wing response to the law-and-order debate dominated predominantly by the right in politics' (2004 p173), particularly since 1979.

The first section of this chapter refers to some of the main criminological theories, beginning with classicism in the eighteenth century. For the sake of completeness, it is worth repeating that we cannot make sense of crime and criminal justice unless we take account of the following variables: access to material resources, class divisions, rich and poor, status and power structures (the radical/Marxist perspective; see Hall *et al* 1978). The feminist perspective within criminology can be located within the same explanatory variables (White and Haines 2004 p115; Heidensohn 1985 and 2002). Furthermore, what is referred to as the republican theory of criminal justice draws attention to the concept of restorative justice, thus standing in direct opposition to the contemporary preoccupation with punishment (White and Haines 2004 p175). Of course all the major theoretical perspectives reviewed in this section have their relative strengths and weaknesses. The significance of the post-Enlightenment master patterns is that they provide probation officers with a variety of explanatory but also competing frameworks. They are important because they enable probation officers to pose questions, generate explanations, and fashion the tools by which certain forms of human behaviour can be approached and interpreted. Consequently they constitute an important starting point in the critical process of analysis and understanding, which should be a central probation task.

However, it can be argued that these theories can only ever be a starting point for probation practitioners. Neither classicism nor the strands of the positivist paradigm can provide a complete explanation for offending behaviour that would address every issue, resolve every conundrum, and answer every question (Radzinowicz 1999). In other words, it must not be assumed that it is feasible to create a perfect fit between any one explanatory paradigm and the behaviour of a particular individual offender sitting in the probation office. All individuals and their circumstances are unique; it is not possible to know with absolute accuracy why or which people will offend; nor can we predict with certainty who is likely to desist (but see Stewart et al 1994; Chui and Nellis 2003). Although criminological theories provide degrees of illumination, suggestive clues, and explanatory possibilities of varying levels of credibility, they have their limitations in explaining one's sense of bewilderment and surprise. For as the quote from Rutter and Giller (1983) makes clear at the beginning of this chapter, there can never be such a thing as an all-encompassing theoretical explanation of crime that could possibly accommodate all the complex variables involved. Consequently, the lesson to be drawn is one of proceeding with caution. In fact it is this note of caution, sounded at the conclusion of this first section, that leads to the suggestion that a framework of understanding for probation practitioners must take into account a number of factors which both challenge and complement this discussion. The task of the next section is to build such a framework within which insightful probation practice comprising five central elements can be pursued.

A framework of understanding for probation practitioners – additional points to consider

1 Autobiography: the challenge of self-understanding

During the years of my involvement in probation work, it has often been repeated in professional conversation and teaching (although noticeably less often over recent years) that the first requirement for anyone aspiring to be an effective probation officer or social worker is the Socratic and theological injunction to 'know thyself'. It is increasingly overlooked (the obvious often is) that in a people-orientated profession the most important resource available to the worker is the self. All of us, upon deciding to join what were classed as the helping professions, had by this point acquired, by various means, a range of intellectual and emotional resources that should subsequently have been refined during training. In fact the self must be nourished and stretched, throughout the course of professional careers, if we want to be of maximum value to others. This means growing intellectually in some of the key disciplines that, for probation and other criminal justice workers, include psychology, sociology, and of course criminology. These provide the worker with some of the conceptual tools and lenses necessary to think about, look through, interpret and understand the behaviour of others. It also means growing emotionally, as well as cognitively, and this is facilitated by reflecting upon feelings generated by doing the job, as well as receiving support and feedback from more experienced members of staff who have travelled along, perhaps for many years, the helping professions route. These are the significant people who have a rich cultural inheritance to transmit, combining knowledge, skill, insight and understanding (Whitehead and Thompson 2004).

Self understanding, that is the form of understanding that is of value to others experiencing difficulties, demands an awareness of the complex influences that have shaped the self and goes some way towards explaining how and why we think, feel and act as we do. These influences include family dynamics, belief system, nature and nurture, perception of reality, values, socialisation, education, how much we are able to feel for others (emotional register), ability to form relationships, where our views of right and wrong come from, behaviour patterns, priorities, our capacity to bend the rules and those times when we have, including those aspects of ourselves we are uncomfortable with and try to hide from others. These are some of the issues to reflect on before we can begin to think about working with, assessing, making judgments about, and understanding, others (Smith 2006). Therefore the point should be established that the self is a required subject of study within the helping professions, running alongside knowledge of the academic disciplines that facilitate theory building.

Perhaps the reader will agree with me (or, if not agree, then be willing to entertain the idea) that it is less easy than we think to arrive at an insightful understanding of the self, particularly when we are, and should be, continually evolving, changing, growing. In this process there could well be discernible links with the past at whatever stage we have arrived, some unifying thread, some foundational value that provides a sense of continuity, coherence, and identity. Living in what sociologists refer to as the late or post-modern period (Tarnas 1991), there is also equally the possibility of experiencing discontinuity as much as continuity, of not being aware of a fixed essence, of being in a constant process of Heraclitean flux within a fluid and uncertain world, as we travel in the direction of some unknown destination. There is a sense in which we are, existentially, inventing ourselves as we go along (Sartre 1973), that we are a mass of contradictions, sometimes feeling as though we are strangers to ourselves, that values are impermanent in a world where God is dead (Nietzsche), and that we are gripped by irrational forces (Freud). Therefore, we are as likely to experience continuity (which can be comforting) as discontinuity (which is unsettling, thus provoking a sense of ontological disquiet). Moreover, my experiences may not be yours; do not experience your self and the world as I do; I am not you and you are not I. These are matters, it can be suggested, for deep reflection for those who aspire to work in the people professions. Perhaps this is one of the reasons why, during training, prospective members of staff were enjoined to spend as much time reading Shakespeare, George Eliot and texts on theology, including the Bible, as texts on criminological theory – because of the insights they provide into the human condition and the promotion of self awareness.

The starting point for trying to understand those forms of behaviour constructed as criminal, which brings us into contact with the discipline of criminology, should arguably begin with self-understanding, particularly for those who earn their living working within the criminal justice system and related branches of social work. The starting point must be the construction of an autobiographical script. In fact, I am minded to advocate the pedagogic point that the first task presented to a trainee probation officer at the commencement of training should be to 'tell me about yourself', rather than write an essay on the history of the probation service or learn how to use a computer. To arrive at an insightful understanding of the self (perhaps the place we arrive at, initially at least, is to understand for the first time that we do not understand) takes a good deal of time and much effort must be expended. Like many things of value that are arguably worth having, self-understanding is elusive and will not present itself easily; it can be a difficult process. But if we are prepared to persist, remain open-minded, be self-critical, and learn as much from our mistakes as from positive and reaffirming experiences, then we will be rewarded with a measure of insight into the human condition that can be of value to others. In fact, the value of the self to others, within the people professions, is proportionate to the level of self-understanding the worker has managed to acquire at a cognitive and emotional level. Effective helpers are those who embark upon, and can also withstand, the risky journey into themselves, who are prepared to excavate the complex layers that form the self, who have experienced emotional disquiet. In fact, I think it is the latter that provides the self with the key to achieving an emotional depth which is a critical resource because it can promote empathy and understanding. Emotional distress, if used creatively, can build those personal resources that enable effective work to be done with others, not necessarily in terms of achieving measurable change but in terms of being able to feel for, understand and appreciate the life of the other. We may not always be able to effect those changes considered desirable in the lives of others (for example, reducing re-offending), but it is of value simply to achieve a measure of understanding as the first step in a process of change. For without self-understanding, it is difficult to understand other people, accurately assess and effectively intervene, which is a central task of probation.

2 Biography: understanding the other

If the task of self-understanding is far from straightforward, although necessary in the helping professions, then how much more difficult and challenging is it to acquire an understanding of the other, the individual with whom the probation officer is working. If the self co-exists with ambiguity, ambivalence, and complexity, then how much more difficult to appreciate, understand, get inside someone else's thoughts, to get a feel for, interpret the motives, feelings and behaviours of others? As the self's thoughts, feelings, values, behavioural patterns and responses have been shaped by innumerable influences over many years, so the other has been subjected to the same process, but not necessarily the same variety or density of experiences (Sutherland's differential association comes to mind). Yet the professional task facing the probation officer and social worker is precisely that of appreciating and understanding, with a view to interpreting and giving meaning to, repertoires of behaviours that will enable assessments to be undertaken, judgments formulated, and decisions made. One of the reasons why it is difficult, if not impossible, fully to understand the other is because in the post-Kantian era (see the next chapter) we have been presented with certain difficulties when disentangling those feelings, thoughts, motives and views of the world belonging to the other from those the subjectivity of the professional worker imputes (I am here adapting the Kantian thesis that knowledge does not conform to objects, but objects to knowledge).

So when I assess and interpret the offender am I describing objectively and therefore with precision what is real and what life is like for the other, or to some degree imposing my view of the world on to the other person? Is it possible to produce an unmediated assessment? Am I engaged in exegesis or eisegesis? When compiling a report for magistrates and judges which should contribute to the sentencing process, is the probation officer describing accurately the nature of reality as experienced by the client; presenting the 'facts' of the offender's life in an objective manner or engaged in theory-neutral and value-free probation work? Or is the worker describing his or her experience of the client, based more on a subjective reading into than reading out of, with the result that the report does not describe the client as him or herself at all (that is independently of the probation officer's experiences)? Therefore, the worker is not communicating some absolute truth about the other, a body of incontestable facts, but rather shades of opinion and interpretation drawn, for example, from the worker's own value base. In other words, the assessment process says as much about the worker as the client. I am not suggesting that this is something done wilfully with the intention of deception, but rather that it is not possible to do otherwise because of the way brains and bodies filter and mediate information through a particular frame of reference. That is why it is helpful to know what it is and where it comes from, to avoid prejudice and discrimination. This is the best we can do and our limitations, interpretations and qualifications should be acknowledged. We are limited in our ability to present the facts, know the truth of the life of the other and ourselves, capture what is real with accuracy, assess, judge, and make decisions. Our knowledge and understanding is less than we think it is, which means we can never know the other as well as we would like. But as far as we are able, we must attempt to enter the world of clients, appreciate and understand their realities. Attempts have been made to do this through ethnographic studies such as those produced by the Chicagoans (Smith 1988); Howard Parker (1975) in *The View from the Boys*; Valier 2002 p45; also the 'appreciative' stance of Matza (1969).

Therefore the probation officer is more involved in expressing an opinion and arriving at an interpretation than in the presentation of 'facts'. There will be a vestige of truth and fact in the assessment process, but its limitations should be acknowledged, both ontologically and epistemologically. Perhaps this is why social work tutors at various universities continue to repeat the importance of 'checking things out' with a view to getting as close as possible to the 'truth' of the other person; to narrow the gap between the self and the other. Colleagues can also be extremely helpful in this process.

When exploring and trying to construct the salient features of another's biography, the point has been established that we are limited as to what we can know about other people and what exists outside and apart from ourselves (see relevant discussions in Chapter 4). At this point we can call upon the assistance of Bryan Magee when explaining the work of Kant. Not only does he help in this discussion, he provides an important framework for what follows when discussing the preparation of reports by probation officers. Magee explains how human beings can only know so much of what constitutes reality. In other words

'on the one hand there is what exists, independently of us and our capacity for experience, and on the other hand there is what we have the means of experiencing; and there could never be good reason for believing that these are the same. The latter is almost certainly narrower than the former, and likely to be very meagre indeed compared to it' (1998 p133).

What we know about anything is limited, determined and mediated by our bodily and cognitive apparatus which, explains Magee, produces end-results determined by its structure. So, for example, a camera provides a photographic image, which is of course different to the actual scene being photographed. The image constitutes a pictorial representation in a form determined by the structure of the camera itself. Consequently it is not the same as the scene, the thing in itself. This idea can be extended to the probation officer and client, when the self is writing about the other through the medium of a court report. The report is a piece of paper with markings on it made by a member of staff using a word-processor. This process creates an image by resorting to words, a linguistic representation; it reflects the person but does not provide an exact copy. This helps to explain why different reports prepared by different authors about the same person can reveal such marked differences, which can say more about the autobiographical details of the authors than the biography of the clients.

To summarise, the probation officer requires an appreciation of the history of criminological theories, beginning in the eighteenth century and continuing beyond the emergence of positivism towards the end of the nineteenth century, then into twentieth century explanations. Such theories provide the worker with a number of conceptual tools and lenses which help him or her to formulate insightful questions when working with offenders. If the worker is not aware of the different approaches found within classicism and positivism and lacks self-awareness; if the worker fails to appreciate the complexities that constitute the other; if there are tensions between positivism and phenomenology; then it is likely that knowledge, appreciation, understanding, insight and awareness could result in distorted assessments, judgments, decisions and images, and these in turn would produce unforeseen consequences. One such outcome could be the promotion of negative labelling and exclusion.

3 Avoid negative labelling

Earlier in this chapter, the reader was introduced to the central thrust of the labelling perspective, which should sound a note of caution for all those who work with people constructed as offenders. The probation system has always worked with offenders and been involved in the business of reducing and controlling crime. The approach premised upon advise, assist and befriend in 1907 was a vehicle for reducing crime through a one-to-one relationship in the community, with religious-minded probation officers. By the time of the Streatfield Report in 1961, the organisation was involved in a sentencing framework that manifested elements of retribution, crime prevention, and of course rehabilitation. By the Crime and Disorder Act of 1998 a much closer relationship was encouraged between agencies, particularly probation and police, manifested in Multi-Agency Public Protection protocols (s115) with a view to managing dangerous offenders who present a risk of harm. Moreover, probation reports for magistrates and judges have been transformed to include an assessment of the risk of re-offending and harm, and offenders placed in one of four categories: low, medium, high and very high. In fact, since the 1991 Criminal Justice Act, probation has assimilated a new nomenclature, reflecting a new political rationality, which has been used to reconstruct the offender and of which we can be reminded at this point:

- Actuarialism, risk, management, containment and control.

- Public protection, dangerousness, seriousness, harm, stricter enforcement.

The 2003 Act includes gradations of harm when assessing culpability – intention to cause harm, knowledge of risk of unintended harm, recklessness, and negligence. These are elements more resonant of a neo-liberal than welfare state (Garland 2001), referred to in the previous chapter.

In fact, the contemporary probation officer has been provided with an extended linguistic repertoire and additional scope to categorise, label, and 'fix' the essence of an offender. This endorses/creates a deviant identity and potentially excludes from the community of the 'normal' those who are deemed to pose a risk to others. Even the probation organisation itself has been through a process of cultural re-labelling with a view to changing the way members of staff think about the job and work with people (see previous chapter). We can remind ourselves of some of the elements of this process as follows:

- From the person as client to offender.

- From the probation officer as social worker to offender manager under NOMS.

- From Probation Service to National Offender Management Service.

- From social work agency to law enforcement organisation.

While multi-agency public protection arrangements procedures take place within the context of an assessment of harm and language of risk, seriousness, dangerousness, and public protection, and while they indubitably deal with legitimate public concerns, there is also the possibility of, inadvertently and unwittingly, negatively labelling the other. The probation service nationally supervises approximately 210,000 offenders (comprising community sentences, pre and post-release licence supervision), a significantly small proportion of whom constitute a level of concern that necessitates action between agencies to keep communities safe (I was writing this in March 2006, when several offenders on community service committed serious further offences and a suggestion was made for a new Violent Person Order). Moreover, there are difficult decisions to be made on serious offenders by MAPPA; much information to evaluate; informed judgments required and decisions expected with a view to preventing further offending. I am certainly not suggesting that such procedures are not required, because it is clear that in each of the 42 probation areas there is a handful of individuals whose behaviour constitutes a serious risk of harm to others – harm of a violent and sexual nature. However, I want to inject a note of caution and preserve a sense of balance because not all offenders constitute a threat of harm to others. Staff need to be aware of the impact of negative labels when applied to individuals and the danger in ascribing a fixed essence and therefore distorting reality, which makes it even more difficult to consider the possibility of individual change. We may recall how David Matza (1964) reminded us that many offenders are not offending all the time, so there is not a wholesale rejection of society's values but rather episodic lapses. This means that agency procedures when dealing with categories of risk and harm must be handled seriously but also with care in equal measure. This point can be illustrated by extrapolating the main points from meetings attended on the subject of risk and harm, distilled as follows.

In October 2005, the probation officer attended a multi-agency risk management meeting under the auspices of local multi-agency public protection arrangements, on an offender who had previously been registered under these procedures as high risk of harm, and who had been supervised for the last six months of his licence. Interestingly, the registration of high risk status was not because he had a record of violence; in fact he was subject to licence having been released from prison after serving a sentence for relatively serious motoring matters. However, and significantly, there had been allegations of domestic violence against a previous partner, in addition to accumulated police intelligence of violent episodes, associated with drugs, which had not been prosecuted by the police or culminated in a sentence of the court. Consequently, the latest scheduled meeting was held and attended by probation, police, social services (because of potential risks to children), and mental health. The rationale of the meeting was to share the most recent intelligence drawn from all the agencies, with a view to arriving at an informed judgment on whether the risk status previously imposed should be extended or rescinded. It should be added that over recent months, since his release from prison, the offender had not been charged with any new offences. It is possible to make a number of observations for further reflection.

- Different agencies with their different culturally determined roles bring different perspectives to these meetings.

- Consequently it is interesting to observe how information is 'framed', presented and then used to arrive at judgments consistent with agency histories and sensibilities.

- The representative from the police concluded that the client was '*very* dangerous' which was arguably difficult to sustain given the 'facts' presented at the meeting – 'dangerous' in certain circumstances perhaps but 'very dangerous'? What exactly is the difference between 'dangerous' and 'very dangerous', when agencies resort to such language?

- It was difficult to know how much weight to attach to the evidence that the client had not re-offended during the licence period. What could be accurately predicted when reflecting on future behavioural possibilities?

While agencies involved in meetings such as this, within the context of public protection, have a duty to make decisions based on all relevant information, negative labelling should be avoided. In other words, when professionals assess the risk of harm they must ensure that they, in turn, do not inflict unnecessary harm by incorrectly labelling and excluding, thus making the situation worse.

Therefore it would be helpful to have a system of checks and balances to avoid negative labelling. This could be achieved by the attendance at MAPPA of the offender's solicitor or some other representative (in the same way as at child protection meetings) which would provide safeguards, in-built checks and balances, thus helping to promote a sense of justice and transparency in the decision-making process.

The client mentioned above was subsequently disenchanted and distressed when informed that he remained on the high risk of harm register. He felt the decision was unjust and questioned the evidence upon which it was based, primarily because he had not re-offended since the last MARMM and was now more settled with a new partner. This adds weight to the suggestion that clients subjected to such procedures should be legally represented. The position can be established that these procedures constitute a sound *principle* for dealing with various behaviours, in all probation areas, which pose a risk of serious harm to self and others. However, it is also possible to be troubled by an opaque *process* which enables one to conclude that justice is not being seen to be done. Therefore the labelling perspective must be taken seriously by probation staff, particularly when reflecting upon MARM meetings under MAPPA procedures.

4 Capturing the social dimension

The first section of this chapter offers much food for thought for those trying to digest the ramifications of different criminological theories, particularly those who work with offenders. These theories range from classical criminology and the refinements of neo-classicism to various manifestations of positivism; from a focus upon individual dysfunction to the importance of the wider social context; from consensus to conflict and radical perspectives. Even though the social circumstances of offenders are pertinent when trying to make sense of offending behaviour (Whitehead and Statham 2006 p146 for an overview from a probation perspective; Stewart *et al* 1994), as well as an appreciation of the offender's varied needs, nevertheless the dominant influence in probation has been towards correcting the individual. In other words, there is something wrong with the individual rather than the social context, but the individual-social dimension has been the cause of not a little tension for probation staff.

Within the modernised probation system created by New Labour since 1997, it is interesting to draw attention to Think First under the aegis of What Works accredited programmes. While the complex needs of probation clients remain an important issue for consideration, the emphasis within Think First is to resolve the offender's cognitive apparatus, because it is assumed that he or she does not think properly, with a view to making the offender more cognitively responsible, as manifested in the ability to make the 'right' decisions. The main reason for crime is framed in terms of a lack of thinking, social and problem-solving skills: consequently the individual needs to be equipped with a repertoire of these skills to make better decisions in social circumstances that remain unchanged. These skills will be taught by staff and must be assimilated by offenders. Greater attention is also paid to managing, containing and controlling various categories of offenders in proportion to the level of harm they are deemed to present, rather than to changing a social environment which can be a significant explanatory variable (Stewart *et al* 1994).

However, a criminology of understanding for probation staff must pay attention to the social circumstances of the clients with whom they are working. The behaviour of the individual must be understood in relation to a number of variables, including family, social environment, school, employment opportunities, relative deprivation, etc. The role of probation within the criminal justice system, armed with such social information, is not to justify, excuse, or collude with forms of behaviour that cause problems for other people. Rather it is to provide a context of understanding for certain forms of behaviour within which to think, collect relevant information, assess, formulate appreciative judgments, and arrive at insightful decisions after considering all the information that seems to be relevant in pursuit of criminal and social justice (often in circumstances of social inequality). At a time when the probation system is preoccupied with the stifling effects of central political control, bureaucratic systems, standardised procedures and processes (see Chapter 2), those who continue to work with individual offenders must not forget that, arguably, the first task is to understand the individual and communicate that understanding to the courts, to enable informed sentencing decisions to be made. This can be facilitated by the distillation of socio-economic information which locates offending episodes within the widest possible parameters.[5]

5 The efficacy of pre-sentence reports – probation officer as artist

When trying to piece together the elements of a framework of understanding, which is closely associated with posing and answering the *why* question of human behaviour (not what have you done but more pertinently why?), the probation officer is required to be more artist than scientist or mathematician. This implies that the probation officer, particularly when conveying information to magistrates and judges with a view to facilitating the sentencing process through the medium of court reports, should paint with words rather than numbers and graphs. Numbers can be used for comparative purposes, to present insights into risk, to suggest lines for further enquiry; a living and meaningful language is required to illuminate the why question. Jenny Uglow expands upon this point in her fascinating book on the novels of George Eliot, which is applicable to the probation officer in the role of information provider. Uglow says that

> 'This is why the artist is so important, and particularly the novelist, who can not only demonstrate through example but has at her, or his command, a concrete, living language full of nuances and half lights, resonant with past experience in a way that the language of the scientist or economist can never be' (1987 p60).

Probation may well have been reconstructed as a business in the way it is encouraged to provide value for money when managing categories of offenders; but its business must also include using the language of the artist to convey an insightful understanding of people with problems.

Despite the fact that court reports include a section addressing the needs of offenders under various headings, social enquiry reports became pre-sentence reports during the early 1990s. Now, of course, we refer to the standard delivery pre-sentence report (an adjournment of three weeks is normally given), but also the fast delivery report (known at one time as a stand down report). The latter could be completed within a couple of hours, but probation can be given up to five days to complete what is a much briefer version of the more detailed pre-sentence report. Although detailed research into the changing nature of reports and information being provided to the courts has not yet been undertaken, there is some evidence to suggest a change of emphasis in the content of such reports (see Chapter 5). This is manifested in the way in which information can concentrate too much on *what* the offender has done, rather than *why* the offender has done it; on *presenting* as opposed to *underlying* problems; language in the service of *description* rather than detailed *analysis*. In my view, the implications of this shift of emphasis, consistent with the tenets of neo-classicism and theme of individual responsibility, are profound. In fact the provision of personal and social information, once culturally rooted in social work and a philosophy of welfare, was the route to providing that form of information, and therefore level of understanding, conducive to the promotion of social and criminal justice. What this means was captured by Benn and Peters when they stated that 'To do justice is to treat men unequally only according to the degree of their relevant inequalities' (1959 p173). For without a detailed, insightful, and meaningful understanding of underlying issues associated with offending behaviour, there cannot be justice; the courts cannot be in a position to do the right thing by reflecting differences between individuals. It is now much more difficult to provide answers to the why question, and focus on delivering understanding, when the criminal justice system has been reconfigured in the direction of delivering various degrees of punishment and when probation has been politicised: that is, when the culture has been reshaped in the direction explored in the previous chapter.

Uglow makes a further contribution by saying that in *Middlemarch*, Eliot 'dramatises the fact that in our lives there are many stories, each of which can have a different 'language' ' (1987 p202). Report writers must spend time thinking about the language or languages required to communicate stories about the lives of offenders so as to promote deep understanding (the Weberian concept of *verstehen*). These languages will include the demands of justice, gender differences, the right to punish and the rights of victims and local communities, in addition to social work values, sympathy, empathy, insight and awareness: a language of sensibility, sensitivity, moral vision and imagination. As Benedict Spinoza stated 'I have striven not to laugh at human actions, not to weep at them, nor to hate them, but to understand them' (Magee 1998 p93). This is the essence of probation practice, which makes it different from other criminal justice agencies.

The provision of information to the courts, in the form of the full pre-sentence report, is fast becoming an expensive luxury which the criminal justice system may not be willing to pay for or even consider necessary any longer. In November 2006 the Home Secretary, John Reid, stated that 'too much money is going on report writing and not enough on practical help' (Reid 2006 paragraph 14). This comment must be understood in the context of a situation where 40 per cent of court reports should currently be in the form of the fast delivery report. Therefore the demands of New Public Management, manifested in the form of throughput efficiency, may well prevail over the demands of justice premised upon the need for comprehensive information, as the transition from pre-sentence to fast delivery reports continues to gather pace. It is envisaged that, eventually, the full pre-sentence report will be the preserve of a handful of the most serious offenders and the fast delivery report will become the norm. This is one of the areas of concern that Chapter 5 will address empirically.

Brief note on the future of probation training

Everything I have tried to cover so far in this chapter has significant training implications. The future education and training of probation officers within the emerging NOMS structure is a matter of concern. At first sight, the future looks reasonably bright because more trainee probation officers have been recruited to the organisation since 1998, and because of the form training has taken within the Diploma in Probation Studies (Whitehead and Thompson 2004; Whitehead and Statham 2006). More recently, the significant increase in trainee numbers has been in anticipation of the introduction of custody plus, a proposal contained in the Criminal Justice Act 2003. However, this new sentence will no longer be implemented according to the Home Secretary's statement of July 2006, which contained proposals for rebalancing the criminal justice system (Home Office 2006). Money earmarked for custody plus will be diverted to more pressing political priorities within the Home Office, namely asylum, immigration and terrorism. Nor will intermittent – or weekend – custodial sentences be implemented.

The point for consideration is this. Within the previous chapter, and reinforced again here, I have drawn attention to the contribution the probation officer can make to the criminal justice system by providing information to sentencers that facilitates both an understanding of the individual and subsequent sentencing decisions. Understanding is premised upon possession of the requisite knowledge and skill, which it is the role of education and training to develop, within a wider process of cultural transmission. However, if, during the course of the next few years, trainee probation officer training is severed from higher education (which was in fact proposed prior to the creation of the Diploma in Probation Studies: see Whitehead and Thompson 2004 p20 for full discussion), then the ability of probation to deliver insightful understandings of offenders will be compromised. Future training could consist of a more superficial form of on-the-job learning, reinforced by the requirement to achieve a codified and evidenced based NVQ. If this happens, the role of probation in court, contained within the NOMS structure and wider criminal justice system, will be more limited, resulting in cultural impoverishment and the likelihood of injustice to offenders.

Summary and conclusion

After considering numerous criminological theories with a view to facilitating a better understanding of the plethora of competing explanatory frameworks, particularly for practitioners, and adding another explanatory layer in the second section of this chapter, the final section turns to consider briefly a number of factors militating against understanding offending behaviour. To some degree pertinent features have already been considered, within a broad historical context, in the concluding chapter of Whitehead and Statham (2006 p251). In fact a number of *forces* between 1979 and 2005 were addressed which have contributed to undermining what is described as the probation ideal. These forces were enumerated as: the politics of Conservatism from 1979 and New Labour after 1997; the politics of spin and the politicisation of crime; American influences; a new relationship between probation and prisons under NOMS; the forces of anti-morality; the phenomenon of bureaucratic managerialism; governance issues; a lack of cohesion within probation and a misunderstanding of management. Nevertheless, it is of interest to say a little more on the contemporary political and organisational dynamics of probation which, it can be argued, are not always conducive to promoting a framework of understanding within which offending should be located. In other words, these are further indications of cultural change.

In the post-Enlightenment period that shaped the modern world, we have already seen how the liberal/classical criminological perspective supported the view that crime is predominantly a juridical category. In other words, people were considered to be largely equal under the law, free to select their own thoughts, and rationally choose how to behave. One of the central themes, explained above, was individual responsibility. Between the 1880s and 1970s a new approach to understanding and responding to crime was shaped, initially associated with the Italian School. This has been described as the period of penal-welfarism (Garland 1985). In fact, and for most of the twentieth century, a combination of reform, rehabilitation, welfare, individual treatment, positive social work help, and a concern with aetiology (the why question), created a framework within which the probation ideal found the space to function.

Since the 1970s, the erosion of consensus and welfare politics has been accompanied by a shift to the political right, which continued after 1997, thus creating a neo-liberal rather than welfare context within which to think about and respond to crime. In other words, it could be suggested that we have witnessed the return of nineteenth-century liberal elements, a renewed focus on responsibility and the justification of punishment. Consequently, punishment as retribution and deterrence have become pronounced features of contemporary penal policy and criminal justice, as evidenced by the Criminal Justice Act 2003 with its guidance on the eclectic and contradictory purposes of sentencing (Taylor et al 2004 p173). Although the notion of offender needs and the provision of help and support have not been expunged from probation work within the criminal justice system, the context and tone for thinking about and responding to offending are discernibly different (Garland 2001); and different means harsher. Therefore social work help (I acknowledge the contradiction) is more likely to be mediated through gradations of punishment, risk, and harm, which is one manifestation of criminal justice modernisation. Within the probation service, these more punitive elements are specifically manifested in the provision of community punishments, more onerous enforcement arrangements, and the benefit sanction in selected areas. Nor should the continuing attractions of prison be overlooked after the announcement in July 2006 of 8,000 more places in response to a prison population which has reached 80,000.

Other lines of enquiry to pursue can be enumerated as follows, one of which has already featured in this book. This is the phenomenon of New Public Management, combining a set of principles which locate probation within a more business orientated environment, bureaucratically driven, and economically conscious. These managerial principles have the capacity to generate conflict with those members of staff who are committed to working with individual offenders within a framework of social work values, and who are also aware of the social context of offending as a precondition to understanding behaviour. Secondly, the NOMS principle of end to end management can be misleading. It is end-to-end management in the sense that a designated offender manager will manage the order from the beginning to the end of the sentence, either in prison, in the community, or both. But it is not end to end management in the sense that the offender manager will have continuous contact, building a professional relationship with an offender over a period of time as happened within the old culture. This is because contestability implies the possibility of inputs from different providers at different stages of the sentence drawn from the public, private and voluntary sectors. In other words, there is a concern that the emerging NOMS structure is more about managing processes as cost effectively as possible, than understanding, building relationships, and spending time with the individual offender.

Finally and briefly, other factors likely to militate against a philosophy of understanding within probation are:

- The likelihood that training arrangements could become professionally impoverished during the next few years.

- The ongoing bureaucratisation and computerisation of probation.

- Focus on aggregates rather than individual offenders.

- The fast delivery report replacing the much more comprehensive social enquiry report.

These are some of the lineaments of a modernised probation system which, it can be argued, militate against the requirement for the profession to have a recognised body of knowledge, skills, and social work values conducive to promoting an understanding of people with multiple difficulties. In other words there is the possibility of a process of cultural and professional impoverishment gathering pace during the next few years within the probation domain, with corresponding adverse effects on the treatment of people who affend within the criminal justice system.

NOTES

[1] When thinking about social contract theories the reader should consult the views of Thomas Hobbes (1588–1678), John Locke (1632–1704) and J-J Rousseau (1712–1778). Where Hobbes is concerned, for example, a distinction is made between a state of nature in which individuals are at war with each other and civilised society which depends upon ceding individual freedoms to establish the conditions for social peace and security. For further information, see Volumes 5 and 6 of Copleston. Attention can be drawn to the following: 'Social contract theories provide an overwhelming critique of pre-modern forms of government and are highly relevant to the development of the rational actor model of crime and criminal behaviour' (Hopkins Burke 2005 p22). Social contract theories supported by the exercise of free will of rational individuals, in addition to the doctrine of utilitarianism, were significant conditions of existence for the emergence of the tenets of classical criminology.

[2] It is helpful to clarify three related points. First, Davies, Croall and Tyrer (2005 p23) identify a number of what they refer to as models of criminal justice: justice model (proportionality); punishment (retribution); rehabilitation associated with the individual treatment-medical model; management/bureaucratic model of speed and throughput efficiency; denunciation and degradation; and finally the radical Marxist model of class based justice. These are the models that arguably one can discern operating within the contemporary criminal justice system. Secondly, this chapter is exploring various explanations of crime, delinquency and offending, within classical and positivist frameworks. It is trying to shed light on the question: why do people offend? Thirdly, I am also alluding to philosophical justifications of punishment. Where these are concerned Barbara Hudson (2003a) says there are two streams of liberalism, associated with two different approaches to punishment. Retribution (Kantian deontologism) – deserts theory looks backwards to punish the offence to restore the balance and remedy the damage inflicted by crime. Consequentialist/Utilitarian looks forward to deter potential offenders, to reduce the likelihood of repetition and therefore shape and control future behavioural outcomes. For as 'Bentham and Beccaria had made clear, the measured severity of sanctions, together with their uniform certainty of application, gave the public reason to know and fear them, and in turn promoted a general effect of deterrence' (Garland 1985 p29). Both punishment as retribution, as well as deterrence theory, can be discovered within the modernised criminal justice system – see purposes of sentencing within the Criminal Justice Act 2003. For an interesting discussion on the merits of retribution, deterrence and reformation, see Dr William Temple's 1934 Clark Hall lecture (Radzinowicz 1999 p122; also see Bean 1981).

[3] In his 1966 book on *Ideology and Crime*, Radzinowicz expatiates on the 12 tenets of liberalism in criminal law (p9f) that I have summarised as follows:

1) Because the law placed restrictions upon individual freedom, there should be as little law as possible.

2) The administration of justice must ensure the rights of individuals are protected against the state.

3) The form of criminal law must define what constitutes an offence and punishment.

4) A written code of law must complement the social contract.

5) The justification/philosophy of punishment was largely retributive because the human rights of other people had been attacked.

6) Severity of punishment must be limited and therefore proportionate to the offence.

7) The punishment must fit the crime and not offender.

8) Penalties for crime must be laid down and correspond to the offences, and inflicted with speed and certainty.

9) Because punishment must be commensurate with the crime committed, there is no place for exemplary punishment or even reform to suit the unique personality of the offender and his circumstances. 'The penologists of the liberal school would unite to proclaim that criminals should be punished strictly for what they have done under the criminal law in force, not for what they are or are likely to become' (p12).

10) Crime is not approached as behaviour which is socially conditioned. All people are equal under the law and so equally responsible for their actions. So the offender, like the non-offender, was a fully reasoning and responsible person who calculates behavioural responses and the likely outcomes – the utilitarian strand of liberalism.

11) Crime prevention is not based upon the creation of agencies to control crime, but rather the punishment of crime within the liberal tradition.

12) Abolish the indiscriminate use of the death penalty.

[4] When turning to the radical/Marxist perspective on crime which explores the relationship between economic conditions and crime, inequality and poverty as explanatory variables, one of the forerunners is Bonger (1916). We can also refer to the work of Sellin on culture conflict; Vold; Turk; Quinney; Chambliss and the way behaviour is criminalised to protect

the ruling class (see Taylor, Walton and Young 1973). During periods of economic difficulties (such as the 1970s) it is argued that crime can be utilised to divert attention from the real source of difficulty for the working class, changing socio-economic conditions. In other words 'the crisis is deflected on to youth, crime and race, away from class relations and on to authority relations' (Downes and Rock 1988 p253). For a full discussion of the Birmingham School perspective: Downes and Rock 1988 p247f; Hall et al 1978.

[5] Offending behaviour must be understood, interpreted and located within a specific context which includes taking account of the social dimension. All probation services should have access to social and environmental data, for their own area, which can be adapted to illuminate court reports. In my own probation area, see the following website for highly pertinent information: www.teesvalley-jsu.gov.uk.

Chapter 4

FROM PLATO TO THE VIENNA CIRCLE: A
PHILOSOPHICAL JOURNEY INTO MEASURING THINGS

'With Galileo, Descartes, and Newton, the new science was
forged, a new cosmology defined, a new world opened to
man within which his powerful intelligence could act with
new freedom and effectiveness. Yet simultaneously, that new
world was disenchanted of all those personal and spiritual
qualities that for millennia had given human beings their
sense of cosmic meaning. The new universe was a machine,
a self-contained mechanism of force and matter, devoid of
goals and purpose.' (Tarnas 1991 p326)

'Nietzsche cherished the colossal power of music and yearned
for the return of a tragic outlook on life that would value
Dionysian wisdom over science. However, he found himself
in the middle of an epoch that was celebrating one scientific
triumph over another. Positivism, empiricism, economism,
and utilitarian thinking defined the age.'(Safranski 2003 p108)

Introduction

The main purpose of this chapter is to embark upon a philosophical journey
into the nature of reality and knowledge from the Greeks to the logical
positivists of the Vienna Circle, encompassing the fifth century BC to the
twentieth century AD. At first (second and even third) sight it may appear
decidedly unconventional to travel in the company of western European
philosophers and their changing ideas, when the subject matter of this
book includes the implications of the transition from the probation ideal
to the National Offender Management Service (NOMS). Nevertheless,
it is considered that this philosophical excursion can profitably be
undertaken to explore a number of salient themes, particularly changing
ontological, epistemological, and axiological perspectives, with a view
to generating ideas and eliciting probing questions that have wider
applicability in the probation domain. In fact, this chapter entertains the
view that an exploration into philosophical ideas has resonance not just
for the criminal justice system, but for all organisations whose rationale
is for people to work with people (for example, social services, nursing,
teaching, helping young and adult offenders). In essence, this chapter is

concerned with establishing a philosophically grounded framework that allows the scope to explore and illustrate significant areas of meaning and value lying beyond a scientifically orientated paradigm, preoccupied with an approach to what is real and what we know, or assume we know, associated with quantification, numbers, and measurement. In other words, and put simply, it is not possible to apply numbers to and measure everything in the social world. Resorting to the notion of *otherness,* as a heuristic device, should facilitate the achievement of this objective, as I hope will become clear as we journey into philosophy. Let us begin to feel our way by initially accompanying Plato.

Platonic inheritance

The view of the nature of reality contained in Socrates, Plato and Aristotle, is as rich as it is complex, with its combination of rationalism, idealism and empiricism.[1] Their's was a rich and complex approach to ontology (what is real) and epistemology (how do we know what is real). Their philosophic vision was not one-dimensional; they believed in this world and also another dimension of reality. There is what can be referred to as a sphere of *otherness* in Plato (that is to serve my purpose in this chapter). Plato's philosophy rested, among other things, on two distinct but connected realms. First, there is the realm of concrete and objective reality, perceived and accessible to the senses (the world of phenomena); secondly, this objective world is underpinned by a metaphysical realm of changeless and timeless essences, referred to as transcendent Ideas or Forms. Plato said that this world, our changing and therefore impermanent world and the objects within it, is an imperfect copy of the ultimate reality that exists beyond it. So for every class of objects – for example houses, trees – there exists, in the metaphysical realm, the perfect Idea or Form of these objects. This is the notion of the archetype, an original model or type in imitation of which other similar things are patterned or derived (an archetype understood as a mould or a stamp).

In Plato's work there is consequently another layer of reality beyond the tangible, objective and observable world of phenomena and sense experience. It is the task of the philosopher intellectually to apprehend, to know, the real as opposed to the fascimile; and the real *can* be known by the philosopher, as Plato claims knowledge it is difficult for us to sustain as a consequence of our western intellectual and scientific heritage that will be explored as the chapter unfolds. As Bertrand Russell said when explaining Plato's philosophy 'opinion is concerned with particular beautiful things, but knowledge is concerned with beauty itself' (1996 p122; and see the difference between knowledge and opinion in Copleston 2003 Volume 1 p151; Field 1969). This can be described for our purposes as a rich, complex and multi-layered ontology and epistemology, presumably different to our own working hypothesis of the world. Moreover, Richard Tarnas helpfully summarises the richness of the approach under discussion by saying that 'intuition, memory, aesthetics, imagination, logic, mathematics, and empirical observation each played a specific role in Plato's epistemology, as did spiritual desire and moral virtue' (1991 p54).

Drawing attention to Plato reinforces and continues the exposition of Tarnas (1991) that the Greek view of reality, with its idealism, rationalism and empiricism, is an ordered cosmos that points to an underlying intelligence which can be known by the philosopher's cognitive faculties. The Platonic/ neo-Platonic vision that permeated what became the Christian world view. For as Tarnas explains (p165), Christianity was a complex synthesis of various currents of thought, including the Judaism of the Old Testament, Platonic and neo-Platonic ideas, elements of Roman culture, Gnosticism and mysticism. There are traces of Platonic ideas in the foundational text of the Christian faith, the 27 books of the New Testament.[2]

Let us remain with Platonic ideas but this time a more contemporary manifestation by turning to some of the work produced by C.S. Lewis in the company of his biographer, A.N. Wilson. If it is possible to illustrate Platonic ideas in theological literature, this can be complemented by referring to the children's novels of Lewis. Wilson explains (1991 p211) that at a certain juncture in his life Lewis questioned whether the world in which he lived, the world of sense experience, is the only world. Therefore is it possible there could be another realm, a spiritual order of reality? In fact could there be another layer of reality that would help human beings to make sense of their lives in this world. Could it be possible to step outside of this world into something other? In *The Lion, the Witch and the Wardrobe* (1991 p220), the second of the seven Narnia books written by Lewis, the author introduces the reader to the story of how four children who are staying with a professor in the country discover a wardrobe which, if stepped through, leads into another world, the world of Narnia; consequently it is a story for children containing the Platonic vision of two realms, thus breaking out of a closed and sterile one-dimensional system of thought.

Orhan Pamuk (2005), in his melancholy and sepia illustrated biographical reflections on his native city of Istanbul, does not directly develop the Platonic theme but should be included here because of the way he illustrates another dimension. Pamuk, the acclaimed novelist from the city called Byzantium at the time Plato lived in Athens, was born on 7th June 1952. The other realm or 'second world' (p21) to which he alludes is not a direct reference to Platonic metaphysics but rather the world of the novelist's imagination, which is in fact critical for the novelist (and other artists) who seizes upon some aspect of the ordinary before transmuting it into an imaginative art form capable of yielding penetrating insights into the human condition. Another reference is worth considering in Pamuk's autobiography. This is his discussion of the work of Resat Ekrem Kocu who conveyed a sense of melancholy when describing the city of Istanbul. Of interest here is Pamuk's description of Kocu's 'failure to explain Istanbul using Western 'scientific' methods of classification' (p153). Kocu's failure was precisely because this once great city which was founded as Byzantium in 667 BC, rebuilt and renamed Constantinople by the Emperor Constantine in 380 AD when he decamped from Rome and travelled east, and became Istanbul in 1453 when seized by the Ottoman Turks, was varied, multifarious, anarchic, and therefore defied rigid classification by western standards.[3]

Augustine and Plato

Bryan Magee refers to Augustine as 'the outstanding figure in philosophy between Aristotle and Aquinas, a period of some 1,600 years' (1998 p50). Magee explains lucidly that it was Augustine who mixed Platonic ideas with the Christian tradition that by this stage was some 300 years old. This was the fusion of a faith that emerged in the Old Testament Jewish world and had revealed truths and later historical events, with Greek philosophical categories (Hick 1993; Kelly 1958). St Augustine, in his *The City of God*, distinguishes between citizens who live in two communities: the Kingdom of God and the nations and states of the rapidly disintegrating Roman Empire of the fourth century AD. So there is a city of God and a city of this world; true values are contrasted with a world of false values. Consequently, it can be said that the influence of Plato has had a long reach within the western philosophical tradition. Frederick Copleston tells us that even if Aristotle emphasised empirical science, he never abandoned Plato and metaphysics. I have already mentioned Platonic and neo-Platonic ideas embodied in theology, but the point can be developed by referring to the early church fathers, the Middle Ages, Renaissance Florence, Thomas More and Alfred North Whitehead in the twentieth century (2003 volume 1 p261-262).

A preliminary point can be established at this stage, albeit ambiguously articulated (I am hinting at something by drawing on various sources rather than spelling it out in detail) that will be taken up, expanded upon, then elucidated and applied within a criminal justice context. In our varied attempts to understand the modern world, including working lives in complex organisations, to discover or create meaning, to establish order and control out of manifestations of chaos, we are arguably disposed to classify, organise, and systematise, particularly within the post-Renaissance scientific and secular age that has produced a distinctive mind-set through which we 'see' the world. It may be suggested that there is a danger of creating a one-dimensional world that attenuates, or even eliminates, this notion of *otherness*. But in defining, reducing and narrowing, with a view to explaining everything in scientific and therefore measurable and verifiable terms (getting at the 'truth' and producing 'certain knowledge'), this process may foreshorten the field of vision and impose false limits, thus distorting the potentially rich and complex nature of reality and human experience. Safranski seems to be hinting at this in his biography of Nietzsche, where music and art forms are contrasted with science, positivism, empiricism, economics and utilitarianism, the latter creating a more sterile landscape.

Living within the confines of the twenty-first century, notwithstanding the philosophical quest of the Greeks and Platonic reach, it is tempting to dismiss the rich ontology and epistemology of the past with its two realms, multi-dimensionality, notion of otherness, metaphysics and transcendence. To some extent we cannot be blamed for our predicament because we carry within us the weight of western European history and learning. We are who we are, the product of our own age, history and culture, people of our own time, the inheritors of the Renaissance and Enlightenment, associated with the elevation of reason and a scientific outlook with its corresponding decline in, for example, religious sensibility and myth hinted at above (Armstrong 2005). It is as though recent decades have provided human beings with the intellectual tools to ask pertinent questions and clarify concepts, as well as giving up a veritable surfeit of information on every conceivable subject. But do we understand more than we did, even though it could be said that we have more knowledge? Are we poorer in spirit, and therefore less human, because we have lost sight of dimensions of meaning and value associated with otherness in the way Richard Tarnas and Safranski suggested at the beginning of this chapter? This philosophical journey provokes the posing of such questions. The point can be conceded that as there are features of reality associated with and accessible through a scientific paradigm grounded in quantification and measurement (science, positivism, induction), it can equally be argued that there are other layers that can be approached by resorting to a language characterised by ambiguity, ineffability, inexpressibility, encapsulated within a sense of qualitative otherness. This point has a resonance for probation which will be explored later.

Into the Middle Ages

We are instructed in our history books of western European civilisation that after the period of the Greek and Roman empires that spanned 1,000 years (fifth century BC to fifth century AD), western Europe entered a dark age that subsequently gave way to the Middles Ages before the Renaissance of the fifteenth century and the creation of the modern world following the eighteenth century Enlightenment. It was towards the end of the Middle Ages that Thomas Aquinas lived (1225–1274). Richard Tarnas (1991) explains that Aquinas put the spotlight on sense experience and concrete things, thus following more in the footsteps of Aristotle than Plato. Plato located ultimate reality in transcendent forms, changeless absolutes and timeless archetypes; but Aristotle believed that this world, our world, is fully real. Notwithstanding the emphasis on concrete things, Aquinas continued to believe in transcendence, the other dimension consistent with the Platonic and Christian world views. Tarnas points out that the epistemologically significant point to emerge from Aquinas is the importance attached to empiricism in contrast to rationalism, idealism, and the transcendent forms of the Platonic inheritance.

Ideas in the modern world

In the fifteenth and sixteenth centuries there was a growing emphasis upon observation of the physical world as the route to knowledge. An important signpost along the way was Francis Bacon (1561–1626) the precursor of the British empirical tradition of Locke, Berkeley and Hume, hailed by Roy Porter as 'the prophet of modern science' (2001 p6). It was Bacon who drew attention to observable facts, scientific method, the collection of data, to produce evidence that can be utilised to demonstrate regular patterns and causal connections with a view to establishing the laws of nature. It is interesting to recall Russell's summary of Bacon: 'although his philosophy is in many ways unsatisfactory, he has permanent importance as the founder of modern inductive method and the pioneer in the attempt at logical systematization of scientific procedure' (1996 p497). It should also be added that prior to Bacon it was William of Ockham (1285–1349) who stimulated the emerging scientific enterprise by giving it a push in an empirical direction (Copleston 2003 volume 3 p153).

With the Renaissance, which attached importance to mathematics and science, a critical point is reached in the philosophical journey briefly described in this chapter in an attempt to look at changing approaches to and conceptions of reality and routes to knowledge. Again it is Richard Tarnas who helps us to grasp this intellectual evolution when he comments that the

> 'assumption that the human mind knows things by intellectually grasping their inherent forms – whether through interior illumination by transcendent Ideas, as in Plato and Augustine, or through the active intellect's abstraction of immanent universals from sense-perceived particulars, as in Aristotle and Aquinas – was now challenged' (Tarnas 1991 p207).

In other words, empirical evidence, the scientific enterprise, was beginning to replace abstract metaphysical speculation as the basis of knowledge. Rather than proceeding upon the basis of rational discussion and argument, or the inner workings of speculative reason located within one's mental capacities, the new method was turned towards observation and looking at the so-called 'facts' in the concrete world of objects. This is a decisive moment that Copleston summarises thus:

> 'The climate of thought in the post-Renaissance world was not the same as that prevailing in the Middle Ages. The change was due, of course, to a number of different factors working together; but the rise of science was certainly not the least important of those factors' (2003 volume 3 p421).

Nicolaus Copernicus, Galilei Galileo, Johannes Kepler and Isaac Newton, who are associated with the scientific revolution, can be mentioned in this context.

In addition to exploring various concepts of reality, ontological and epistemological constructions, and different approaches to knowledge (theological, philosophical and scientific), the beginnings of modern science created a fundamental shift in understanding of the functioning of the physical world, associated with Copernicus and Galileo. This can be described as a shift from a geocentric paradigm (earth at the centre of the known universe) to heliocentric (sun at the centre). Our understanding of the universe was turned on its head as the inherited conception of an immovable earth was displaced by Copernicus, who put the sun at the centre and postulated that it is the earth that moves (a full revolution on its own axis every 24 hours and a revolution of the sun every 365 days). As a result, Copernicus was placed on the list of banned books created by the Roman Catholic church which, in its passion to defend biblical 'truth', was inadvertently and unwittingly sustaining error. Galileo as well as Copernicus, could have paid with his life for his ideas because he supported the Copernican theory prior to appearing before the church authorities in Rome. In fact he was forced to abjure the Copernican heliocentric theory (Sobel 2000).

One of the reasons for the disquiet of the church authorities in light of the emerging science was that Copernicus and Galileo constituted a direct challenge to the Christian world view of the time, its beliefs and traditions, its Bible stories understood literally, and its lack of will to adopt an open mind when confronted with new ideas, albeit radical new ideas. The new science, with its different route to knowledge, began to pick holes in established dogmas, traditions, authorities and power structures. The idealist, theological and metaphysical approach to knowledge was under threat because it could be stated that this approach was actually distorting, and therefore misrepresenting, the real world the new science was trying to understand, interpret and explain. The new science emphasised the observation of objects in the world, facts, phenomena, and sense experience; the world was set on the path to becoming an impersonal machine that could be understood through natural and impersonal laws. For Galileo, the language of the universe could not be understood unless it was properly comprehended: it 'is written in the language of mathematics, and its characteristics are triangles, circles and other geometric figures without which it is humanly impossible to understand a single word of it...' (Galileo as quoted in Grayling 2005 p168). Additionally Kepler wanted to solve the mystery of the cosmos by using mathematics to demonstrate its Pythagorean harmony. This was how the world took shape in the post-Renaissance and scientific revolution period.

Prior to continuing the story of the scientific and empirical tradition and its implications, it is necessary to pause here to reflect that the rationalist tradition did not suddenly disappear as a result of the newly emerging science. If empirical science was beginning to challenge inherited conceptions of reality and knowledge, and therefore traditions associated with the Greek world view, the Christian vision, and the dogmas of the church, what was the basis of certain knowledge? Could there be a response to Renaissance scepticism?

Descartes and rationalism

One of the central tasks of Descartes (1596–1650) was to establish the basis of certain knowledge. Ever since the Greeks, western philosophy had focused upon two fundamental questions that may be said to encapsulate the subject matter of the discipline:

- What is real? – The ontological question.

- How do we know what is real? – The epistemological question.

Of course the equally searching Socratic question should be added to these two:

- How should people live and what should they do?

This is the axiological question confronting those who work within the people professions. If it is possible to be deceived by the senses (empirical tradition), as Descartes suggested, how can we know and what can we know? Descartes began his quest by doubting everything but what, one might ask, is left over after engaging in this process? Is there anything beyond doubt? Descartes tells us he could doubt everything except the fact that he was experiencing, was actually aware he doubted. Tarnas helps us by clarifying that everything can be questioned and doubted

> 'but not the irreducible fact of the thinker's self awareness. And in recognising this one certain truth, the mind can perceive that which characterises certainty itself: certain knowledge is that which can be clearly and distinctly conceived' (1991 p277).

So it can be postulated that the location of true and indubitable knowledge is the reasoning mind itself. As Russell neatly puts it, the Cartesian 'I think, therefore I am, makes the mind more certain than matter…' (1996 p516), establishing knowledge in thought, reason and subjectivism, which is part of the philosophical doctrine of rationalism. The rationalist believes in the supremacy of reason providing the route to knowledge, along with an acceptance of *a priori* or innate ideas and self evident truths. Furthermore, Descartes relied on mathematics to provide 'a model of clarity, certainty and orderly deduction' (Copleston 2003 Volume 4 p17).[4]

Based upon this chain of reasoning, and for illustrative purposes, Descartes said that as he turned to empty the contents of his mind he had the idea of a good God, a perfect Being. Consequently, he inferred that God exists, was certain God exists and advanced arguments to support his contention. Descartes said that God had put the idea of himself into human beings and that

> 'the idea of God has to be caused by an infinite substance. But there is only one infinite substance, namely God. So, given an idea of God, God must exist to cause the idea. Descartes has an idea of God. So God must exist' (Sorell 2000 p69).

This rationalist approach to knowledge, located in the continental philosophical tradition represented by Descartes, Spinoza and Leibniz, is of course different to the sense experience and empiricism represented by the Renaissance, subsequently taken up by Locke, Berkeley and Hume, and already encountered in Aquinas, Bacon and Ockham. Prior to expanding upon the developing empirical tradition, it is interesting to return briefly to Bacon, whose application of the scientific method enabled him to conclude that 'rationalist thinkers were like spiders who spin their webs out of matter secreted inside their own bodies; their structures are impressive but everything comes from within, and lacks sufficient contact with external reality...' (Magee 1998 p75). It was Bryan Magee, in conversation with the philosopher and sociologist Ernest Gellner during the 1970s, who stated that before Descartes 'people didn't know much, but by comparison with present-day attitudes they were sure of what they thought they knew, whereas after Descartes they knew a great deal more but were a lot less certain about it' (1978 pp289–290). Before moving on it should be acknowledged that Descartes was a philosopher and also mathematician of distinction (Grayling 2005 p205).

Empiricism

The point made by the rationalist tradition was the doctrine that knowledge is acquired by the exercise of reason. Empiricists rejected the concept of innate (*a priori*) ideas and the rationalist route to knowledge. They believed that the mind is a *tabula rasa* at birth and knowledge is really derived from sense experience, which is the tradition of Locke, Berkeley and Hume. In other words, knowledge comes to us from without rather than being located within. By the time of David Hume (1711–1776), during the Age of Reason in the eighteenth century, Tarnas explains that it was the sceptical Hume who rejected the grand metaphysical claims of philosophical rationalism and its deductive logic. He also had problems with the notion of causation that had been accepted by Locke and Berkeley (Ayer 2000 p24), the inductive method, that metaphysics is really a myth and so religious belief can be discredited, that we know much less than we think we know and that, in fact, there cannot be any certain knowledge at all about anything. Consequently, there are problems with both the rationalist and empiricist basis of knowledge:

> 'With Hume, the long-developing empiricist stress on sense perceptions, from Aristotle and Aquinas, to Ockham, Bacon and Locke, was brought to its ultimate extreme, in which only the volley and chaos of those perceptions exist, and any order imposed on those perceptions was arbitrary, human and without objective foundation...For Hume all human knowledge had to be regarded as opinion.' (Tarnas 1991 p339; Humean scepticism acknowledges contingency in the sense that patterns, shapes, uniformity, cause and effect are not discovered in the world or mind but rather imposed by habit and custom.)

Magee states that 'If we could stop just at this point, Hume would stand before us as an unmitigated sceptic, a man who denied that we could be sure of anything, whether it be the existence of God, or of the external world, or of our own continuous selves, or indeed of any reliable connections between anything and anything else in the world of fact' (1998 p135).

Remaining with the issue of causation, which at first sight appears uncomplicated, it was Hume who questioned the assumption that B is caused by A. Causal connections are not observed but are rather a sequence of events. Bertrand Russell explained by saying that

> 'objects have no discoverable connection together; nor is it from any other principle but custom operating on the imagination, that we can draw any inference from the appearance of one to the experience of another' (1996 p605).

Thus Hume's empirical scepticism undermines the view that it is possible to establish scientific laws, logical proofs, based upon particular observations with the rejection of induction. With David Hume the point had been reached, epistemologically speaking, where everything is contingent; one can only know phenomena and cannot go beyond them; all we are in possession of is a mass of chaotic impressions and sensations; order in the world between things is not arrived at by describing how things really are, but rather something imposed by the mind. Therefore by 'showing on the one hand how an uncritical trust in reason had foundered in dogmatism, and on the other by reducing pure empiricism to absurdity, he had paved the way for Kant' (Ayer 2000 p26).

Kant's synthesis

Help was at hand in the person of Immanuel Kant (1724–1804) who provided a fusion between rationalism and empiricism (although Copleston questions whether we can in fact approach Kant in terms of a synthesis of the rationalist and empirical traditions: 2003 Volume 6 p428). This fusion, in the *Critique of Pure Reason* (see discussion in Tarnas 1991; Magee 1998; Kuehn 2001; Copleston 2003) is approached by arguing that claims to knowledge cannot go beyond sense experience, and yet knowledge is partly *a priori* and not inferred inductively from experience. So what are described as the innate categories of the mind are involved in giving shape and order to reality. Sense experiences are screened, filtered, or sieved, through the *a priori* structures of the mind. In other words, the mind, human subjectivity, is actively involved in ordering and processing, thus supplying 'the concepts and means of which we understand experience' (Russell 1996 p642). The Copernican revolution in Kantian philosophy is not that knowledge conforms to objects, but that objects conform to the cognitive apparatus of the mind. As Scruton puts it 'Self-consciousness requires that the world must appear to conform to the categories' (2001 p39). After Kant it is no longer possible to know the transcendent realm of reality that Plato talked about and thought possible (*noumena*). We know things only as they appear to us, not as they are in themselves, unmediated (Magee 1998 135). Kant would say that it is not possible to know, for example, that God exists. This would be an epistemological claim too far. This does not mean, however, that God does not exist, rather that there is no way of knowing or discovering whether or not this is in fact the case. Yet Kant postulates that belief in God is necessary in order to act as a moral being in the world, so there is a justification for belief in God on moral grounds. Nevertheless, there cannot be any certainty, hence the distinction between faith and knowledge in the disciplines of religion and philosophy.

To complete this reference to Kant, Manfred Kuehn explains in his detailed biography of the philosopher that Kant is attempting to answer three questions: What can I know? What ought I to do? What may I hope for? (2001 p241). Importantly, following Hume, a critical distinction was being made between the very essence of things as they are in themselves (*noumena*), and things as they appear to us (*phenomena*). In other words, there is the world and everything in it, and our experience of this world, but the two are not the same. Kuehn summarises the Kantian position by saying that 'we can never know what holds the world together in its innermost being, or what things are apart from our conceptual apparatus. We cannot even know who or what we ourselves ultimately are' (2001 p246).[5] It is helpful at this stage to call upon Tarnas again (1991 p282) to summarise the intellectual tenor of the 'modern' world that had been emerging since the Renaissance, scientific revolution, Kantian synthesis, and the Enlightenment of the eighteenth century:

1) God is no longer needed to explain the world in which we live, having moved beyond religious and metaphysical speculation.

2) A growing emphasis upon the material rather than spiritual.

3) Science is taking priority over religion which means that almost everything can be explained rationally.

4) The world does not have an order derived from or imposed by God, rather it can be conceived of as an impersonal machine (deism) that operates according to fixed laws that can be discovered empirically.

5) Knowledge is primarily derived by observation but we know much less than we claim to know. In fact what we assume as knowledge could well be interpretation and informed opinion.

6) A radically new cosmological understanding derived from Copernicus and Galileo.

7) The subsequent impact of Newton; Darwin (man not at the centre of a biblically ordered universe); Freud (religion is a childish illusion).

8) The independence and emancipation of man from religious beliefs and the profound implications of this for morality, values and ethics (Nietzsche).

Following this brief ontological and epistemological survey based upon important intellectual developments which takes into account Plato's two realms, Greek and Christian world views, and the growing importance of empiricism and natural science in modern times, it is important not to lose sight of the dimension of the *other*. Hans Kung, the radical Catholic theologian, when expanding upon the *other dimension*, reminds us that Descartes, Spinoza, Leibniz, Voltaire, Lessing and Kant, in addition to Copernicus, Galileo, Kepler and Newton 'would never have thought of forthrightly denying any dimension beyond that of mathematical-natural scientific reason' (1976 p86; but see Dawkins (2006) for an alternative perspective). This is a salient issue for us to bear in mind. The point Kung was making during the 1970s was that reality is not one-dimensional but multi-dimensional; there are different ways of approaching the nature of reality that should embrace the layers represented by Plato, scientific method, secular and religious perspectives. In other words, reality is kaleidoscopic in nature, in that it is complex and multi-faceted. If we are disposed to focus on one facet at the expense of others, for example the 'truths' disclosed by modern science, we could easily distort the nature of reality, the very thing we are trying to understand. To illustrate the dangers of such a position let us turn to the positivism of Auguste Comte and later the Vienna Circle (positivism was influential between the 1850s and early 1900s).

Standing inside the Vienna Circle

Comte (1798–1857) is credited with coining the term sociology and being the progenitor of positivism (the tradition traced through Montesquieu and Condorcet in the eighteenth century and later Saint Simon and Durkheim).[6] In broad terms, positivism (we have already begun to dip our toes in this stream by alluding to the empirical tradition) is the doctrine which states that knowledge, what we know, is based upon sense experience, which means proceeding on the basis of observation, experiment and measurement (measurement will preoccupy us later). Comte believed that knowledge has developed through three stages – first, the theological with its belief in supernatural beings, then the metaphysical, which is a refinement of the theological, and finally, the positivist which is scientific. Reality therefore consists of what can be observed and knowledge is limited to what is accessible to the senses. It is not possible to proceed beyond this, which means there is no place in this ontological and epistemological framework for theology, speculative metaphysics, rationalism and idealism. Importantly, Comte was influential in the study of society rather than the individual. He wanted to produce knowledge to establish the invariant and predictive laws of the social world that would stand alongside Newton's laws explaining the physical world. In other words, he wanted to establish a science of society, the sociological tradition later pursued by Durkheim. The significance of positivism within the context of this chapter is that, as a scientific paradigm, it denies any validity to forms of knowledge beyond those which can be obtained by the inductive method (Bryant 1985; Farmer 1967).

After Comte, in the 1920s and 1930s, came the logical positivists of the Vienna Circle. The group was founded by Maurice Schlick and comprised philosophers, scientists and mathematicians. It developed its thinking against the background of the analytical philosophy of Bertrand Russell and was also influenced by Ludwig Wittgenstein (1889–1951). This was a scientific approach to reality, again rooted in the empirical tradition, which articulated the view that meaningful statements are those which can be empirically verified (Bryant 1985). The radical implications of this paradigm include the idea that theological discourse, metaphysics, aesthetics, ethics and values are rendered meaningless because they do not meet the stringent test of empirical verification. This is a greatly simplified summary of logical positivism, but it helps to explain the Vienna Circle's approach which is an attenuated perspective on the nature of reality. Significantly, the Vienna Circle represents a shift from the philosophical agenda that addressed the big questions of existence, the nature of the world, ontology, epistemology, time and causation (Magee 1998), and puts the spotlight on clearing up linguistic and conceptual muddles. Logical positivism is concerned with analysis and clarification; the meaning of what we think and say, rather than the creation of a metaphysical system that purports to account for everything.

Copleston helpfully adds to this discussion by saying that since the Renaissance in the fifteenth century, the intellectual context for philosophy has been provided by the empirical sciences (2003 Volume 11 26). Nevertheless, it is important to acknowledge that (and this is a Kungian position) science, theology and metaphysics provide human beings with different types of knowledge. However, the application of scientific method has created a way of thinking which says that 'all that can be known can be known by means of science' (p30) which is the intellectual climate nourished by logical positivism. Copleston claims that logical positivism is the heir of Renaissance science and that the atmosphere created by empiricism, scientific method, and logical positivism has been inimical to those areas of life considered to be beyond the objective and scientifically factual – religion, faith, art, music, moral values and metaphysics. Although the influence of the logical positivists declined after 1945, the point can be advanced with Copleston that the development and growth of empiricism as the scientific route to certain knowledge and truth, in addition to the industrial revolution and the creation of a more technical civilisation along with its economic values 'has produced a type of mind which is naturally closed to the Transcendent…' (p32): in other words, that is closed off from the notion of the possibility of otherness. However, he goes on to state that 'if human culture is not to descend into an arid wilderness of materialism, it is important to remember that there are other levels of experience and knowledge than that represented by empirical science' (p43).

A similar point is made by Hans Kung, whom we touched upon earlier in this chapter. When composing his influential theological work during the 1970s, he reflected at one stage on the different routes by which twentieth-century man has attempted to become human: for example, through political-social revolution (Marxism) and then again through technological revolution. Kung's point is that neither science nor technology provide human beings with a comprehensive, all-encompassing view of reality. Arguably, science deals only with one facet of what is real. And let us not forget that science sometimes goes catastrophically wrong. This kind of thinking represents a reductionist ontology and epistemology, which is a perspective that has resonance with what this book is attempting to address and counter in relation to the probation domain. In other words logical positivism and scientific thinking more generally are tantamount to an approach that attenuates otherness by limiting, narrowing and reducing the complex nature of reality while moving towards one-dimensionality. At this point I want to broaden the correctives to the scientific paradigm we find in Kung and Copleston, by turning to additional illustrations of otherness, beginning with religion.

Religion as a dimension of otherness

One of the central propositions of this chapter is that it is not possible to measure everything scientifically. Arguably, therefore, one illustration of this proposition is to refer to the religious imagination contained within numerous traditions – Jewish, Christian, Islam, Hinduism in India, Buddhism and Taoism in China, and so on (see Kung 1976; Freeman 1999; Graves 1985; Armstrong 1993). The point can be advanced that the primary subject of religion (the word God will have to suffice here), is not someone or something that can be discovered at the end of a chain of deductive reasoning, or that is accessible to empirical observation. God is not a constituent element of a logical argument or a component in a mathematical equation, whose existence can be proved beyond doubt, like dealing with something that can be weighed, quantified and measured. Arguably, God does not constitute an object amenable to Cartesian reasoning or Newtonian science about which a general law of existence can be established. The reality of God, or Being itself (if I can be permitted to resort to this expression), touches upon issues of deep existential meaning, purpose and value for human beings, which are to be approached by a leap of Kierkegaardian faith (Carnell 1965), not the presumed certainties and unambiguous truths purported to reside with science. It is not possible to philosophise or logically argue Being into existence; to think otherwise is to fail, some would claim, to grasp the essential nature of this enquiry. This is because God comes into the domain of the qualitative and ineffable, myth and mystery, feeling and faith, including the realm of ambiguity. Religion, therefore, belongs to a dimension of otherness which is other than the scientific paradigm.

Further illustrations of otherness

It is interesting to continue the religious theme by referring to Rudolf Otto, who said that

'Taken in the religious sense, that which is 'mysterious' is – to give it perhaps the most striking expression – the Wholly Other, that which is quite beyond the sphere of the usual, the intelligible, and the familiar, which therefore falls quite outside the limits of the 'canny', and is contrasted with it, filling the mind with blank wonder and astonishment' (1958 p26).

According to Otto, the Holy is what is sacred, numinous, Being; in other words the ineffable. He illustrates the numinous by referring variously to religious emotion, expressions of piety, and the atmosphere surrounding religious buildings. From a peaceful tide to something that can be thrilling and vibrant, the soul returns once again to a more ordinary state.

In similar vein, Martin Buber (1970) talks about 'I and Thou' in contrast to 'I and It' relations. The former can be conceptualised as a subject-to-subject relationship, the latter as subject-to-object. In I–Thou relations one person engages with the totality of the other person within a context of mutual reciprocity and unity; if I–It prevails the context is depersonalised and it is more person-to-object, in relation to isolated aspects of the other person. In this case, the person becomes a 'thing' or impersonal category: a label of some description is imposed by one person upon the other. Importantly for Buber it is Theos, as the eternal Thou (the other), who sustains I–Thou, person-to-person, subject-to-subject, relations.

Hans Kung has not only written many stimulating books on theology. In his slim volume on *Mozart* (1992) he invites the reader to detect traces of a transcendent otherness in the sphere represented by music. It is also interesting to refer to Anthony Storr's *Music and the Mind* (1992). Storr explains how music is able to communicate with people at an emotional level, with a depth and intensity beyond the language of science. The language of science and analytical philosophy deals in concepts and levels of proof to demonstrate what is and is not the case empirically, with a view to establishing the indisputable truths of existence and reality. Music, literature, poetry, and the arts in general operate at deeper levels, which are emotionally evocative in their ability to tap into areas of human emotion and experience beyond science. Storr clarifies that music affects people both physically and emotionally through the composer's structure and arrangements of the notes. Although it is possible to measure the time it takes to complete a musical performance, trying to measure and quantify its emotional impact, its deeper meaning, misses the point.

Brian Sewell, the art critic, on his pilgrimage from Paris to Santiago de Compostela (the subject of a television series in 2005) engaged in a critique of buildings, cathedrals and paintings he encountered along the mediæval pilgrim route. At the beginning of his pilgrimage he described himself as a lapsed Catholic who, until this point in his life, had been comfortable with his loss of faith. Yet as he followed in the footsteps of those earlier pilgrims, retracing his own steps from 40 years ago when he first made the journey, he began to feel uneasy with himself. At one point, he described his scepticism about being a sceptic. He was 'moved' by his pilgrimage; his emotional state altered; he was affected by the experience, yet did not seem able to provide a rational basis for his altered condition. This does not mean he wanted to revert to how he thought and felt 40 years ago and recapture lost faith, even though he could envy the faith of the faithful en route. Is this an experience of Otto's Wholly Other, a sense of the numinous; is this Buber's eternal Thou interacting with Sewell's 'I'? Does this represent yet another illustration of otherness, of something of profound meaning and value which has an ineffable quality, not easy to measure or to encapsulate within the scientific paradigm?

Pascal in the seventeenth century (Pascal 1966; Cailliet 1944) left room for the heart alongside mind and reason. Notwithstanding the Copernican revolution within Kantian philosophy, he wanted to abolish knowledge to make room for belief and a mystical reality beyond sense experience. The scientist Einstein also referred to the mystical. The politician Dennis Healey who, as Chancellor during the 1970s, spent much of his time working with numbers, commented that 'Oxford, the war, and politics all taught me the limitations of scientific reason as a guide to human beings. Fortunately I have always found the arts an inexhaustible source, not only of pleasure, but also of knowledge and understanding' (1992 p136).

In spite of all the discoveries and benefits of science, technology, and human reason since the Renaissance, and the ability of philosophy to analyse, question and elucidate language, ideas and concepts of an ontological and epistemological nature, it is suggested that a disparate collection of other disciplines – religion, theology, music, painting, sculpture, architecture, poetry and literature – invites the question of whether science can ever be the last word, the final arbiter, on the rich and complex nature of reality. Can the scientific paradigm, with its emphasis on quantification and measurement as the basis of knowledge, incorporate the sum total of, and therefore the deepest meaning and value within, the human experience? Does such a paradigm provide a single master vision that is capable of incorporating all that is real and significant? Many illustrations of otherness take issue with this scientific perspective. The scientific advances of the sixteenth and seventeenth centuries did not totally expunge religious beliefs. Scientific advances did not mean that Galileo and Newton, for example, 'regarded physical science as the sole source of knowledge' (Copleston 2003 Volume 3 p289).

In one section of Alan Bennett's *Untold Stories* (2005), the reader is provided with an analysis of painting. Standing before numerous paintings during the course of his life, Bennett confesses not to having had a sensation of 'rapture, or any physical sensation'. Nevertheless, he says he likes certain pictures rather than others because of an ineffable 'glow' (and he cites Bellini's *Agony in the Garden*, Giorgione's *Il Tramonto*, Catena's *Portrait of a Young Man*, and Antonello's *St Jerome in his Study* as good examples). Bennett says it is difficult to be precise about what he means by glow 'but, whatever it is, all I can say is that I know it when I see it, which is of course intellectually not very respectable or communicable' (p457). This is a good example of the notion of the ineffable.

It is clear that there is a considerable ontological and epistemological gulf between the Greek Platonic vision of reality of two realms and what it was thought could be known, contrasted with the scientific, empirical and positivist traditions that established a narrower basis for understanding reality and thinking about what it is possible to know and the process by which knowledge is established. The end point of this tradition in this chapter finds its fullest expression in the Vienna Circle. Nevertheless it would be remiss if this chapter did not refer briefly to the eighteenth/nineteenth century (counter) Romantic movement, with its multi-dimensional rather than one-dimensional approach to the nature of reality. It can be argued that, although the intellectual tradition associated with science, quantification and numbers, has liberated the mind from superstition and misleading metaphysics, paradoxically this mind-set also has the capacity to create a less than balanced and therefore human world. In other words, it can simplify but also distort. Hence the Romantic movement's reaction to the Enlightenment, because the former drew attention to a spiritual dimension, transcendence, feeling, the artistic and the imaginative, including intuition. Romanticism was dealing with something other than the zeitgeist of reason. Consequently

> 'Romantic poets, religious mystics, idealist philosophers, and counter-cultural psychedelists would claim the existence of other realities beyond the material and argue for an ontology of human consciousness sharply differing from that of conventional empiricism' (Tarnas 1991 p375).

It is therefore helpful to contrast the following categories:

- Materialism v idealism

- Mind v soul

- Head v heart

- Reason v faith

- Science v humanism

- Apollonian v Dionysian

- Concrete v abstract

- Quantitative v qualitative

- Age of Enlightenment reason v Romantic sensibilities
- Obvious v more ineffable features

Tarnas continues the discussion by adding that, with the arrival of the post-modern mind in the twentieth century (as opposed to the construction of the 'modern' from the Renaissance), there is no longer any underpinning, overarching, or unifying theme. In other words we are no longer in the grip of either the Greek or Christian world views which had a powerful influence in their own day. There is not even one scientific world view upon which everyone can agree. Consequently the post-modern world is not founded upon the certainty of one reality. The intellectual landscape is characterised by something much more unsettling: relativism, diversity, fallibility, interpretations rather than facts. The notion of what is real is constantly changing and being constructed, reconstructed, and deconstructed, by the post-Kantian human mind. A lucid summary of this perspective is provided by Tarnas when he says that

> 'In virtually all contemporary disciplines, it is recognised that the prodigious complexity, subtlety, and multivalence of reality far transcend the grasp of any one intellectual approach, and that only a committed openness to the interplay of many perspectives can meet the extraordinary challenges of the post-modern era' (1991 p404).

This has resonance for the remainder of this chapter.

This journey into the history of philosophy, which incorporates illustrations of *otherness*, poses questions, stimulates thinking and generates ideas, creates a framework within which to analyse developments in probation and wider public sector people-based organisations. Otherness has been used as a heuristic device to explore (literally to find, to flush out) dimensions of meaning and value that, it is suggested, can be found in interstices beyond scientific method and the positivist enterprise. This line of enquiry is pertinent to probation, particularly in light of developments since the 1980s (see Chapter 2).

Thinking critically about probation

Since Descartes (of course it is possible to go as far back as the Greeks), important philosophical questions have been, and continue to be, centred around: What can I know? How can I know? Just what is the extent and basis of human knowledge? It can forcefully be argued that within the world of probation since the 1980s, and the emerging NOMS structure since January 2004, the ontological, epistemological and axiological basis of the organisation has increasingly been pared down to what can be quantified and measured. In other words, the organisation is based on a more restricted form of (politically acceptable) knowledge, associated with a narrower approach to accountability, increasingly derived from numbers. The potentially rich and complex nature of what was fundamentally a people-based organisation with a distinctive mission, which must therefore make room for both quantitative and qualitative features, has been attenuated. Primarily as a result of increasing political pressures over recent years, probation has been transformed to focus on certain organisational features rather than others. It has elevated, for example, national standards, cash-linked targets, audit trails, quantification, computerisation, and a penchant for numbers linked to risk assessments via OASys, obscuring those features of a more qualitative and ineffable nature from its field of vision. Complex human dynamics associated with a people-focused organisation, aetiological issues (why do people offend), in addition to debates surrounding ideals, ethics, values, and a personalist/ relationship oriented philosophy within which to understand and work with individuals (McWilliams 1987), are now less important. To put this another way, the qualitative and ineffable dimensions of *otherness* have been seriously weakened. So what could some of these ideas suggest for probation? How can aspects of this philosophical framework be applied to the probation world? Can anything be learned from the discussion that would make us exercise a degree of caution and re-evaluate the current predicament?

1 When two realms become one

When applying some of the ideas generated by this journey into the history of philosophy to the very different and, it could be argued, totally unrelated domains of probation, NOMS, and the wider criminal justice system (including other people-based organisations within the public sector), the first point to extrapolate is that there are two distinctly separate yet interconnected realms. These are not the two realms contained in the philosophy of Plato and the neo-Platonists, but something much more simple and mundane, although by no means insignificant. In probation work it is possible to proceed on the basis that there is a dimension of reality which can be represented by numbers, quantification and measurement. Additionally, there are qualitative features which reflect the fact that organisations, like probation, work with people and that the complex nature and contingencies of people-work cannot be captured, in their totality, by generating and applying numbers, pursuing audit trails, and producing statistical tables. This is not a metaphysical point, but rather an attempt to appreciate the multi-faceted nature of probation work in the round.

Developments since the 1980s have elevated the quantitative dimension at the expense of qualitative features, due to a weighty and so far unstoppable combination of political power, central control, New Public Management principles, expanding bureaucracy, and a growing obsession with accountability and explication of the probation task by recourse to mathematics. This reshaping was initiated at the level of central government before being implemented and cemented in place by bureaucratic positivists, with the inescapable implication that probation activity can in fact be quantified. Consequently organisational goals and corresponding managerial tasks have become dominated by target achievement assisted by the use of computers, analysed in Chapter 2. But it does not have to be like this: the job could be justified and evaluated in a different way that was less reliant on numbers; there could be a greater recognition of those qualitative aspects that, it can be argued, undoubtedly complement the quantitative. Arguably there could and should be a much better balance between the quantitative and qualitative realms of practice which, over recent years, have been disrupted. The point is that observation can result in the quantification of certain probation tasks, thus making a case for the use of numbers. On the other hand, observation can be used to make qualitative judgments about practice issues located in a realm beyond quantifiable measurement, precisely because of the people-orientated nature of the job. So there are two distinctive yet related realms that cannot be reduced to one, which can be explored in further detail as follows.

2 Quantitative measurements contrasted with qualitative observation

This chapter has tried to explain, with the valued assistance of certain distinguished philosophers and their equally distinguished interpreters (Richard Tarnas, Bertrand Russell, Frederick Copleston and Bryan Magee), that a certain pattern of thoughts has evolved since the scientific revolution that created the modern world. This pattern of thoughts has drawn attention to a route to knowledge, and corresponding approach to the nature of reality, that is predominantly empirical. In other words, it proceeds on the basis of observation and the collection of so-called facts.

124 *Modernising Probation and Criminal Justice*

Of course Copleston and Kung, for example, inject a note of caution when faced with the temptation to reduce knowledge of what is purportedly real to the parameters of the scientific paradigm. It is unhelpful to be dogmatic, and more sensible to keep an open mind, by acknowledging that there are different routes to what could be classified as different kinds of knowledge (bear in mind the degrees and levels of knowledge in Plato; Copleston Volume 1 152). This is an argument for a multi-dimensional rather than one-dimensional approach.

Where the recent history of the probation service is concerned it has, it may be suggested, got itself into a conceptual muddle by confusing measurement and observation. These two concepts are linked, but there are important differences that need clarification. It is evident, and this point can be conceded, that certain aspects of probation activity lend themselves to quantitative measurement and subsequently audit arrangements associated with performance management and accountability. This approach is linked to an organisational approach based upon objectives, targets, and measuring performance against the benchmark of national standards. However, it can be restated with equal force that it is not necessary to proceed on this basis; there could be a qualitative approach to employee accountability or, and this is more likely, a balanced approach through synthesising the two very different positions. Yet it must be remembered that there are fields of activity, fundamental to people-based organisations, which lend themselves to qualitative observation and judgment more than numerical quantification. These are the qualitative features which can be observed rather than measured, for example, by an experienced practice development assessor (PDA) when supervising, coaching and evaluating the work of trainees; the same reasoning can be applied to the role of middle managers in both probation and social services, when evaluating the work of staff in their teams. It is the PDAs' and managers' responsibility (Whitehead and Thompson 2004) to help trainees and other staff acquire and then develop a range of qualitative and ineffable people skills that can be listed as follows:

- Assessment and intervention skills.

- How to interview and ask the right open and closed questions at the right time to collect relevant information.

- How to engage with and establish relationships with people to facilitate assessment.

- Insight and awareness as aids to understanding.

- Intuition, imagination and creativity.

- Empathy and feel for people and their circumstances.

- How to listen actively.

- Understanding and appreciation of complex human problems.

- Sensitivity and patience.

- Ability to make balanced judgments based upon relevant information.

- Exercising discretion.

- Ethical basis for practice – what is the right thing to do.

- Expression of certain values – respect for persons etc… (axiology).

- Therapeutic imagination and artistry through reflection (Schon 1987).

- An understanding of both the 'What' and 'How' of practice' (Whitehead and Thompson 2004 p207).

- Simply *being* with people as a primary value and end in itself, rather than always *doing*.

Furthermore, the NVQ is an instrument which should be seen as part of a wider managerial and bureaucratic system devoted to quantifying, measuring and evaluating probation tasks which have become increasingly codified.[7] Experienced PDAs should be clear that probation practice cannot be reduced to even the most sophisticated system of measurement by the allocation of numerical values to all spheres of work. Therefore a clear distinction must be established between what belongs to different quantitative and qualitative dimensions; measurement and observation; bureaucratic demands and the essence of the professional task. At present, managers could be failing to observe and acknowledge quality work undertaken by staff because it does not fall within the narrow bureaucratic parameters created by political priorities, particularly since 1997.

3 Otherness and ineffability in probation

This leads to the heuristic device of *otherness* that is a connecting thread in this chapter. The point to establish is not to charge probation or NOMS in the twenty-first century with a lack of transcendence in the sense that the probation service is not Platonic, religious or metaphysical enough. This is not the point to which I wish to draw attention, notwithstanding the nineteenth-century religious origins of the organisation. Probation's otherness, increasingly attenuated by the emphasis upon quantification, is rather the doctrine of the *ineffable*. Certain features of the job are difficult to pin down; indirect and vague rather than obvious; difficult to capture with precision; not easy to define; and hence incapable of precise numerical measurement (see the examples cited above). Otherness is the acknowledgement of ambiguity; of subtle and nuanced perspectives; of something that is located within a dimension of reality beyond the scientific paradigm. Otherness is also associated with the notion of professional competence and what it means to be a probation officer, which includes being as well as doing. But it must be asserted that a combination of factors including centralised political power structures, changing ideology, and the emergence of bureaucratic positivists, have been responsible for the creation of a computerised, target driven, number crunching culture that has radically transformed an organisation that once had a better understanding of qualitative, ineffable and personalist features.

This can be illustrated by saying that in certain spheres of operation the probation officer task (re-designated offender manager since 1st April 2006) is dominated by the insatiable demands of computers for increasing amounts of numerical data. From conversations with a number of probation staff (mainly during 2006), it can be estimated that 80 per cent of each working day (some staff inform me it can be less than this, but others remarkably more) is devoted to working at a computer terminal, as an office based data-entry operator, rather than spending time in face to face contact with the clients. A number of newer staff stated that they joined probation with the understanding they would be working with people (a reasonable assumption one would think), yet to their frustration find themselves feeding data into computers. The emergence of the computer has radically transformed probation's working practices and created a new culture linked to ideological transformation from the rehabilitative ideal to risk management, with far reaching implications for clients and staff.

4 Weberian rationalisation and bureaucracy

Steve Bruce reminds us that the three well-known founders of sociology, Durkheim, Weber and Marx, all presented a central idea of how the post-Enlightenment modern world differed from the pre-modern world. For Durkheim, it was the breakdown of moral regulation, solidarity, and shared norms, associated with rapid socio-economic change during the nineteenth century. For Weber, it was the controlling idea of bureaucracy and rationalisation. For Marx, of course, it was class conflict (1999 p31). Weber looked at the emergence of the modern world with its industrialisation, relativism, and saw how the promise of Enlightenment reason and scientific progress created an iron cage of bureaucracy (Morrison 1995; Gerth and Mills 1948; Bendix 1960; Garland 1990). Weber's work on bureaucracy and rationalisation has much to teach probation and has implications for the wider developments across the public sector since the 1980s. Weber drew attention to four dimensions of rationality, one of which is formal rationality. This concerns the application of rules, laws and regulations in the spheres of economic, legal and scientific institutions and bureaucratic forms of domination. Ritzer and Goodman (1997) explain that formal rationality has six characteristics that clearly resonate with recent developments within the probation services:

- Calculability – emphasis on quantification and measurement.

- Efficiency – maximum outputs for minimum inputs (NPM).

- Predictability – imposing national standards to reduce local variations.   ·

- Human beings replaced by technology and computers.

- Control over uncertainty – reducing autonomy, discretion and individual judgments.

- Irrationality – the unintended consequences of rationality.

They proceed to say that 'One of the irrationalities of rationality, from Weber's point of view, is that the world tends to become less enchanted, less magical, and ultimately less meaningful to people' (1997 p223).

Having had the experience of working for the probation service since the late 1970s, I have observed at first hand how bureaucratic systems, processes, and new ways of thinking (a different rationality), have assumed a stranglehold over the organisation, particularly during recent years. There seems to be an inordinate capacity for a bureaucratic form of organisation to expand, swallowing up and infecting everything within it. It has an unstoppable quality and, once bureaucratic systems have been introduced, they cannot easily be dismantled; they never seem to have enough information – bureaucracy constantly feeds upon itself to create new ways of generating data, forms, audits, measurements. But this type of organisation also has the capacity to turn in upon itself and become self-serving, an end in itself, more committed to the demands of accountability *per se* and seeing its primary task of working with people as a means to an end, the pursuit of targets for their own sake. The National Offender Management Service has the classic features of bureaucracy and some of the characteristics are:

- Creativity, imagination and discretion of staff stifled.

- Policies, systems, processes and procedures elevated before people and the ability to make intelligent judgments about individuals.

- Surfeit of rules and regulations that continue to expand.

- Mechanised and routinised nature of the job.

- Arid environment and authoritarian top-down mechanisms of control.

- Bureaucratic management rather than moral/charismatic leadership.

- Attenuating the human dimension and importance of social work relationships.

- Reduction of autonomy and judgment.

- Quantity before quality.

- More technically efficient but less motivation, job satisfaction, meaningful activity.

- Centralisation of power structures.

In other words, it can be argued that peering through a Weberian lens helps one to see the increasingly rational and bureaucratic nature of the modern/post-modern world. This is a world characterised by a form of reason that attempts to eradicate all traces of irrationality; it produces efficient and economic modes of action within organisations. The position is expressed by David Garland (in fact I cannot improve upon his way of stating the point and it echoes Ritzer and Goodman) when he says that society and organisations have become more effective, but in doing so have paid a heavy price because at the same time they have become 'less emotionally compelling or meaningful for their human agents' (1990 p179). MacRae echoes Garland when he says that

> 'The spontaneous affections of the heart, the hatreds of the moment, the comely and honourable ways of tradition, are all forbidden. Reason illuminates all being with a shadowless and clinical light before which fly poetry, faith and myth' (1974 p86).

It is the disenchantment of the modern world: the banishment of magic from things by rationalisation, bureaucracy, 3Es (economy, efficiency, effectiveness), reason, and the input-output mentality. Such developments are inimical to probation, as well as other organisations, as people-orientated professions.

5 Paradox of clarification and attenuation

This point has already been made but it can be further refined here. The scientific and empirical mentality since Bacon has drawn attention to a process of ontological and epistemological elucidation. This process has resulted in the clarification of the approach to and thinking about the nature of reality, what it is possible to know, and the basis of such knowledge. Yet it can be argued that this process of clarification has in fact attenuated, narrowed, reduced, refined, and omitted; it has also arguably distorted, misrepresented and misinterpreted the nature of the reality it purports to capture. It has been suggested in this chapter that logical positivism is the culmination of this philosophical journey. In other words the empirical mind-set that yields clarification by attempting to produce its predictive laws within the physical and social worlds, is at the same time in danger of creating a one-dimensional closed universe, a narrow system of thought that is short of imaginative efficacy. So it is possible to be reminded of:

- How Kocu failed, according to Pamuk, to explain Istanbul because he resorted to western scientific methods of classification that did not leave room for eastern variety, disorder and anarchy.

- The Romantic rebellion against Enlightenment reason.

- Kung's discussion of a spiritual dimension of reality beyond science to which Copleston and others have contributed by giving their consent.

The paradox of the modern mind is that it can clarify, yet arguably distort, the nature of reality, at one and the same time, by casting doubt on and even eliminating what purports to lie beyond scientific method. Hence the need for greater openness to the possibility of richness and things being more complex and multi-layered than, at first sight, we are prepared to accept. The philosophical point which needs to be re-emphasised is the argument that there are dimensions of meaning and value that can be explored and illustrated beyond the scientific enterprise of quantification and measurement. In other words the positivist paradigm denies the validity of forms of knowledge beyond those acquired by the inductive method which this chapter has questioned. This undoubtedly applies to contemporary probation and other people-based organisations, as explored towards the end of this chapter. To put it simply, people with problems cannot be reduced to a rationality that solely relies upon number, weight and measure.

Summary and conclusion

The main purpose of this chapter, worth repeating in this concluding section, is to create a philosophical framework beginning with Plato and culminating in the logical positivists. The reason for this is to explore ideas of an ontological, epistemological, and axiological nature which have always been central to the philosophical enterprise, but which are also applicable to the probation domain. Some of these ideas have wider applicability to all organisations that purport to work with people – for example social services, health, education. Within a historically grounded and dynamic framework of changing conceptions of and routes to knowledge, and competing views on the nature of reality from the Greek world view through to Renaissance science, the emergence of the modern and post-modern world, a variety of perspectives have been explored. Paradoxically the emergence and development of the scientific enterprise that continued into the nineteenth century with the positivist paradigm of induction, quantification and measurement, attempted to clarify and demystify the remit of what can be known, yet at the same time attenuated possible layers of knowledge, experience, meaning and value, of a more qualitative and ineffable nature. It is not possible to apply the scientific and positivist paradigm to all phenomena but this does not mean that what lies outside this paradigm does not exist, or is of little value. One should think in terms of different types and hierarchies of knowledge, and different methods for accessing quantitative and qualitative layers. I have contrasted the different intellectual climates represented by

Enlightenment reason and Romantic sensibility; the arrival of an iron cage of bureaucracy, reason, science, and technology at the expense of emotion, feeling, meaning and value within human relationships.

During the course of this journey I have introduced a number of examples from a variety of sources, which invite the reader to think beyond operating with a single vision lens. I have pursued the heuristic device of *otherness*. This device is a corrective mechanism because it prises open the mind to possible layers of reality, different types of knowledge and meaning. Recourse to this device has a particular resonance for the probation service, today, in the first decade of the third millennium, as a consequence of developments since the 1980s.

Over recent centuries, specifically those preoccupied with science, attention has increasingly been drawn to the central role played by number, weight and measure (Porter 2001). Scientific and technological developments in the physical sciences of chemistry, biology and physics; the evolving science of society in the works of Comte, Montesquieu, Condorcet, St Simon, Durkheim, Fourier, Proudhon, Bentham and Mill (Ritzer and Goodman 1997); and the application of the same inductive methodology have all suggested that it is possible to establish predictive, causal, and invariant laws of the natural and social worlds. This process and methodology relies upon mathematics as the means through which knowledge of the world is obtained.

From as early as the sixth century BC, the Pythagoreans were interested in mathematics and the way in which phenomena such as the relationships between things, proportions, and even musical intervals could be expressed by recourse to numbers. Reality was thought to have an order and structure where everything fits harmoniously together, as in mathematics and geometry (Magee 1998; Storr 1992). It was suggested at the beginning of this chapter that Plato's theory of knowledge relied upon Forms existing objectively and independently of the human mind. According to Plato, the most important clue to understanding these Forms was to be found in mathematics, both of which were considered to be transcendent entities (Tarnas 1991 p11). Throughout the centuries, beginning with the Greek period, mathematics has been a significant intellectual discipline in the provision of knowledge, closely associated with the philosophical enterprise.

The emergence of Renaissance science and the acquisition of knowledge via repeated empirical observations focused attention on the importance of objective 'facts' as the basis for arriving at certain knowledge (critically questioned by Hume), which of course relied upon the use of numbers. Mathematics was central to the development of a new theory of the universe associated with Copernicus, Galileo and Kepler, and for Descartes the subject was fundamental to the search for truth and certainty. In fact, Descartes 'wished to give to philosophy a clarity and certainty analogous to the clarity and certainty of mathematics' (Copleston 2003 Volume 6 p393). Newton explained gravity by numbers, and the *Principia Mathematica* of 1687 changed our understanding of the physical world, based upon mathematical equations. If Newton attempted to provide certain knowledge of the world via mathematics, and was undermined by Hume's scepticism of the mind's ability to do this, it was Kant who synthesised Hume and Newton, scepticism and science, rationalism and empiricism. According to Kant, mathematics was the model and route to certain knowledge (Tarnas 1991). Finally, numbers were important to the logical positivists and mathematicians who belonged to the Vienna Circle. During the twentieth century, the computer became an important instrument for handling large amounts of numerical data, even within people-based organisations. Therefore it can be claimed that mathematics and the manipulation of numbers have been an integral component of our developing knowledge of, and theory building in, the modern world.

Michael Cullen (1975) states that a statistically-based approach to the study of social problems can be traced to the 1660s, when data on social and economic matters were collected. Cullen cites William Petty (born 1623) for whom a science of society was premised upon 'number, weight and measure' (p6) and the focus upon quantification and its association with social reform, such as in the field of public health. It is equally interesting to note that the word 'statistics' was first used in English in 1770, but was in vogue by the 1820s in relation to quantifiable surveys. Yet, and this point is pertinent to the theme of this chapter, Cullen reminds us that as late as 1842 J.R. McCulloch rejected the idea 'that everything in statistics may be estimated in figures' (p11). Only in the twentieth century did the word statistics become solely synonymous with numbers. The point being made by Cullen is that, in the early years, 'statistics' was an elastic term and that it took some time before it was precisely defined in the way it is understood today. Initially, it carried within it the notion of facts about the state (state-istics), which of course incorporated the use of numbers, but not only numbers.

In a fascinating book on the nature of political power and techniques of governmentality, Nikolas Rose (1999) includes a pertinent essay on numbers. He clarifies how numbers are used for measuring things, quantifying aspects of social life (number of crimes committed each year, determining how long it should take to complete certain tasks in the workplace, prioritisation, formulating judgments, making decisions, and expressing an opinion). Governments and organisations increasingly function through numbers by which they audit, make comparisons, impose tax codes, determine population trends, and quantify births, marriages and deaths. The importance attached to numbers is neatly encapsulated when Rose states that

> 'The organisation of political life in the form of the modern 'governmental' state has been intrinsically linked to the composition of networks of numbers connecting those exercising political power with the persons, processes and problems that they seek to govern. Numbers are integral to the problematisations that shape what is to be governed, to the programmes that seek to give effect to government and to the unrelenting evaluation of the performance of government that characterises modern political culture' (1999 p199).

The same point can, with equal force, be applied to the probation services. A combination of numbers and computers has, arguably, radically transformed its social work culture.

Furthermore, as MacRae (1974) points out when discussing the writings of Max Weber, and here I paraphrase as well as embellish the point being expressed, the sum total of human events within the modern world, the world that has been taking shape for hundreds of years – who people are and what they do, how people think and what they feel and believe, and the desire to explain what exists – cannot be reduced to or encapsulated within any one ontological and epistemological approach, any one branch of science. The complex nature of reality, encompassing diverse human events, cannot be reduced to number, measurement and quantification, because this approach fails to provide an all-embracing vision, a form of total knowledge 'for the world is too rich' (MacRae 1974 p64). There are dimensions that belong more to the realms of qualitative and ineffable otherness, lying beyond the reach of numerical expression. This point is as relevant to the domain of philosophical enquiry into ontology and epistemology, as it is to probation work with people who offered.

I would like to make one final point before moving on. I am indebted to the single volume work of Richard Tarnas for helping me to structure this chapter, and he has accompanied us throughout this philosophical journey. Towards the end of his book, *The Passion of the Western Mind*, he informs us that the scientific certainties associated with Newton in a former age had, by the twentieth century, become more provisional than absolute following the work of Einstein, Bohr and Heisenberg (1991 p359). In fact, Popper and Kuhn suggest that the scientific paradigm cannot provide us with certain knowledge, but rather interpretations. Therefore Tarnas injects a note of caution to the weight we place on the findings of empirical science. The post-modern mind is associated with fluidity, ambiguity and pluralism, is more relative and uncertain, and we now find ourselves not in the region of certainty, but in a region of numerous possibilities and opinions. In other words, the post-Kantian mind is constantly involved in shaping, constructing and reconstructing reality, as opposed to describing unambiguously and 'reading off' what can be directly observed. Therefore

> 'In virtually all contemporary disciplines, it is recognised that the prodigious complexity, subtlety, and multivalence of reality far transcend the grasp of any one intellectual approach, and that only a committed openness to the interplay of many perspectives can meet the extraordinary challenges of the post-modern era. But contemporary science…is more conscious of its epistemological and existential limitations' (1991 p404).

By applying this philosophical journey to the probation domain, it is being suggested that a synthesis is urgently required between number, quantification and measurement, and an acknowledgement of the existence of qualitative and ineffable features. Too great a reliance upon numbers attenuates a multi-layered and complex sphere of reality and can distort understanding of the nature of people-based organisations. Moreover, numbers may not deliver the certainties one assumes in the new computer age, at the expense of professional assessments and judgments. Just as there are dimensions of meaning and value that can be explored and illustrated within a philosophically orientated framework outside the positivist-scientific paradigm, so there are dimensions of meaning and value, of a qualitative and ineffable nature within people work, which are beyond the efficacy of numbers. This exploration into philosophical developments associated with ontology, epistemology and axiology, is both framework and analogy for thinking about what probation has become, in which *otherness* can be utilised as a heuristic device to pursue neglected features.

NOTES

[1] Rationalism is from the Latin *ratio* meaning reason. Within the context of this chapter it is the epistemological position that *a priori* reason, that is innate ideas existing independently of and prior to experience, has the efficacy to grasp fundamental truths about the world and therefore nature of reality; truths, principles, axioms of the nature of reality which can be grasped by the intellect, independently of sense experience. According to Scruton, rationalism is a God's eye view of reality. In other words 'Rationalism derives all claims to knowledge from the exercise of reason, and purports to give an absolute description of the world, uncontaminated by the experience of the observer' (2001 p21). By contrast empiricism is from the Latin *experientia*, from which the word experience is derived. Therefore this alternative route to knowledge is based upon sense experience and observation. For example Copleston states that 'The first aspect of scientific method, namely observation of the empirical data as a basis for induction, for discovering causes, was stressed by Francis Bacon' (volume 3 p289).

[2] Two interesting texts for pursuing this topic in more detail are: John Hick's *The Metaphor of God Incarnate* (1993) and J.N.D. Kelly's *Early Christian Doctrines* (1958).

[3] Orhan Pamuk (2005) discovers the key to understand Istanbul in the concept huzun which is a term used to explore the melancholy associated with the faded glory and spiritual loss of a city caught between East and West: spiritual East that is fading and modernising West that is on the march.

[4] In addition to explaining rationalism compared to empiricism (see Note 1 above) so it is equally important to distinguish between the related concepts of deduction and induction. Therefore deduction is the view that one can arrive at certain truths about the world through a process of logical and deductive reasoning, premised upon innate ideas and truths. For example this is the Cartesian route from self-consciousness and inner certainty of one's own existence to the external world (Grayling 2005 p280). Deductive reasoning proceeds from the general to the particular. By contrast, induction has its roots deep within the empirical tradition. In other words the inductive-scientific method proceeds on the basis that the world of objects outside our heads can be observed and therefore grasped and known. By the observation of phenomena one can collect observable facts in a theory neutral and value free way. The accumulation of such facts, based upon repeated observations and experiments, can result in the manifestation of regular patterns which are amenable to measurement and quantification with a view to establishing the predictive, causal and invariant laws of the physical but also the social worlds – the methods of

natural science applied to the social sciences. In other words observation of particular occurrences culminates in the postulation of a general law.

[5]   The Kantian position can be further illustrated by referring to Urmson and Ree who explain that 'the framework of ideas which it was the positive task of metaphysics to elucidate was thought by Kant as the framework of things only as they appeared to beings with our cognitive constitution, not of things as they were in themselves. What was ultimately real was unknowable' (1991 p205). Additionally Copleston says that 'The world of experience, the phenomenal world or reality, as it appears to us, is not simply our construction, a dream as it were; nor is it something given; it is the result of an application of *a priori* forms and categories to what is given' (2003 Volume 6 p58). The *a priori* categories include space, time, and causality (Kuehn 2001 chapter 6) which, from a Kantian perspective, are not objective realities existing in the world, but rather imposed mental constructs.

[6]   Comte was to influence Herbert Spencer and Durkheim in the direction of studying society scientifically. In other words the application of the methods of natural science to society (social science) with a view to establishing predictive laws. For Durkheim the subject matter of sociology is to study social facts because the realm of the social has a reality which exists independently of individuals.

[7]   The term codification requires explanation within a probation context. Codification arranges, for example, items of knowledge in a systematic order. It is a process which determines the parameters of a subject by compiling definitive lists illustrated by the 12 NVQ units which remain an integral component of the Diploma in Probation Studies. It is the type of knowledge which is defined, prescriptive, static, and can be specified in advance of practice situations. Codified knowledge can be quantified and measured. Nevertheless codification can be contrasted with the notions of contingency, artistry (Schon 1987), and surprise which are important features of probation work. Stevenson puts it like this: 'The capacities to contribute, innovate, create, adapt, solve problems, fit in, add value, ask and solve the right questions, and so forth are often difficult to express, and it is usually difficult to work out how they might be acquired or transferred' (2001 p650). See discussion in Whitehead and Thompson for further information (2004).

Chapter 5

MODERNISING PROBATION AND CRIMINAL JUSTICE: SOLICITORS' PERSPECTIVES

'And my stance is that of a dispassionate observer, the aim being to investigate issues with which one is passionately involved, but with a detachment that permits one to grasp complexities and to minimise the projection of one's own wishes and fears onto the phenomenon.' (Garland 2004 p163)

The main purpose of probation 'is to provide and to organise, to staff and to structure, punishments for offenders outside of the custodial setting. So to offer a variety of sentences which provide a rehabilitative component, a punitive component such as unpaid work, and a supportive component for the offender.' (quotation from a solicitor)

Introduction

Previous chapters have examined and reflected on numerous manifestations of cultural change within the probation service. More significantly, the central preoccupation with cultural change has been closely associated with New Labour's modernising agenda since 1997. In fact, *Modernising Government* was the subject of a command paper presented to Parliament in March 1999 by the Prime Minister and Minister for the Cabinet Office. It makes interesting reading in 2007, particularly in light of the changes wrought throughout the public sector over the last decade. It was always my intention to support the related themes of modernisation and cultural change by undertaking empirical research. However, I did not envisage, initially at least, the nature of the research featured in this chapter, which I will now explain.

The obvious way to gather data for my research would have been to interview a number of probation officers to talk to those most affected by the cultural changes which have undoubtedly occurred. If some earlier work had researched aspects of probation practice towards the end of the politically challenging 1980s (Whitehead 1990), then it would have been of interest to do something similar on this occasion, thus enabling comparisons to be made over a period of nearly 20 years. Undoubtedly, this approach would have been of value. However, an unexpected opportunity to discuss aspects of cultural change within the probation service and wider criminal justice system with a different group of professionals was presented, located at Northtown Magistrates' Court, situated in an inner city area of the north-east of England. To be more precise, during 2006 I was able to interview a number of defence solicitors about their understandings, perceptions, awareness and experiences of developments within probation. I reasoned that solicitors were well placed to further my research because they have daily contact, work closely with, use the services of, and discuss the lives of clients with probation staff, particularly in those cases where reports have been prepared. It seemed reasonable to assume that solicitors would have a dispassionate and more independent view of probation-related matters, being on the outside looking in, than probation officers would, being on the inside looking at themselves. Consequently, the first phase of this research project focused on the views of solicitors. The second phase, undertaken during 2007 and beyond, will extend the scope of the project to include barristers and judges, magistrates, district judges and clerks, with a view to building a multifaceted account of modernisation and cultural change in the probation service and wider criminal justice system.

Over many decades, various forms of empirical research have been undertaken within the criminal justice system on numerous subjects, including crime rates, types of offences and their aetiology, sentencing practices of the courts and the proportionate use of different sentences, the effectiveness of sentencing, the work of various criminal justice agencies such as probation, prisons and police, and the impact of different legislation. One only needs to peruse the diverse collection of Home Office Research Studies since the 1970s for findings on these and other related subjects: www.probation.homeoffice.gov.uk; www.homeoffice. gov.uk/rds/index.htm. Further references on criminal justice research topics can be found in a set of papers included in Noaks and Wincup (2004); Baldwin and McConville on plea bargaining (1977); Baldwin (2000); Brown on *Magistrates at Work* (1991); Shapland's work based on a small sample of barristers, judges and recorders on reports to courts (1981). The research into measuring the satisfaction of courts with the probation service (Home Office Research Study 144 1995) could also be mentioned here. Nevertheless, I have not been able to find any specific research on recent cultural changes in probation, primarily based upon interviewing solicitors who work within the magistrates' courts system of England and Wales.

The solicitors based at Northtown Magistrates' Court are busy people, many of whom undertake a range of tasks within the court building each week: interviewing their clients on the court landing to take instructions prior to hearings before a bench of magistrates or district judge; obtaining and reading crown prosecution advance disclosure packages; collecting, verifying, and questioning evidence derived from the police; visiting the Bridewell; appearing in court; completing legal aid forms; and of course liaising closely with probation and other court staff. These tasks are sandwiched between visiting their offices at the beginning and end of each working day. It is far from easy for the prospective researcher to gain access to this group of professionals, whose main task is to represent their clients in criminal proceedings. This helps to explain the paucity of research data using solicitors as respondents. Consequently, I became a privileged researcher when I approached as many potential respondents as I could during the summer of 2006 with a view to gaining their permission to commence interviews during the autumn. Practically all those I approached signalled their willingness to take part. This was the first major hurdle surmounted.

Before commencing the interviews, I ascertained that approximately 13 local firms of solicitors appear on an almost daily basis at Northtown Magistrates' Court, providing in the region of 36 solicitors. It was my aim to interview as many as I could to provide as comprehensive and accurate a picture as possible. By the end of 2006, I had been able to interview 31 out of 36 solicitors, with the result that 12 out of 13 firms were represented in the research. I am grateful to all those who gave both permission and time, many of whom took full advantage of the opportunity to express their views and concerns on issues of deep professional significance for them. Given the nature of the work undertaken each day by these solicitors, I knew that time constraints would be a factor in the research. I had a maximum of 40 minutes per interview to collect the data; some of the interviews were conducted during the respondents' lunch period. Prior to the interviews the respondents were aware, and became intrigued, that I wanted to talk to them about cultural change in probation, a theme which would overlap with modernisation and lead them to reflect on probation reports and the NOMS agenda. Furthermore, the design of the semi-structured interview schedule comprised a total of 14 questions. Most of the data collected, taped, and later transcribed for analysis was qualitative. However, I designed the research to produce a limited amount of quantitative data, some of which is reflected in the tables below.

Respondents' profile

Profile (N=31): Table 5.1 Age of solicitors

Age	Number	Per cent
20 to 29	4	12.9
30 to 39	9	29.0
40 to 49	9	29.0
50 to 59	6	19.4
60 to 69	3	9.7
Totals	31	100.0

Age

The average age of these 31 solicitors is 42.4 years. In fact the inter-quartile mean figure (calculated by excluding the seven youngest and seven oldest) is not too dissimilar at 41.9 years.

Gender

This was a concern during the early stages of the research because I hoped for a balance between male and female respondents. Within the probation service itself there is a much higher proportion of female officers than male, despite the fact that there are more male than female offenders. On the other hand, out of a total of 36 solicitors, only 7 (19 per cent) were women. As the research continued, I had the opportunity to interview four of these seven. Four of a total of 31 respondents at Northtown Magistrates' Court amounts to 13 per cent. This was not the gender balance I had hoped for.

Ethnicity

All my 31 respondents identified themselves as white British. Out of a total of 36 solicitors, I could have interviewed only one with a different ethnicity. However, as it transpired, this solitary respondent could not be included in the 31.

Table 5.2 Number of years working as a solicitor

Years	Number	Per cent
1 to 9	13	41.9
10 to 19	9	29.0
20 to 29	5	16.1
30 to 39	4	12.9
Totals	31	99.9

Number of years as a solicitor

The average number of years spent working as a solicitor is 14.4. The inter-quartile mean score is 12.8 years. Looking at the data presented in Table 5.2, it could be suggested that the 13 located in the first band (one to nine years) would have little of interest to say about cultural change within the probation service because they have not worked in their profession long enough to formulate views and make comparisons. However, only 6 out of 31 (19 per cent) had worked as a solicitor for fewer than five years, and in fact they asked me whether they would be able to make a worthwhile contribution to the research. I reasoned that all 31 respondents, from the 41.9 per cent in the first band to the 12.9 per cent in the 30 to 39 age bracket (it should also be acknowledged that nine solicitors (29 per cent) had over 25 years' experience and one of these had worked at Northtown Magistrates' Court for 36 years) would have something of value to say about probation and criminal justice matters. This proved to be the case during the interviews. I was concerned to include as many solicitors as I could with a range of experience, even at the risk of diluting the data. With this profile in mind, it is time to turn to the solicitors' understandings of the probation service.

Understandings of probation

During the course of this research, I asked the solicitors about their understandings and perceptions of the purpose of probation (what is the organisation for and why does it exist). Responses to this question included:

- The provision of insight into the lives of offenders.

- Prevent re-offending.

- Manage and monitor offenders in the community.

- Punishment.

- Alternatives to custody.

- The provision of help.

- To contribute to the sentencing process within the courts.

Additionally, and interestingly, 16 out of 31 resorted to the language of reform (1) and rehabilitation (15) to pin down their understanding of the rationale of probation. These two words, particularly rehabilitation, were used more consistently than any others by the solicitors, and they did so without any prompting from the researcher: the questions posed did not include either of the words 'reform' or 'rehabilitation'. This does not mean that the solicitors rejected any association between probation work and punishment (observe the findings in Table 5.3), because some of them expressed the view that rehabilitation can be effected through community punishments. Nevertheless, one respondent clarified his understanding of probation by stating that

> 'I think as a whole the profession is in a situation where it deals with the rehabilitation of offenders and ultimately that's my view of the probation service. They are there to assist the court in aiming to rehabilitate offenders, hence (pre-sentence reports are prepared) with a view to trying to rehabilitate offenders and to provide information along those lines that would assist the court...'

As the interviews progressed, the solicitors were asked in more detail about their understanding of probation. The various agencies which comprise the criminal justice system – police, prisons and Crown Prosecution Service, all of which have their own distinctive histories, cultures and values – were mentioned. The respondents were asked to list the features, which, for them, defined the essence of probation, and were invited to complete a tick box containing various statements. The resulting quantitative data are presented in rank order in Table 5.3.

Table 5.3 Features which should define the essence of probation

		Number	Per cent
1	Understand why people offend	30	96.8
2	Awareness of offenders' personal and social circumstances	29	93.6
3	Promote criminal and social justice through court reports containing relevant personal and social information	28	90.3
4	Values of tolerance, care, compassion and decency	25	80.7
5	Advise, assist and befriend	24	77.4
6	Empathy	20	64.5
7	Deliver punishment in the community	18	58.1
8	Manage, contain and control offenders	18	58.1
9	Social work ethos	17	54.8

10	Keep offenders out of custody	14	45.2
11	Public protection	13	41.9
12	Rigorously enforce court orders	7	22.6
13	A robust, tough and punitive approach	1	3.2
14	Victim support	0	0

As would be expected, from a group of independent professionals who are not averse to speaking their minds in court, the 31 solicitors did not always tick the same boxes. Over half were comfortable with the notion of punishment in the community, as illustrated by the following: 'I've also ticked 'deliver punishment in the community' because I think sometimes offenders need to be punished, and I think if they can be punished in the community then that's for the best'. The same proportion accepted the association of probation with managing, containing and controlling offenders. Few defined the essence of probation in terms of public protection, fewer in terms of rigorously enforcing orders, and only one respondent resorted to the language of a robust, tough and punitive approach.

When turning to enforcement (about which more will be said) three respondents advocated a more flexible approach than the current one under the Criminal Justice Act 2003. One advocated such an approach on the grounds that greater flexibility would be more consistent with a social work approach to understanding offenders and searching for explanations of behaviour. Another asked if it would be possible to construct another step, prior to formal breach proceedings, which involve a return to court and the imposition of more onerous requirements. The third stated: 'It seems that there is a culture of you are breached, we're not going to tolerate it, and you'll be further punished for the breach'. On the other hand, one respondent said when completing the tick box that

> 'I've ticked that it should rigorously enforce court orders because that is very important. The next one underneath, that is to have a robust, tough community approach to offenders, yes in relation to enforcement but I think the boxes (on the other left side of the page): values of tolerance, care, compassion and decency and an awareness of an individual's circumstances – I think they are more important. I'm sure that at some point certain offenders will get to the point where there has to be a robust, tough community approach but that should not be the starting point.'

Yet another respondent could accept that offenders should be managed rigorously by probation 'otherwise it will have no credibility at all'.

A different respondent clarified that the left hand column of the tick box is associated with probation (social work; values of tolerance, care, compassion and decency; empathy; an understanding of why people offend; an awareness of an individual's personal and social circumstances; advise, assist and befriend; keep people out of custody; and promotion of criminal and social justice). It is the right hand column (punishment, public protection, rigorous enforcement, a robust approach, manage, contain and control offenders) which has been introduced by the government. Therefore 'it's become that but it's not in my perception of what it should be. Now I'm not saying it's wrong but it's gone too far and probation was never set up to deliver what it is now expected to deliver'. Developing this theme one respondent commented that 'Robust, tough, punitive approach to offenders – well there's enough people with that mentality in other agencies so I don't see the punishment approach as being part of the probation service ethos, in my opinion'. Finally 'I have always thought, well not always but certainly since the 1980s, that the probation service as a law enforcement agency is wrong and is gradually being pushed and cajoled into corners where I don't think they should be'.

Not all 31 respondents accepted that the essence of probation is associated with a social work ethos (17 (54.8 per cent) thought that it should be), nor is it overwhelmingly the case that it can or should keep people out of custody (14 (45.2 per cent) said probation should). Different opinions were expressed, different boxes ticked and various comments made. In other words, these solicitors did not share the same perceptions of probation, as shown by Table 5.3. However, and this is arguably the central point: the data presented above suggests that the solicitors' understanding of those features which define probation work are weighted more towards one set of ideas than another, illustrated by the rank order presentation. When the respondents were invited to think about cultural change in probation, that is to compare their understandings of what probation should be with what it has become, the following data are instructive.

What has happened – evidence of cultural change

During the course of this research I was not only interested in understanding the solicitors' understandings of the rationale of probation – this is my understanding, as a solicitor, of what it should be. I was also interested in any differences between their understanding of what they think it should be and what the service has become, according to their experiences and observations of cultural change. Therefore the respondents were presented with another set of statements which enabled them to identify the cultural changes of which they were most aware. The results are presented, again in rank order, in Table 5.4.

Table 5.4 Cultural changes solicitors are most aware of

		Number	*Per cent*
1	Rigorous enforcement procedures	21	67.7
2	From advise, assist, and befriend to punishment in the community	20	64.5
3	Target driven organisation	18	58.1
4	From social work help to law enforcement agency	17	54.8
5	Focus on managing the risk or re-offending and harm	17	54.8
6	Public protection	14	45.2
7	Benefit sanction	11	35.5
8	More concerned with victims than offenders	6	19.4

1 Rigorous enforcement procedures (21/31 67.7 per cent)

National standards for the probation service were first introduced in 1988, initially for community service orders (now unpaid work), but expanded to cover other areas of practice in 1992. Since then these standards have progressed through various manifestations, and in the process procedures have been tightened. In the national standards of 1995, offenders could receive two final warnings before proceeding to the intention to breach stage, which resulted in a return to court after the third failed appointment. By 2000–2002, this had been reduced to one final warning before intention to breach at the second absence – from three to two strikes and you are back in court. The Criminal Justice Act 2003 introduced the notion of more onerous requirements if breach proceedings allowed the order to continue, rather than revocation and re-sentence. This was a significant development because, under the Criminal Justice Act 1991, the court had the power to deal with breaches by issuing a verbal warning. This was no longer considered legal under the 2003 Act. An argument can be made for greater discretion and flexibility in certain cases when appointments are missed, notwithstanding the political position that probation is now a law enforcement (as opposed to social work) agency: 'It is what we are: it is what we do' (Boateng 1999).

According to the data presented in Table 5.4, 21 solicitors referred to developments in enforcement as an indicator of cultural change. This is illustrated by the following comments.

> First 'In connection with (this tick box) I have noticed that there is far more rigorous enforcement and less tolerance is afforded. It seems that probation officers are now having to adopt a more aggressive approach, for what reasons I'm not quite certain, but it often alienates the individual (client) as well, that's what I've been finding.'

Another respondent commented that

> 'You've set rigorous enforcement procedures; my only complaint with probation is that you do appear to want to bring people to court for breaching orders. I can understand that you get a lot of people breaching them and a lot of people who say I was at the doctor's, that I've got this and that, but it does seem that people get brought to court quite easily for missing say one or two appointments, but maybe there could be more dialogue between the probation service and the person before you have to involve the courts.'

A third respondent stated

> 'I think there should definitely be enforcement of court orders, but the question of how rigorously they should be enforced I find a difficult concept because I have found the increasing approach of more and more probation officers is to enforce court orders more rigorously than they did in the past. It seems that perhaps they are not as understanding of personal circumstances as to why someone has to be breached.'

It could be suggested that the Criminal Justice Act 1991, which allowed for verbal warnings, was more enlightened than the 2003 Act. In this kind of people work, probation staff need flexibility and discretion; they need to make intelligent judgments rather than imposing rules in a blanket fashion.

It should be acknowledged that one of the outcomes of this modernising policy change is that those offenders with the greatest needs and problems are the ones most likely to fail and therefore end up being breached (Hedderman 2003). This, in turn, increases the possibility of a custodial sentence for non-compliance with a community order; a sentence which was not considered appropriate when the order was initially imposed. Are rigorous enforcement procedures contributing to the escalating prison population? Additionally, should a clear distinction be made between non-compliance in terms of not keeping appointments, and offending whilst subject to a community order? From the standpoint of seriousness, the latter is more significant than the former.

2 From advise, assist, and befriend to punishment in the community (20/31 64.5 per cent)

Section 4 of the Probation of Offenders Act 1907 stated that one of the duties of the probation officer was to advise, assist, and befriend the probationer. Arguably this duty is resonant with the ethos of probation as an alternative to punishment or even sentence of the court. Offenders made the subject of probation were released from court into the care of the probation officer. However probation was reconfigured to become a retributive punishment in the community as a consequence of developments towards the end of the 1980s, culminating in the Criminal Justice Act 1991. This was part of a government inspired strategy to make community sentences more credible for magistrates and judges with the aim of controlling a potentially burgeoning prison population. Twenty respondents alluded to this significant shift in probation as a clear indicator of cultural change:

> 'I'm hesitating at the first one, advise, assist, and befriend, to punishment. I do think that there has again been a change and probation seems to be at times more concerned with punishment and overseeing punishment of offenders, but again that differs from officer to officer and quite often from offender to offender.'

Another solicitor said 'There are three that strike me and yes that's a real shift in what I see as a cultural change, from advise, assist, and befriend, to punishment in the community.'

A third respondent said that 'It seems that there is very much the emphasis on punishment in the community and getting its pound of flesh'. Finally 'My recent experiences have been that I'm quite alarmed to which it seems, particularly younger probation officers, have shifted towards an emphasis, I think, on punishment in the community or imprisonment'. Since the creation of the National Probation Service in 2001 the service has been defined more in terms of 'enforcement, rehabilitation and public protection' than 'advise, assist and befriend'. Such a shift of emphasis is considered more illustrative of a modernised service.

3 Target driven organisation (18/31 58.1 per cent)

In this discussion of cultural change I do not want to repeat the critique of targets found in Chapter 2. Suffice to say that targets, both measurable and cash-linked, are the tools by which the political centre has seized control over and redefined the public sector in terms of performance and accountability. Unfortunately, they are a blunt rather than sophisticated instrument within people based organisations, precisely because they do not allow for a detailed consideration of qualitative and ineffable features. It is clear from Table 5.4 that for 18 respondents the development of targets is indicative of cultural change as the following comments reveal. First, is the insightful comment that

> 'Target driven, again it is very unfortunate but this new and different approach is all about targets and that is very, very misleading. Target driven organisations tend not actually to be representative of the way things are, but target driven also means undue pressures on good probation officers who clearly might do a very good job but if they are not ticking the boxes in the right way they might not do so well in the organisation...'

A second respondent initially touched upon enforcement before warming to the theme of targets:

> 'The enforcement procedures, I've sort of put that in very much with the target driven organisation which is one of the changes in the service. In the reports you get nowadays, they are quite statistically based with elements of risk and harm put in...I used to feel when I first started that the first reports I saw had more gut feeling and gut instinct, but the probation service must be becoming more mathematical and calculated rather than actually focusing on the clients now.'

Finally, one respondent was aware of numerous cultural changes and stated that 'Yes and target driven organisation. I suspect...targets and the rules are imposed from above and there seems to be less leeway given to officers to take consideration of people's personal and individual circumstances...'

4 From social work help to law enforcement agency (17/31 54.8 per cent)

For many decades after 1907, the probation system was associated with an attitude of help (as well as Foucauldian discipline). The probationer was released into the care of the probation officer, it was something other than punishment (Garland and Sparks 2000) and part of the helping professions in the post-war welfare state as the probation officer was understood as the social worker within the court system (Home Office 1962). In fact the probation officer was a trained social worker assisting people who offend with a range of personal and social problems (Smith 2006). Nevertheless, Table 5.4 reveals that 17 respondents were aware of the cultural change from social work to law enforcement agency. This can be illustrated by the comments of one respondent who said that 'I think my perception of the service is that it has become more of a law enforcement agency…it is more so now than it was'. Another respondent was clear that 'from social work help to law enforcement agency I do perceive a shift. It's a tool that the probation service is becoming to beat up the offender with to some degree…".

5 and 6 Focus on managing the risk of re-offending and harm (17/31 54.8 per cent) and public protection (14/31 45.2 per cent)

It is perhaps unnecessary to say a great deal about these two related indicators of cultural change because of the detailed discussion in Chapter 2 on targets, risk, and the associated theme of public protection. Table 5.4 reveals that 17 referred to managing risk and 14 to public protection as indicators of change. One respondent took up the theme of public protection by saying that it

> 'seems more pronounced. Certainly the phrase is used more often now than it used to be and it's probably going to become more and more important when we hear about all the headline stories of those committing heinous offences whilst subject to probation, and I think it's unfair that the probation service is criticised because the only way to protect the public, as a guarantee, is never to let someone out of prison.'

7 Benefit sanction (11/31 35.5 per cent)

The withdrawal of state benefits from selected offenders who do not comply with community orders, in four specific probation areas under sections 62–66 of the Child Support, Pensions and Social Security Act, has been addressed in some detail elsewhere (Whitehead and Statham 2006). Concerns expressed during interview about this measure can be illustrated as follows, starting with the first respondent who began by saying: 'There is no doubt that we know there are experienced probation officers whose hands are tied in how they have to deal with clients and they are not being allowed to deal with clients according to their own knowledge and experience which is terribly frustrating.' Where the benefit sanction is concerned, this respondent's experience is that for some probation officers it 'is completely and utterly wrong for a person who may have breached because of their own inadequacies and vulnerability and have then wrongly been punished...'.

A second respondent said that

> 'So far as the benefit sanction is concerned, I think that is a horrible thing, a horrible development. It seems to me to fly in the face of all logic that those in government deem those living on the breadline, who statistically are more likely to get into trouble due to unemployment, poor housing, poor education etc... should be additionally punished by having their benefits potentially taken away, where those in work and therefore in fact in a better position...That has definitely been a change for the worse.'

It is difficult to understand, from a probation perspective that is, why such a policy persists in Northtown, which is one of the most deprived areas of England and Wales.

8 More concerned with victims than offenders (6/31 19.4per cent)

The attention paid to victims of crime has been steadily growing since the Criminal Injuries Compensation Board was established in 1964, followed by the creation of Victim Support in the 1970s. This led to the Victim Charter published by the Home Office in 1990 that ushered in further developments during the 1990s. Today the probation service has its own victim liaison officers who establish contact with the victims of the more serious sex and violence offences to keep them informed about their perpetrators (for example release from custody). While this has been a substantive change within the probation and criminal justice system (see discussion in Easton and Piper, 2005, Chapter 6), only six of the respondents identified the issue of victims as an indicator of cultural change. It was suggested that dealing with victims is not the role of probation, but of other organisations.

Finally, when thinking about cultural change, a solitary respondent referred to the employment of a grade of staff without probation officer training as a significant development in Northtown. This was perceived as tantamount to 'de-skilling' the profession. Another respondent said that the attention given to domestic violence cases was also indicative of profound change. I will turn to this in the discussion on court reports which follows.

What is the purpose of probation reports?

McWilliams (1983) arrived at the view that by around 1889 police court missionaries were already involved in pre-sentence investigations, long before the Probation of Offenders Act 1907 had established the probation system. The 1926 Probation Rules endorsed that the role of the probation officer was to make enquiries. During the 1930s, Le Mesurier (1935) devoted a specific section in her book to reports. After the Streatfield Report of 1961, social inquiry/enquiry reports (SIR) increased in number (Bottoms and Stelman 1988), and the Criminal Justice Act 1991 transmuted the SIR into pre-sentence reports as probation became a punishment in the community. Section 158 of the Criminal Justice Act 2003 states that a report is prepared 'with a view to assisting the court in determining the most suitable method of dealing with an offender'. Moreover, section 160 refers to *other reports* – that is other than the full pre-sentence report. In the past it was possible for the probation service to deliver a stand-down to magistrates and judges (verbal information following a brief interview). More recently, this became a specific sentence report (a truncated version of the full report delivered in writing). Currently, the fast delivery report (FDR) is the only alternative to the standard delivery pre-sentence report. Again, the latter is a truncated version of the full report which contains a series of tick boxes, in addition to space for explanatory text. The full pre-sentence report is prepared over 15 working days in the more serious cases where the courts require 'full' information and where the following issues are pertinent: domestic violence, public protection, child protection, sexual and violent offences, in addition to Schedule 1 offences. The target for FDRs is currently set at 40 per cent of all court reports. Fast delivery reports should be completed on the day they are requested and/or within five working days rather than 15.

Therefore, there is a long history of the probation system providing information to sentencers. Modifications have been made over recent years, including the introduction of national standards which specify that reports must be written under the headings offence analysis, offender assessment, assessment of risk of re-offending and harm, and culminate in a conclusion containing a clear recommendation for sentence. It can also be argued that, in the right circumstances, the FDR format saves both time and money. Interestingly, in a speech delivered at HMP Wormwood Scrubs on the 7th November 2006, the Home Secretary, John Reid, stated that 'too much money is going on report writing and not enough on practical help' (paragraph 14) by which I think he was alluding to the full report. Consequently, this research asked numerous questions about court reports, as such documents have some salience where solicitors' clients are concerned. Initially, I wanted to elicit the respondents' views on the purpose of reports before turning their attention to the FDR format specifically.

The standard delivery/pre-sentence report

When reflecting on the comprehensive standard delivery report (PSR) it is helpful to use some of the respondents' own words, beginning with the following statement:

> 'In my opinion it is to give sufficient background information for the court to form an opinion as to how best to sentence somebody, so it should paint a full picture of the defendant's background, personal circumstances, things related to the offence which it's sometimes difficult to get from a defence perspective. You (probation) sit down from a different perspective and personal details should be brought out in the report which is relevant to that person and relevant to the magistrates when they come to decide sentence. And the conclusion of the report should be, in my view, to make a recommendation or suggest some way that the probation service can assist the offender'.

Interestingly, more respondents used the term 'circumstances' than any other to clarify their understanding of the purpose and content of reports. In other words, the report should include information on the 'personal circumstances' of an offender, which in turn is conducive to providing a 'full picture' of the person, to assist the court to determine the most appropriate sentence, including punishment. Another respondent clarified the purpose of a report as 'to provide the court with background information relating to the offender with an emphasis on trying to understand reasons for offending'.

Another respondent said that

> 'The report has a number of functions: the first is to be able to advise the magistrates as regards the likelihood of the person re-offending and his response to a particular sort of order. The report writer has the opportunity of working in-depth with the client and will have the experience to know what issues there are and how they need to be addressed. I can stand up and I can say this is clearly a case where probation is needed and the magistrates will not take my word for it and therefore the report serves to underpin what are the solutions... As far as I am concerned that's the extent of it.'

Yet another stated that 'The purpose is to assist the court with sentencing options, looking into the background of the offender, finding out how it happened, why it happened, whether there are any issues that needed to be dealt with, social, domestic, etc…and to come up with an appropriate recommendation for sentencing that would be of assistance to the court.'

The author had the following exchange during an interview with one of the solicitors:

PW   'What is the purpose of the probation court report?'

R   'To assist the court'

PW   'Would you like to say anything else or is that your answer?'

R   'I don't think they are as well written now as they used to be. I don't think they are written as personally as they used to be.'

Finally, one respondent, not known for his extreme views, was quite trenchant in his assessment of court reports:

'I'm not quite sure what the probation service's purpose is on reports. It seems to me to ensure the maximum severity of punishment and it does that by a series of means, such as I've noticed recently there's a complete failure of any positive aspects of the defendant's behaviour. I find this very concerning and it's led to a situation now where defendants do not trust the probation service. It is said to me over and over again that the probation service has changed, defendants don't trust them, they see them as the enemy and last week it was said to me by an extremely violent man that the next time he saw a particular probation officer he would 'rip his face off' and that is not the sort of comment that I would have heard some years ago. And that isn't I think a change in the defendants, rather that it's a situation brought on by the change of attitude of the probation service and my people who are already isolated and estranged from the system, their only real way in, if you like, was with the probation service and that door I think has been pretty much closed.'

It is important to add at this point that the tenor of this reply is relatively extreme and accordingly untypical. Significantly, this respondent associated probation reports with punishment, which will be expanded upon below as another important indicator of change. However, first I want to turn to how my respondents understood the FDR rather than the full report.

Fast delivery reports

This is a selection of comments on the FDR:

> 'Well the FDR is to do…it quicker. It seems that if it's quicker it's better, but that's not always the case and I think sometimes valuable information is missed through rushing things through.'

> 'FDRs I think have a place but it is clearly the obvious case possibly can be dealt with by way of an FDR. But I'm only a fan of it for the right case, for the right purpose. A lot of magistrates and judges, I think, jump to an FDR simply because they want to make progress. Everything's driven by 'let's try and make progress today' and sometimes at the cost of the offender, the victim…I actually think that more time or care is needed. It's amazing how much information is still picked up on an FDR, now I've seen the tick box exercise is very thorough, but there's still things that can be missed and still things that concern me about it.'

> 'Yes well I can only see the aim of the FDR as being to improve everybody's statistics in terms of how quickly cases are disposed of, because it is meant to contain as much information as the SDR, or at least to cover the same sorts of areas, personal offender mitigation, etc…and it's meant to provide sufficient information, together with the advocate's, for the courts to reach a sentencing decision. And yet if it is the case that a full three week adjournment is being lifted, because of other commitments, to sit down and speak with somebody at length, then I really do think that the only purpose of an FDR is to improve statistics.'

> A 'snap-shot rather than an in-depth consideration of the problems that somebody has…a cursory look.'

> 'I haven't got any problems with an FDR actually, although you might challenge me on that, in this sense that generally speaking the FDRs are there for perfectly straightforward cases where there are no issues. So, for example, domestic violence, mental health, would not be regarded as being appropriate cases.'

One respondent stated that the FDR is about 'a quick analysis'; another 'just cheap justice' because it saves on money and time. Importantly, for another, although the FDR is about speed, 'well it has to be a good thing'.

'My personal opinion is that the purpose of the FDR is to move people through the criminal justice system very quickly indeed for the purpose of demonstration by the government to the public at large that they are being seen to be tough on crime and the causes of crime and I personally find it very frustrating sometimes that there are issues that need to be covered in a full standard report that aren't covered in an FDR. And I sometimes feel that the probation service are being pressurised themselves time-wise to knock out a report quickly for the benefit of the court and not for the benefit of the individual.'

'Again it depends on whose point of view we're talking about. From the courts' point of view I think it benefits them to show a quick result, so it's sort of statistic driven and maybe get some credit for that. It's also, on a positive side, it has to be right. If someone's in immediate need of assistance, or even punishment, or a combination of the two, then the sooner that's delivered the better. I agree with that, but having said that I think a lot of reports are rushed. I don't think they go into sufficient detail and this sometimes works in favour of the defendant and sometimes against him, but generally speaking except in the simplest possible cases I'm not sure that they are a particularly good idea for society in general.'

Interestingly, three solicitors were positively disposed towards FDRs for financial management reasons, of which the following is representative:

'I have found it very helpful because from a financial point of view, the quicker the case comes to a conclusion then that's financially advantageous to us so rather than have a case adjourned for three weeks for a PSR, to adjourn a day or less for an FDR is certainly beneficial to us. So I think it's to speed the court process and get people through the system which is better for us, better for the courts to get to a conclusion quicker. I think the defendants enjoy it being concluded quicker, so I find them very helpful.'

By contrast one solicitor expressed the view that the FDR process can be construed negatively, particularly if he has to wait around for the document to be completed. This has become a pertinent issue in circumstances where waiting time allowances could be removed. Therefore from the advantages of financial management to the disadvantages of time management: 'To expedite matters full stop...From a legal point of view it's a nightmare because it means we have to sit around for perhaps up to two hours until the FDR is completed. I'm not bemoaning probation at all but that's the practical effect of an FDR.'

In summary, it was acknowledged that the probation service and courts are under pressure to expedite cases to meet government targets and utilise resources efficiently. Fast delivery reports can be used for appropriate and straightforward cases, and efficiency is not necessarily tantamount to compromising justice. Such reports can be advantageous not only for the criminal justice system (speed) but may also enable defendants to receive help more quickly. However, the advantages of FDRs are qualified by the following points:

- Valuable information could be missed.

- They are not conducive to providing a thorough background assessment.

- A cursory look at personal and social issues may not be in the best interests of the client.

It should be acknowledged that, if there are concerns about the appropriateness of the FDR, both probation and solicitors can argue the case for a full report. Consequently, there are built-in safeguards. Nevertheless, there is tension between the political demand for the financial benefits associated with speed (the NPM agenda) and achieving criminal and social justice for individuals premised upon the provision of all relevant information. Consequently, and as part of the discussion about FDRs, the solicitors were asked to consider in more detail whether they thought this type of report was more concerned with achieving efficiency/throughput targets than justice for individual offenders.

Table 5.5 Do you think the FDR (tick box format) is more concerned to achieve throughput efficiency targets than justice for individual offenders?

	Number	Per cent
Yes	23	74.2
No	0	0.0
Ambivalent	8	25.8
Total	31	100.0

These are some of the replies to this question:

'I think the tick box system has always been no more than an auditing system and cannot be evidence of the competence of the report writer and can't be evidence of the competence of the investigation as such and for me the tick box system doesn't fill me with a great deal of confidence.'

'The FDR is cheap justice, that's what it is. If we can get the case listed on the same day, the plea goes in on the same day, and all the defendants are pushed to do that, that's why you get credit for an early guilty plea, so it's a thing about saying well done, patting you on the back. It's cheap justice.'

'I'm absolutely convinced of that, absolutely convinced of it. It affects your figures, it affects the Crown's figures, and it affects the court's figures. My figures don't matter a damn in that context and your management of the process of the criminal justice system is seen to be more efficient if you can get matters completed on the same day, the next day or the day after on the back of an FDR.'

'It's certainly a ticky box form which is designed for efficiency and targets...I don't find it detrimental to the defendant...and you've got the option of going for a full PSR.'

'Undoubtedly and the reason being is again speed through the system. Statistically it looks good for the government and the Lord Chancellor's Department.'

'I think it goes for the efficient aspect personally. I think to do justice to the offender more time should be given to their needs, to their requirements that can be given when an FDR is simply a matter of ticking a box answer than qualifying it. But I think in the main an SDR would address the offender's needs rather than a FDR.'

Therefore these responses reflect a tension between what could be considered right and appropriate for the individual, and the exigencies of a system for processing people expeditiously.

Table 5.6 Are reports demonstrating less understanding of offenders' personal and social circumstances?

	Number	Per cent
Yes	20	64.5
No	6	19.4
Ambivalent	5	16.1
Total	31	100.0

Garland and Sparks make the following pertinent comment on the notion of understanding:

> 'The posture of 'understanding' the offender was always a demanding and difficult attitude, more readily attained by liberal elites unaffected by crime or else by professional groups who make their living out of it. This posture increasingly gives way to that of *condemning* criminals and demanding that they be punished and controlled' (2000 p17).

Moreover, Fred Jarvis, when reflecting on the qualities looked for within prospective probation officers, emphasised 'flexibility of mind and a capacity for listening to and understanding others' (1974 p268). With this in mind, the following responses are of interest:

> 'Yes I do, if I think of a typical report you now have quite a short comment on the offence itself, you have a strange and frankly unintelligible statistic about offending, the graph, which I feel is completely pointless. That kind of information that's come into a report I think has detracted from the more substantive knowledge and discussion of the client by the probation officer and of necessity has restricted if you like the more considered final recommendation.'

> 'Yes, that's something that I've mentioned before, that reports have become very statistical and computer displayed with your bar graphs... I think that reports are generally looking at the offence more now than the causes of it...'

> 'Definitely, definitely. I am certain of that. There has been, in the time that I've been practising, there has been a complete change in the tenor of reports and whereas before it was commonplace to read a degree of understanding that was obviously intended to explain the offending, not to mitigate and not to excuse it, but to explain, issues like that I think are routinely ignored or just mentioned in passing.'

> 'Yes I would say it has. Perhaps in the old days probation officers were social workers to some extent as well and looked at the social aspects, whereas now I don't know if the courts aren't as interested or other reasons, not as much going into the background and trying to explain why the offending is happening. So yes, I agree with that and the change has been that it is more to do with the offence and the risk of further offending, rather than exploring what might be the reasons for this and how to address the root causes rather than simply looking to punishment for the offence.'

It is important to balance the above by including the following observations:

> 'I don't think they are showing less understanding of an offender's personal circumstances or indeed social make up...Managing risk certainly but I do find that often reports are quite good at explaining offenders' lives and the difficulties that they have dealing with day to day life in disadvantaged circumstances. Certainly a lot depends on the experience of the probation writer.'

> 'I think if anything they are demonstrating greater understanding of offenders. I don't think reports should be about the offender's CV and I can never understand why large parts of reports, particularly full PSRs, deal with the person's upbringing, because usually very little of it is going to have anything to do with the offence itself...'

These latter comments are not representative of the 31 solicitors interviewed but should be included to demonstrate that all of them do not perceive the probation world in exactly the same way. It was also of interest to find out whether solicitors think probation reports to the courts have become more punitive. Table 5.7 poses this question:

Table 5.7 Have reports become more punitive?

	Number	*Per cent*
Yes	21	67.7
No	3	9.7
Ambivalent	7	22.6
Total	31	100.0

Back in the more rehabilitative and welfare orientated 1960s, the Streatfield Report (Home Office and Lord Chancellor's Office 1961; also see Bottoms and McWilliams 1986) resulted in an expanded use of court reports. At this stage in the history of the probation system the purpose of reports was to provide three main types of information: first, social and domestic background information relevant to the courts' assessment of culpability; secondly, information on an individual offender to check a criminal career; thirdly, to assess the likely effect on an offenders' criminal career of probation or some other sentence (Bottoms and Stelman 1988 p23).

The issue of probation officers proposing custody during this period was more delicate than currently, primarily because a more social work orientated service operated with the values of care, respect for persons, and hope in the possibility of individual change.[1] Moreover, and centrally, it should be acknowledged that from a historical perspective, probation was qualitatively different to a punishment (it was not prison and it was not a punishment in the community). In fact, the 1980s were the alternative to custody decade for probation. During the 1980s Bottoms and Stelman (1988) suggested five possible justifications for advocating a custodial sentence in probation reports:

1) In the best interests of clients.

2) In the best interests of society.

3) Being realistic.

4) Tactical sentencing – recommend custody to ensure the shortest possible period in custody when it was inevitable.

5) The defendant prefers custody to probation.

However, after discussing these justifications, Bottoms and Stelman arrive at the conclusion 'that in almost every case the probation officer or social worker should not make a direct or indirect custodial recommendation' (1988 p49). The advice of Bottoms and Stelman (given less than 20 years before completing this book in 2007) dates from a different era. The Criminal Justice Act 1991 signalled a different probation and criminal justice culture. A more punitive culture has been created since 1993 and the 'prisons work' debates; during the 1990s, probation was recreated as a law enforcement rather than social work agency; and we have become less squeamish about resorting to the language of punishment. Furthermore, during the 1980s, McWilliams (1987) argued that in the post-rehabilitative era three schools of thought emerged to fill the vacuum, namely the managerial, radical, and personalist. They were united by a commitment to the probation service providing alternatives to custody. However, since 1993 the organisational goal of alternatives to custody has largely been replaced, as probation has become an alternative form of punishment. In other words probation and prison provide varying degrees of punishment. This theme was taken up by the 31 solicitors who had much to say about their perception of reports. Several respondents thought these had become more punitive:

> 'Yes, generally they have. More and more the conclusion or recommendation in a report is a custodial sentence and for a long period of time I didn't see that in a report unless there was absolutely

no alternative at all. It is now suggested by probation officers and on some occasions is very, very inappropriate. In particular domestic violence reports seem to be written quite often with an agenda being that the defendant is a very bad person and has to be punished.'

'Oh crikey, yes…I have seen of late, two or three years mainly, reports that are actually being extremely negative and that was not the purpose of the report author or the probation service and I have actually seen reports phrased in ways that gives very little choice to the courts and really are recommendations for custody…'

'Yes, particularly in so far as violent offences are concerned. In my view it seems that the probation service are taking almost, well some are taking a pro-active view in terms of looking into background, speaking to the domestic violence unit and putting in information that in my view is prejudicial so far as a particular incident is concerned.'

'There has been a change in culture and the answer to that is yes. There was a time when the probation service would never recommend a custodial sentence and I find it disturbing that those recommendations are being given now. I haven't got a problem with the probation service saying we cannot offer anything to this man, but to say we think this man should go to prison doesn't sit comfortably with me.'

'Yes absolutely. I have had full reports in the year 2006 which have given me grave concern, two of them because I honestly believe, I genuinely believe, that the author had written the report designed to engender punishment by the court…they were both domestic assaults…I have no doubt and I will go as far as to say that I think there are one or two people in the probation service who are behaving as if they are prosecuting that particular offence.'

Other respondents were more ambivalent:

'That's perhaps more complex. I would say not markedly but I think there is a range of community penalties that are now available to a sentencing bench that has increased the punishment level of many of the reports.'

'There are more instances now of reports that are more punitive than was the case in the past. I'm not necessarily sure that's a bad thing. I think there's a sense of realism about reports now which on occasions is well merited. I think the reports now seem more prepared to say what would have been the unthinkable several years ago.'

PW 'Could you give an example of that?'

Respondent: 'Reports are now more willing to talk in terms of punishment and the sanction of custody as an appropriate sentence, whereas I feel ten years ago that would have been a collector's item.'

These respondents answered 'no' to the question of whether reports have become more punitive.

'No, I wouldn't say that at all. What we do see more now is a recommendation saying that the author of the report can see no alternative other than custody which never ever used to be the case. I think perhaps a more realistic approach when it is a no hope case, which we all understand, but of course that does not make the job of an advocate any easier, although sometimes it may do, but no, I don't think it's more punitive.'

To summarise, of the 21 (67.7 per cent) who thought that reports had become more punitive, 13 (61.9 per cent) equated punitiveness with recommendations for custodial sentences. This factor alone is a significant cultural change where probation practice is concerned. Five of the 21 (23.8 per cent) illustrated punitiveness by raising domestic violence cases. Over recent years domestic violence cases have been given a much higher profile (Whitehead et al 2003). Some years ago the attitude amongst professional groups was likely to be dismissive – it's only a domestic – and therefore should be left to the parties involved. The present position is to attach a much higher priority, so much so that Northtown Magistrates' Court has its own designated domestic violence court. However, this is a source of tension between the probation service and solicitors if a defendant is appearing before the court for motoring matters, or in fact any offence *not* related to violence in general and domestic violence in particular. Solicitors would argue that mention of previous domestic violence, or any other form of violence for that matter, is irrelevant. This argument is logical and persuasive. However, it is the probation officer, not the solicitor, who is entrusted to undertake a computer based risk assessment of re-offending, also harm, in relation to all offenders. Consequently, if the probation officer, when undertaking enquiries, uncovers previous incidents of domestic violence, then it can reasonably be argued that such information informs the risk of harm assessment. Such information is relevant to evaluating risk of harm (probation perspective); yet irrelevant to the current and unrelated offence (solicitor perspective). Such differences between the two professions within the criminal justice system require resolution through dialogue to promote an understanding of each other's responsibilities.

One last point concerns the emotive issue of custodial sentences within the context of a rising prison population and whether probation officers should propose custody in court reports. Even in circumstances where, it is argued, probation values should be reformulated, Nellis and Gelsthorpe (2003) advocate retaining the legitimate pursuit of alternatives to custody for the following reasons: first, the democratic ideal of keeping restrictions on liberty to a minimum; secondly, to reduce the damage that custody can inflict on people; thirdly, because community orders can facilitate bonds and attachments to society which are damaged by custody. Furthermore the What Works literature (Chui and Nellis 2003) justifies keeping offenders out of custody on the grounds that community programmes are more effective at reducing re-offending than custodial sentences. In fact the latest figures are that 67 per cent of adults leaving prison and 80 per cent of young people leaving young offender institutions re-offend within two years of release. It also costs £37,500 and £70,000 per year to accommodate adults and young offenders respectively in custodial facilities (House of Commons Official Report 2007).

Summary and conclusion

I have been associated with the probation service since the 1970s and experienced many changes from the inside, particularly over the last ten years (1997–2007). It is not surprising that my main research interests focus upon the related themes of modernisation and cultural transformation, and these themes remain my concern as I attempt to build a multi-faceted picture comprising the perceptions of court clerks, magistrates and district judges, in addition to barristers and judges at the Crown Court. This chapter presents the results of interviews with 31 solicitors at the Northtown Magistrates' Court in one local criminal justice system in the north-east of England. Although numerous and sometimes conflicting opinions were expressed by these respondents, the evidence allows me to conclude that there is also consistency.

It was never assumed, nor would it have been right to assume, that these respondents would share identical perceptions of probation work. Nevertheless, it can be suggested that a higher proportion associated their understanding of probation with one set of ideas than another. This is supported by the findings contained in Table 5.3:

- The importance attached to *understanding* why people offend, including *empathy*.

- Providing information on background personal and social *circumstances.*

- Promoting *criminal and social justice* via relevant information (hence the expression of concern over the Fast Delivery Report).

- *Values* of tolerance, care, compassion and decency.

- The importance of *advise, assist and befriend* alongside probation's association with a *social work ethos.*

Consequently these features are more important to the respondents than:

- Punishment in the community.

- Manage, control and contain offenders.

- Public protection.

- Rigorous enforcement procedures.

- A robust, tough and punitive approach to those who offend.

There is some evidence that a number of the solicitors are concerned about the political process that has brought about modernisation and cultural change, and the nature and tone of such change. A number of them lamented the transformation of the probation service, from one type of organisation to another, as illustrated by their responses to the questions. Table 5.4 reveals a number of discernible shifts in emphasis with which the solicitors could identify, the implications of which should be considered carefully by those who are responsible for the criminal justice system:

- Towards more rigorous enforcement procedures.

- From advise, assist and befriend to punishment in the community.

- From social work help to a law enforcement agency.

- Managing risk of re-offending and harm.

- Recognition of the emergence of a target-driven organisation and the implications of this.

Another indicator of change is the perception that some probation officers are more willing to propose custodial sentences in reports, as illustrated by concerns over domestic violence cases. It is not possible, given the parameters of this research, to quantify just how many reports contain a proposal for custody compared with previous years. Nevertheless, as probation officers of a certain age and trained under a more social work/welfare orientated culture leave the service, and are replaced by officers trained since 1997/98, then it is possible that there could be fewer qualms about probation's engagement with community punishments and custodial sentences.

My main preoccupation is with modernisation and cultural change and their implications in probation and the wider criminal justice system, and I have tried to allow the respondents to speak on these subjects for themselves, with minimum of input from me. This research-based chapter is not intended to produce a policy document advocating change, but the Northtown Probation Service, if disposed to do so, could use these findings as a basis for reflection on the direction of professional practice. It is perhaps also possible that, over recent years, area services within the National Probation Service have been so preoccupied with national standards, quantification, targetry, audits, computers, and the expansion of bureaucratic systems of accountability – the accoutrements of modernisation – that not enough time has been devoted to the implications of these developments for professional practice.

Finally, the development of NOMS and even more legislation contained in the Offender Management Bill (the latter had its third reading on 28th February 2007) questions whether the process of modernisation and cultural transformation of recent years is at an end, or could be reversed. On the contrary, where the Offender Management Bill is concerned, Gerry Sutcliffe, Parliamentary Under-Secretary of State for the Home Department, has clearly stated that 'The Bill is necessary to change the existing culture' (House of Commons Official Report 2007 column 962). There is no end in sight to modernisation and cultural change in probation, a public sector service which has had more than its share of change over the last two decades, particularly since 2001.

NOTES

[1] One should not get carried away with the view that in previous decades probation officers did not recommend custodial sentences. This point can be illustrated by turning to what purported to be the alternatives to custody decade of the 1980s. During this period Bill McWilliams alludes to a study of social enquiry reports by Stanley and Murphy in 1984. In fact this was an extensive survey which revealed that in adult cases sentenced to imprisonment the authors 'found that in a high proportion the probation officer had not recommended a non-custodial measure, but had either recommended prison or had made no recommendation' (1987 p115).

Chapter 6

CONCLUSION: FURTHER REFLECTIONS ON MODERNISATION AND THE PROBATION IDEAL

'The logics and technical requirements of audits displace the internal logics of expertise. The emphasis on defined and measurable goals and targets in the work that professionals do with their clients is an element within a much wider reconfiguration of methods for the government of specialist activities.' (Rose 1999 p154)

Question posed by researcher: 'How do you envisage the future of probation within NOMS, and the wider criminal justice system, during the next five years?'

Solicitor: 'I am concerned because it seems to me that the system is now driven, almost to the exclusion of everything else, by speed. But the interests of justice are being driven over rough shod and that the input of the probation service is going to be, and the defence as well, as a group, ignored...So I'm concerned for the future, both for the probation service and my profession, for the same reason I think. We seem to be just being swept along.'

Introduction

The probation system established with Home Office support in 1907 under a reforming Liberal government was qualitatively different to the much more complex organisation that has been evolving since the 1980s, particularly during the decade beginning in 1997. In fact, the early missionary pioneers would hardly recognise the latest construction. This is mainly because recent years have been characterised by centralisation and bureaucratisation, accompanied by computerisation, culminating in de-professionalisation, destabilisation and organisational fragmentation. The creation of the National Probation Service in 2001 and the Halliday Review of sentencing as the precursor of the Criminal Justice Act 2003, quickly followed by the Carter Review of correctional services which resulted in proposals for a National Offender Management Service, have promoted far-reaching changes and elicited concerns at different levels (Hough 2006). Consequently, at both a theoretical and empirical level, this book engages with the related themes of modernisation and cultural

167

change within probation and the wider criminal justice system. Some of the more troublesome features of the process of modernisation can be reprised as follows:

- From attempts at meaningful understandings of behaviours to measurements and audits.

- From interpretative assessments to integers via computer technology.

- From appreciating individuals to regulating aggregates of risk and harm.

- From a profession characterised by autonomy and discretion, professional responsibility and accountability, to an expanding bureaucracy with centrally imposed standards.

- From the knowledge and skills required by a social work profession, including building relationships, to achieving cash-linked targets.

- From local governance and leadership to a national service subject to endless change with no recognisable end in sight.

Against the backdrop of rapidly changing events, this final chapter devotes more space than earlier chapters to some elements of macro level change over the last two decades. These include politics and New Public Management, criminological discourse, criminal justice and penal policy, and the National Offender Management Service. Of course, there are other determinants of cultural change as follows:

- The wider framework of public sector reforms in health, education and police.

- Tax and spend balance and the funding of public services according to treasury priorities.

- Nil growth for probation over the next few years from April 2008 determined by the treasury.

- Government's priority to control risk and harm, and protect the public.

- The Criminal Justice Act 2003 and central themes of persistent offenders, dangerousness, punishment in the community, prolific and priority offenders, and rigorous enforcement of orders made by the courts.

- Changing ministerial priorities and the effects of different Prime Ministers and Home Secretaries on probation, in addition to the impact of regional offender managers.

- Local community safety partnerships and priorities of criminal justice boards.

- Delivery and performance issues monitored by the Number 10 Delivery Unit.

- The ongoing salience of cash-linked targets and punitive sanctions for local services if they are not met.

In its centenary year, probation, and the wider criminal justice system, are affected by a range of other factors, some of which are included in a significant document that has its origins within the Prime Minister's Strategy Unit (Cabinet Office 2006):

- A regime of tougher sentencing since 1997 which has seen the average custodial sentence at the Crown Courts increase from 20 to 30 months.

- An expanding prison population that reached 80,000 by the end of 2006, but which is projected to rise to 100,000, if not more, by 2012.

- The courts are imposing more community sentences, but these are replacing fines rather than custody.

- Re-offending rates over a period of two years following the imposition of a community sentence are 53 per cent, and for custodial sentences 67 per cent.

Approximately 100,000 offenders are responsible for 50 per cent of all crimes (I think attention is being drawn here to the police apprehension of offenders from a certain section of the community, rather than white collar crime or the crimes of the powerful) (Lea and Young 1984). With these factors in mind, I now turn to determinants of change at a macro level in the first section of this final chapter.

PART 1: FURTHER REFLECTIONS ON MODERNISATION AND CULTURAL CHANGE

Politics and New Public Management

The first of four consecutive election victories for the Conservatives, in May 1979, established a new political climate. This was manifested in the form of new government priorities (Rose 1999), which in turn created the prism through which crime and offenders were re-conceptualised in a neo-classical direction. This decisive step, synonymous with Thatcherism, was articulated in terms of the need for more law and order, the fight against crime, greater individual responsibility, and the demand for more authority and discipline. Mrs Thatcher herself stated that 'the most direct way to act against crime is to make life as difficult as possible for the potential and actual criminal' (1995 p558). This did not mean that every vestige of welfare and penal modernism associated with the post-war democratic consensus was abandoned (Garland 2001). However, it did signal a return to more nineteenth-century liberal than twentieth-century welfare themes (the latter persisted from the 1900s to 1970s). This shift to the political right established a different framework within which to think about the viability of, and also to practice, the probation ideal. In other words, government practice was responsible for shaping new ways of thinking and behaving in the public sector, including probation and the criminal justice system, in relation to the new political framework after 1979 (Rose 1999 p4). The first serious glimpse of this occurred with the Criminal Justice Act 1982 and then specifically during 1983/84 (Home Office 1984). Traditional social work values associated with the probation ideal were put under pressure (Lloyd 1986) and the new political style began to de-couple the phenomenon of rising crime from wider social conditions in the Thatcher-Reagan dominated 1980s (Brake and Hale 1992).

The political tone of the post-1979 period became associated, as the 1980s progressed, with the principles of New Public Management which, according to Hood (1991) had been emerging since the late 1970s in the form of curbing public expenditure, privatisation, automation and technology. Notwithstanding a much greater emphasis on law and order during the early 1980s (and associated themes of toughness, more police, harsher penal regimes), crime continued to rise. Additional expenditure on the criminal justice system did not equate with greater effectiveness in the post-rehabilitative era (McLaughlin et al 2001), hence the demand for greater accountability through the application of NPM principles: more emphasis on allowing managers to manage, greater standardisation, measures of performance in the form of objectives and then measurable targets, quantification, a focus on inputs, outputs and results rather than procedures and outcomes, competition to raise standards, lower costs and the principle of more for less (Power 1997).

The NPM agenda initiated by the Conservatives during the 1980s was continued by New Labour after 1997 as part of its modernising agenda – the principles and mechanisms for managing, regulating, and controlling public services. For as McLaughlin et al state, new labour came to accept the managerial reforms of the Conservatives as necessary developments. In other words, they were 'acts of modernisation that improved productivity, delivered better value for money and enhanced quality of service' (2001 p306). Such acts of modernisation facilitated far reaching cultural change in the public sector, including probation, which had previously been characterised by administration, but also professionalism (Stewart and Walsh 1992 p508). However, it has been questioned whether the public services – specifically organisations that work with people with varying needs and problems – can be turned into and run like a business which sells things to customers within a competitive market place (McLaughlin 2001 p303; Rose 1999 p150). Managers in the people professions have become auditors of business forms of accountability in which the 'logics and technical requirements of audit displace the internal logics of expertise'. In other words, the professional role has been radically transformed; experts turned into bureaucrats; 'financial vocabularies, grammars and judgments have infiltrated the very terms in which experts calculate and enact their expertise' (Rose 1999 p153). This constitutes a significant managerial and organisational transformation within the probation service.

Criminological discourse

As any assiduous student of criminological theory is aware, there is a confusing plethora of competing explanations of those forms of human behaviour classified as criminal, from classical and neo-classical to various manifestations of positivism, from deviant subcultures in the 1950s, labelling during the 1960s, radical left-idealist perspectives in the 1970s, to the latest manifestations of neo-right control theories (see Chapter 3). One of the indices of change recounted in Garland's *Culture of Control* (2001), illustrative of the new pattern of crime control which has been emerging since the 1980s, is what he refers to as the 'transformations of criminological thought' (p15). This epistemological transformation must be seen within the context of the new politics of the 1980s, that is not the post-war welfare state and social democratic consensus but the arrival of a more right wing neo-liberal state. This point can be expanded because it has profound implications for the context within which probation operates.

Within the political framework of the welfare state, which included elements of positivist thinking from the 1900s to the 1970s, offending behaviour was largely configured in accordance with a set of ideas that sustained an approach to criminal behaviour largely as a response to individual and family malfunctioning. Therefore it was assumed that increased material prosperity and welfare state assistance, combined with a criminal justice system orientated towards welfare and the rehabilitative ideal, would address the issues, right the wrongs, and help offenders to rejoin mainstream society. However, since the 1980s, offenders and their offending have been politically and criminologically recast as phenomena requiring a more authoritarian response, discipline, punishment and control, rather than welfare assistance. This is because offenders have, in these more neo-classical and conservative times, been held more responsible for their own behaviours which, it is believed, can be positively reshaped in the direction of conformity more effectively by retributive and deterrent punishments than by social work help. In fact, rather than wasting time searching for the causes of crime and the complex motivations of offenders, one should acknowledge offenders' rational choices and routine activities.

Garland draws attention to the normality and routine aspects of crime – 'criminologies of everyday life' (2001) – which require managing, containing and controlling, rather than understanding. Do not focus on why people commit crime but on what they have done; punish the offence rather than bothering too much about the person behind the offence. According to this type of criminological discourse, offenders can be justifiably and legitimately punished for what they have done, both in the community and by custody. The language, imagery and way of thinking about offending, which have disorientated the probation service, come from this form of discourse. It should be acknowledged that such shifts in criminological emphasis do not constitute a complete break with older ways of theorising about and responding to crime, as I mentioned earlier. It is more that the emphasis has shifted, rebalancing the way in which we think about, respond to, and make sense of behaviours. Probation has not escaped these influences.

It should also be acknowledged that there is a 'fit' between the NPM target culture and the changing criminological context that has evolved since the 1980s (Garland 2001; White and Haines 2004). If crime in a more neo-liberal, rather than welfare state, frame of reference is perceived as a normal social fact, a phenomenon that does not require a deep aetiological explanation because it belongs to the normal occurrences of everyday life, and if crime is something freely chosen by rational actors who calculate the costs-benefits of different behavioural routines, then the organisation of probation within this criminological context fits with NPM principles. These principles are concerned to manage, contain, control and regulate human behaviour as economically and efficiently as possible. This constitutes a transition from performance and accountability – judged in terms of social work outcomes, provision of appropriate help, support and understanding to facilitate rehabilitation – to a neo-liberal and neo-classical criminological context of maximum outputs for minimum inputs, which provides a rationale for a target-driven culture. In other words, do not agonise about the person or pose the 'why' question, but focus instead on managing the presenting behaviour of different categories of risk according to the doctrine of the 3Es.

Probation, according to this way of thinking, is not the only organisation that can be expected to achieve centrally imposed objectives and targets. Within the NOMS and contestability framework, practically any organisation which can put forward a viable business plan designed to achieve government targets as efficiently, economically and effectively as possible could be awarded the interventions contracts by regional offender managers. This is the rationale which lies behind the Offender Management Bill proceeding through Parliament in 2007, which could complete the demise of probation during the next few years.

Criminal justice and penal policy

The period under discussion (primarily the last 25 years) was preceded by a more settled period when the criminal justice system, direction of penal policy and the role of the probation service were largely free from the conflicts which were later to spill over between the main political parties (Downes and Morgan 1997). Within a more welfare orientated criminal justice system, there was a greater emphasis upon the possibility of positive rehabilitation rather than negative punishment, supported by the politics of the post-war welfare state. The scholarly contributions made by David Garland to this subject remind us that it was precisely within the context of penal-welfare that the criminal justice domain operated according to two main axioms: a) social reform and rising affluence would, over time, reduce the necessity to offend; b) the state was responsible (not the market place) for the welfare, treatment and also the punishment of offenders when this was required (ideally as a last resort). Significantly, the ideology of rehabilitation 'was the hegemonic, organising principle, the intellectual framework and value system that bound together the whole structure and made sense of it for practitioners' (2001 p35).

For some time now, the notion of rehabilitation has become one element among many within a more ideologically diverse criminal justice system. This proposition can be illustrated by first referring to the not altogether intellectually compatible purposes of sentencing set out at section 142(1) of the Criminal Justice Act 2003: punishment, deterrence, reform and rehabilitation, public protection, and reparation. Secondly, the phenomenon of crime can be approached through the application of different lenses. There is an incompatible and hybrid system in operation which no single lens is currently capable of capturing in its totality: yet each lens may be said to reflect a significant facet of the hybridised whole. Davies, Croall and Tyrer identify several ideologies, or lenses, within the contemporary criminal justice system:

- The justice model.

- Punishment (retribution and deterrence) which has been a significant feature under New Labour since 1997.

- Vestige of rehabilitation and individualised treatment, the acme of which was during the 1960s.

- Management-bureaucratic model of efficiency, value for money, and targets (NPM).

- Denunciation and degradation.

- Marxist model of class-based justice to punish miscreants from the working class – the rich get richer and poor get punishment thesis (2005 p23).

I would support the view that all these models can, to varying degrees, be found within the Northtown criminal justice system.

It is worth reiterating that the developing eclecticism of these disparate models should not be allowed to obscure the fact that the system has become more punitive over recent years. For example, sentencing is tougher, reflected in an increase in average length of custody at the Crown Court; the prison population is projected to rise from 80,000 at the end of 2006 to 100,000 by 2012; there is a harsher attitude towards the enforcement of community orders (Cabinet Office 2006). Reviewing the period from the 1970s to the rise of New Labour during the 1990s, Cavadino and Dignan (2002) identify three main penal strategies or credos: 1) punitive law and order; 2) managerial, administrative and bureaucratic; 3) humanitarian elements. They argue that from 1979-93 elements of 1) and 2) were in evidence, yet without totally eradicating 3). From 1997, they identify all three strategies at play. Against the backcloth of New Labour's second election victory in 2001, they correctly state that 'At present, despite the promiscuous mixture of philosophies and approaches contained in the government's penal policy, the trend is still towards greater and harsher punishment, and more and more use of imprisonment' (Cavadino and Dignan 2002 p342; see also Kennedy 2005; Seldon 2004; Tonry 2004; and the Cabinet Office document 2006 for future possibilities in a punitive direction).

National Offender Management Service

The expectations generated by the prisons-probation review announced in July 1997, two months after New Labour assumed office, caused a frisson of consternation. Intriguingly, they were not pursued at the time, but were resurrected in the Carter Review of 2002-2003 (Carter 2003). The rationale of what was undoubtedly a significant development, emerging only a short time after the upheaval associated with the creation of the National Probation Service in 2001, was intended to bring to an end what was referred to as the silo mentality within prisons and probation. Hough et al (2006) suggest there are three main themes underpinning Carter: the ongoing modernisation of the criminal justice system associated with the principles of NPM (already alluded to); the desire to maintain the prison population below 80,000 (which has already failed); and to address the lack of coordination between custodial facilities and community corrections. Organisational and ideological changes and managerial and bureaucratic developments have been salient features within probation since the 1980s. Such changes have persisted and been taken to a new level by New Labour in line with the principles of NPM, measurable targets, and the creation of competitive markets in the public sector. Another of Carter's modernising aims is to raise the game of public services, as manifested in the split between offender case management procedures and the delivery of interventions. The latter opens up the possibility of additional public, private and voluntary sector involvement as correctional services are offered to the market. Will Securicor become responsible for unpaid work? Will Global Solutions be given the contract for hostels? Will another agency be writing court reports by 2010?

If area probation organisations constitute the primary public sector service entrusted with the delivery of, for example, community service from the mid-1970s and hostel provision over many decades, the NOMS structure will enable other agencies to make a pitch for contracts meted out by regional offender managers. But as Hough et al presciently comment:

> 'We do not know whether the provision of correctional services through networks of providers from the statutory, voluntary and private sectors will result in fragmentation that far outweighs the unifying effects of combining the prison and probation services' (2006 p6).

In fact, Hough et al raise four main areas of concern worth serious reflection and monitoring:

- Whether NOMS will attract legitimacy and public support.

- The notion of responsibility and accountability if and when there are numerous providers of interventions.

- The issue of culture, values and professional relationships between the different providers.

- The very real danger of the fragmentation of services in a market driven environment.

It is worth reflecting further on some of the possible dimensions of fragmentation. In what I have already referred to as the old culture of probation – pre-modernised, pre-managerial, pre-bureaucratic and pre-computerised – there was arguably a much greater sense of cultural unity than prevails in the centenary year and is likely to evolve during the next few years. There was a much clearer focus upon the professional probation officer as an officer of the court, whose duties were encapsulated in legislation and statutory probation rules. Another significant manifestation of cultural unity was the closer association between all grades of staff who were engaged in a common enterprise, in other words united by a more social work value-base in their work with offenders. I have already cited the example of how senior and even chief probation officers held limited caseloads up to the early 1980s, which would be unthinkable in today's more bureaucratic service. However, as a result of a number of factors, including the decline of cultural transmission, bureaucratisation, and computer technology, I would argue that there is currently more cultural fragmentation than unity. The following examples demonstrate this point.

Staff fragmentation

The organisational structure of the probation service in its centenary year is marked more by heterogeneity than homogeneity. Modernisation has created a situation in which members of staff occupying the upper reaches of the organisation – from chief officers (civil servants appointed nationally, not locally, who arguably have divided loyalties between central political demands and local needs) and other senior managers/ directors, to civil servants and National Probation Directorate, including government ministers – operate in zones far removed from staff working on the front line with offenders. There is a greater distance between hierarchically demarcated grades of staff than previously. Consequently, there is a danger that disconnected spheres of operation will facilitate mutual misunderstandings, rather than promote cultural unity rooted in a sense of common purpose, underpinned by shared values, experiences, loyalties and trust. This has potentially serious implications for the upper reaches of the organisation in terms of legitimacy and credibility. In other words, members of staff who work with people who offend psychologically need those above them to appreciate and understand the work they do. This is particularly important when some senior managers may never have worked as probation officers themselves; those who have done the job, but perhaps a decade ago, have no direct experience of computerised probation work and the significant reduction in professional autonomy and discretion. In what should be a people-based organisation, tensions are generated if there are widening divisions between managers operating in discrete managerial zones and practitioners in practice zones, who are striving to respond to the needs of individual offenders in a target driven organisation. Additionally, the cultural differences between practitioner and managerial grades are much more pronounced than formerly. The result is various subcultures operating within the contemporary service, in the grip of their own demands and priorities.

Arguably, those who work in the upper reaches of the organisation are less affected by modernisation than those who work directly with offenders. The latter have witnessed a marked decline in their professional status, associated with loss of autonomy and discretion. Paradoxically, it is senior managers who have the most to lose because they can be more easily replaced than practitioners in a culture of market competition.

Fragmentation of people knowledge and skills

Another feature of fragmentation is the employment of staff trained under different regimes, for example the Diploma in Probation Studies since 1997-98 and, before that, the Diploma in Social Work courses at various universities. Currently, the organisation includes staff trained under both regimes, although those trained under the latter are becoming fewer and will eventually disappear. Notwithstanding a number of concerns associated with probation training over recent years (Whitehead and Thompson 2004), there is still scope, even since 1997-98, for trainee probation officers to consider the requirements of a body of social work knowledge and skills, although the culture has been modernised to place more emphasis on criminal justice law enforcement priorities, as acknowledged by a number of solicitors in Chapter 5. Arguably, Think First has been facilitative in this sense (Chui and Nellis 2003).

However, the dimension of fragmentation under discussion concerns the expectations of trainees at the beginning of their training, their assumptions and reasonable expectations about the nature of probation work, contrasted with the job they find themselves having to undertake upon qualification. It is possible that for the foreseeable future, training arrangements will allow the acquisition of a body of knowledge and skills to engage, motivate, understand, and work with people with many personal and social problems. Yet the organisation as it is currently configured demands that staff are more office based, that they become computer operators and bureaucratic technicians. Therefore instead of being provided with opportunities to refine a repertoire of people skills after initial training, current political and bureaucratic priorities are concerned more with technical efficiency and meeting targets than with the person behind the offending. This has profound implications for motivation, morale, and also effectiveness. Organisational structures are not conducive to facilitating those people skills required by probation staff.

Fragmentation within NOMS

It may reasonably be assumed that the attenuation of a so-called silo mentality following the creation of NOMS on 1st April 2006, between probation and prison, will enhance organisational unity. This is to be achieved through the case manager role, which provides the glue within a process of what is referred to as end-to-end management. In other words, this model consists of a designated offender manager (formerly probation officer) providing continuity from beginning to end of the sentence, within a seamless supervisory process. However, this does not necessarily mean that the offender manager will be the only person providing weekly contact and input throughout the sentence. Instead, the offender manager role can increasingly be perceived as a broker of services between public, private and voluntary sectors/providers, following the move towards contestability. Therefore the case manager is not so much involved in supervising and working with the person (although to some degree this will continue) as facilitating a bureaucratic process for the management of risk between various providers.

This model is unlikely to endear itself to staff who would like to do purposeful work with their caseload and who want to be committed to their local service; nor is it likely to endear itself to offenders who have been known in recent years to complain about the unsettling effects of frequent changes of supervisor, long before NOMS appeared on the scene. In other words NOMS could create a level of fragmentation rooted in the weakening of the personal relationship, based on professional trust, between supervisor and offender, which arguably should be at the heart of practice and which must be given time to develop. Put simply, workers cannot influence offenders unless they have contact and spend time with them. Managing offenders is not the same as supervising them.

Interlude: integrating some research findings

During the course of interviews with the 31 respondents, I was interested to find out whether they had heard of NOMS. Therefore:

Table 6.1 Do you have any understanding of NOMS?

	Number	Per cent
Yes	5	16.1
No	26	83.9
Total	31	100.0

Responses from the five solicitors who declared some awareness included:

> 'I don't have a great deal of understanding of it. I've had a few clients... well my understanding is that people are identified as requiring that type of supervision and it's a multi-agency thing.'

> 'I've made no enquires as to exactly what they do but I would guess that they are a quango set up as a spiffing good idea in order to allow somebody to justify their existence really.'

> 'Is that the crime initiative that might be coming in or has come in? I only heard the term the other day, so I don't really know a lot about it, although from what I understand it is some kind of private initiative that is trying to impose itself on probation, which is why I understand probation have been set targets and if those targets aren't met then NOMS may take over I think; I'm not entirely sure.'

Table 6.2 Have you heard of contestability?

	Number	*Per cent*
Yes	0	0.0
No	31	100.0
Total	31	100.0

Interestingly, none of the 31 had heard of contestability (the only unanimous reply to the questions in the interview schedule). Two of the more interesting replies were:

> 'Is there such a word as contestability? Sounds like a civil service invention. The civil service invent things like this but yes I've never heard of it before to be truthful.'

> 'Contestability? No, sounds like some government buzz word, doesn't it?'

Within the macro level framework established in the first section of this chapter, the next section therefore argues for the lineaments of a probation system that cuts across the grain of where it finds itself in 2007. Accordingly, I want to develop four substantive areas:

- Refine the essence of the probation ideal.

- Probation as a profession not computerised bureaucracy.

- A profession with objectives rather than targets.

- The role of probation information in the criminal justice system.

PART 2: BEYOND MODERNISATION AND CULTURAL CHANGE

Refining the essence of the probation ideal

An earlier piece of work (Whitehead and Statham 2006 pp280-282) attempted to give some shape to the features which would constitute the probation ideal. At this point in the final chapter, I would like to refine these features, which would play their part within the criminal justice system:

- Probation staff should be as concerned as politicians, sentencers and local communities about the impact of offending behaviour upon victims and the consequences for the offenders themselves and their families. In other words, offending is not condoned or colluded with (a left realist more than left idealist approach).

- Probation should focus upon individuals and their potential for positive change, rather than impersonal aggregates and risk categories. William Temple said in the 1930s 'We are not what we appear, but what we are becoming; and if that is what we truly are, no penal system is fully just which treats us as anything else' (in Radzinowicz 1999 p124).

- Probation should work alongside other agencies to keep offenders out of the formal criminal justice system for as long as possible, which implies a better 'strategic fit' with, for example, social services, education, and youth justice. Once inside the system, the negative effects of labelling should be prevented, and the damaging effects of custodial sentences avoided. Therefore the imposition of custody should be delayed for as long as possible. Only the most seriously harmful and dangerous offenders should be committed to custody, which arguably has not been government or even probation policy for a considerable period of time. Probation has the potential to mitigate the worst punitive excesses of the criminal justice system by being allowed to work with offenders in the community.

- The essence of probation includes the values of tolerance, decency, human feeling, care and compassion, which are deeply rooted in an insightful understanding of the human condition. There is an ethical dimension to probation practice, any diminution of which would impoverish the workings of the wider system of justice.

- Not only should members of staff be clear about *what* they should be doing, but also *how* they should be doing it. Probation staff should be working with people who offend within the context of relationships. What this means will be clarified in the next section on probation as a social work profession.

- Probation should acknowledge that offenders can be victims of complex family backgrounds and unpropitious social circumstances. Hopkins Burke (2005), in his useful text on criminological theory, operates with three main paradigms: the rational actor model (classical and neo-classical); predestined actor model (variants of positivism); the victimised actor model. It may be suggested that it is the third model which has some relevance where probation practice is concerned.

- Probation makes an important contribution to the notion of establishing a fair and just society by its commitment to equal opportunities, diversity and anti-discriminatory practice.

- The probation ideal has the potential to understand and explain human behaviour and address those factors considered to be associated with episodes of offending. In other words, it advises, assists, befriends and helps people. Primarily through the provision of personal and social information contained in court reports, probation staff have a critical role to play in interpreting the behaviour of those who offend. This role could be damaged if the FDR supplants the full PSR, largely for reasons of economy. The objective of speed before justice should be treated with caution.

These are some of the elements which constitute the essence, the distinctive features, of the probation ideal. If these do not continue to have a foothold within systems of criminal justice, it could be argued that probation is in danger of becoming a redundant organisation and perhaps an extension of the Crown Prosecution Service, more involved in the prosecution and punishment of offenders. It should be clear that probation has a distinctive role to play within the criminal justice system and that unless this distinctiveness is maintained the entire system of justice will become impoverished.

Support for the position advocated here can be found in the work of Cullen and Gilbert on *Reaffirming Rehabilitation* (1982). The rehabilitative ideal about which these authors write, which has points of overlap with the tenor of the probation ideal, has of course in the past been criticised because of its theoretical shortcomings, which are discriminatory in nature, but also inconsistent with the principles of justice. There was a downside to the rehabilitative ideal which led to a sustained critique by Bottoms and McWilliams (1979), who replaced the treatment/medical model with their non-treatment paradigm. On the other hand, a number of positive elements are arguably attached to the rehabilitative ethic which Cullen and Gilbert preserve. Over recent years (since the 1980s), although the language of reform and rehabilitation has not disappeared from the criminal justice system or underpinning legislation, the dominant penal philosophy has increasingly equated justice with punishment. Back in 1982, against the background of the decline of rehabilitation and the corresponding rise to prominence of the justice model of corrections, Cullen and Gilbert advanced four reasons for not abandoning the rehabilitative approach. These can be paraphrased and embellished as follows:

- First, the rehabilitative approach puts a moral obligation on the state to care for the offender's needs and welfare (in opposition to a contestability philosophy). On this point, it is of interest to turn to the position of Radzinowicz: 'Detention, control and care of prisoners should not be parcelled out to entrepreneurs operating according to market forces, but should remain the undiluted responsibility of the state' (1999 p432).

- Secondly, the rehabilitation approach represents an ideological position which opposes the new-right's stance that more punishment-repression is equal to justice and will reduce crime. Increased punitiveness does not equal enhanced effectiveness; more punishment does not mean better justice.

- Thirdly, reform and rehabilitation continue to receive support, albeit more limited at present than previously, as a goal of the criminal justice system. For example, rehabilitation remains one of the five purposes of sentencing under the Criminal Justice Act 2003.

- Finally, and centrally, the rehabilitative ideal if complemented by the probation ideal is associated with a set of humanitarian impulses and values within the criminal justice system which challenge the prevailing ethos.

It may be argued that the balance between competing ideologies changes over time; attitudes towards retribution, deterrence, and rehabilitation are negotiated and re-negotiated within changing political contexts (look at the period between 1979 and 2007). Notwithstanding the ascendancy of the punishment ideal, the probation ideal represents a set of values which makes a contribution to just outcomes. If the prevailing wisdom of the age is that justice = punishment, serious attention should also be given to the position that both criminal and social justice include the ethics of rehabilitation and the application of the probation ideal within a personalist framework; which leads to the next point.

Probation as social work profession not computerised bureaucracy

The central proposition is the untimely one (indubitably pre-modernised) that probation should be synonymous with a social work profession comprising a body of trained professional practitioners. These professionals can be identified by the way they draw upon distinctive bodies of knowledge, skills and experience, the latter gained from working with people. The acquisition of the first two elements should begin during initial training and opportunities should be provided over subsequent years for their enrichment. The knowledge base is provided by, for example, a critical approach to psychology, sociology, criminology and law; skills amount to an ability to engage and work with people with problems which reflection, experience, and importantly feedback and guidance from mature practitioners, can facilitate. These elements combine to equip the thoughtful practitioner to be a responsible and accountable professional, responsible for his or her own thinking, able to formulate judgments, make decisions and respond to each individual case on its merits, rather than operate within a fixed set of standardised and routinised procedures, regulatory systems and bureaucratic processes. Professional practitioners should be imbued with the confidence to learn from success and failure (of course more from the latter than the former if handled correctly) which often go hand-in-hand in people-based work like probation. An enabling managerial framework would expect the highest standards of performance from its staff, but would also trust its staff to be professional, unfettered by the burdensome restraints of centrally imposed bureaucratic systems which carry the threat of sanctions for target failures. The latter is no way to trust or respect an organisation or the people within it.

It can be argued that, as a consequence of the modernising developments described throughout this book, the service has, in moving away from its social work roots, been impoverished by a lack of attention to probation as a social work profession. Within this modernised manifestation of the profession, much greater priority is afforded to ensuring that computer records are up to date, than to creating opportunities for staff to develop professional expertise which, in turn, would facilitate an insightful understanding of clients. In an interesting paper, David Smith (2006) argues that those elements of probation practice from the more rehabilitative, treatment and social work era of the pre-modernised 1960s and 1970s are in fact similar to recent criminological themes of a more psychoanalytical orientation. This psychoanalytical tradition draws attention to a number of features, including the notion of social work relationships, which were a significant features of probation work for many decades. This requires amplification at this point.

Social work relationships

The four Departmental Committee Reports of 1909, 1922, 1936 and 1962 had much to say about the development of the probation system. I suggest, after re-reading these documents, that the common theme which binds them together is the importance attached to the relationship between the probation officer and probationer. As early as 1909, fewer than two years into the system, the following neatly sets the scene:

> 'The value of probation must necessarily depend on the efficiency of the probation officer. It is a system in which rules are comparatively unimportant, and personality is everything. The probation officer must be a picked man or woman, endowed not only with intelligence and zeal, but, in a high degree, with sympathy and tact and firmness. On his or her individuality the success or failure of the system depends. Probation is what the officer makes it' (Home Office 1909 paragraph 28).

It can be extrapolated, although the ideology of probation was transformed significantly during the twentieth century from a theology of saving souls to a more scientifically secular form of casework, that the ability of the officer to establish relationships was the framework through which advice, assistance and friendship were delivered (McWilliams 1983, 1985, 1986 and 1987). This was endorsed by the fourth and last Departmental Committee (Home Office 1962) which stated that:

> 'Casework, as we understand it, is the creation and utilisation, for the benefit of an individual who needs help with personal problems, *of a relationship between himself and a trained social worker*...It is a basic assumption of all casework that each person is a unique individual

whose difficulties are the product of complex and interacting factors. The caseworker thus needs the fullest possible insight into the individual's personality, capacities, attitudes and feelings and he must also understand the influences in the individual's history, relationships and present environment which have helped to form them' (Home Office 1962 p24, emphasis added).

By 1964, in the second edition of Florence Hollis' *Casework: A Psychosocial Theory*, the centrality of the casework relationship was being advocated as the medium for developing a fully functioning individual beset with problems of a personal and social nature. Moreover, it was through a social work relationship that the personalist values of human worth and acceptance could be expressed. Accordingly Traux and Carkhuff (1967) emphasised the importance of empathy, genuineness, and warmth in successful therapeutic relationships. This nomenclature is no longer at the heart of practice values.

Specifically within a probation context, Ian Sinclair's (1971) research into 46 approved probation hostels revealed that failure rates with offenders varied from 14 per cent to 78 per cent, and that these marked differences were only partially accounted for by previous convictions and social histories. He found that successful hostels had staff who combined emotional warmth, kindness, and an understanding of residents' problems, in addition to administering hostel rules in a fair and consistent manner. More recently, Cherry and Cheston (2006) drew attention to face-to-face rehabilitative relationships as a central component within a model regime for approved premises. This contrasts markedly with the current emphasis upon monitoring and surveillance. Next, and briefly, Jarvis drew attention to such features within the context of probation training (1974), and Martin Davies (1985) emphasised the quality of the social work relationship as the starting point of practice. Joyce Lishman (1994) stated that the essential ingredients of building a social work relationship are genuineness, warmth, acceptance, encouragement and approval, empathy, responsiveness and sensitivity. At the turn of the millennium, Peter Raynor, when reflecting on the meaning of casework throughout the history of probation, came to the view that it was a 'process of therapeutic work in which the offender's needs and motivation, characteristically hidden by 'presenting problems', could be revealed through a process of insight facilitated by a relationship with a probation officer' (2002 p1173).

In an interesting collection of papers dealing with aspects of probation practice since the late 1990s, Chui and Nellis (2003) discuss the transition in probation from the one-to-one casework era, through the decline of the rehabilitative ideal, to the What Works agenda accompanied by the renaissance of rehabilitation. Even cognitive-behavioural work must take into account the research into those ingredients which create the conditions for effective helping, based upon social work relationships. In fact, in McNeill's paper on desistance from offending it is stated that it 'requires engaging, active and participative relationships characterised by optimism, trust, and loyalty, as well as interventions targeted at those aspects of each individual's motivation, attitudes, thinking and values which might help or hinder progress towards desistance' (2003 p160). In other words engagement skills, relationships, responding to the needs of individuals, and the contemporary jargon of pro-social modelling, are some of the components of effective probation work.

Finally, David Smith (2004 and 2006) reinforces many of those features associated with psychosocial social work practice, largely abandoned in the more sociologically-orientated 1970s, yet revived in the 1990s. He suggests that elements of probation work from the psycho-dynamically inspired 1950s and 1960s find an echo in some recent criminological themes, including the attention that is once again being drawn to the quality of the worker. In other words the quality of the probation officer, including the ability to form relationships, is more important for determining success/ failure than methods employed within supervision (which takes us back to the 1909 Departmental Committee cited above). Even the What Works agenda gives credence to the quality of the relationship between probation officer and client, respect for persons and emotional warmth, looking for positives, expressions of concern and support, and attending to needs within a personalist framework.[1] Smith challengingly concludes that:

> 'The reconstruction over the past ten years of the probation service (in England and Wales) as something other than a social work agency entails the risk of forgetting what may be of positive value in the history of probation practice, as well as what is best treated as an example of what to avoid' (2006 p372).

For as one research respondent observed 'I've seen the probation service change...I feel that many years ago there was a more one-to-one personal basis between subject and supervising officer. When I spoke to someone (an offender) 20-30 years ago they knew their probation officer by name.'

It can be concluded that there is a body of work which draws attention to the central importance of relationships within social work orientated probation practice. These relationships should be underpinned by knowledge, skills and experience. Effective work cannot be undertaken unless practitioners spend time engaging people with problems. However, politicised processes of modernisation and cultural transformation manifested by bureaucratisation, targets and computerisation have damaged rather than facilitated what should be the central elements of professional practice. In fact, the cornerstone of such practice, social work relationships, has been undermined by organisational structures that demand office based bureaucratic technicians, facilitating organisational processes and maintaining systems. The fundamental requirements of practice are consequently in danger of being forgotten, which will adversely affect the effectiveness of the probation officer as helper and public protector.

A service with broad objectives rather than targets

It is not necessary to examine either objectives or targets at length here, because Chapter 2 provides a critique of the contemporary target culture. There are, of course, different ways of approaching the issue of objectives and targets within people based organisations along a continuum: an argument for broad objectives rather than targets can be located at one extreme; a better balance between broad objectives and limited amounts of targets somewhere in the middle; and of full support for a cash-linked target culture at the other extreme. But, as discussed in Chapter 2, several pressing problems are associated with targets within probation, which is not a business in the way that other organisations, particularly in the private sector, purport to be businesses making and selling objects/things for profit. As McLaughlin et al point out in their helpful paper on the principles of New Public Management in the criminal justice system:

> 'the attempted imposition of key aspects of the Conservatives' wider managerial agenda (that is in the 1980s) provoked considerable resistance from criminal justice professionals who argued that criminal justice, a public sector good, could not be run or managed like a business selling products to customers in a competitive market place' (2001 p303).

Yet this is the ethos which has gathered pace since 1997.

Moreover, a quantifiable and measurable cash-linked target culture has the potential to skew judgments and decisions about, for example, advice on sentencing provided by probation officers to sentencers. Two examples of this should suffice. First section 148(2) of the Criminal Justice Act 2003 makes it clear that the requirements attached to a community order must be 'the most suitable for the offender' after considering individual needs and the seriousness of the offence. However, if the organisation predicts halfway through the year that it is unlikely to achieve its target for the Drug Rehabilitation Requirement (DRR) by the following March (end of the financial year), thus risking financial sanctions, then it could be forced into making skewed decisions which contradict the intentions of the Act. This, in turn, could result in setting up some offenders to fail a DRR because they are not suitable for this specific requirement and also the prospect of appeal against sentence on the basis that it was not the most suitable, having regard to all the circumstances, for the individual in question. In other words, a target culture can result in questionable decisions being made, professional integrity compromised and the achievement of targets being put ahead of all other considerations.

Secondly, the current target for FDRs is 40 per cent of all reports prepared by the probation service. While the point can be reiterated that, in certain circumstances, FDRs can be justified and will not be prepared on offenders who are deemed to be serious (where there are issues of public protection, serious offences involving risk of serious harm, mental health issues and domestic violence), again, decisions and judgments are in danger of being skewed to meet service targets. The FDR is prepared to meet the target, rather than because it is the right or most appropriate thing to do, according to professional rather than business criteria. Again there are profound tensions between the demands of professional practice and the demands of centrally imposed bureaucratic processes within a modernised organisation.

The FDR and full PSR within a professional rather than bureaucratic organisation should proceed on the following basis. Targets constitute a problem within people-based organisations and, as one solicitor respondent commented in Chapter 5: 'Target driven organisations tend not actually to be representative of the way things are'. The emphasis should be placed upon giving the professional probation officer the autonomy and discretion to make a judgment on the most suitable report for the individual, having regard to all the circumstances and mindful of the probation ideal.

Probation information – criminal and social justice through trialectics

For the Greeks, dialectics were a process of arriving at truth via argument (Socratic process). Many centuries later, Hegel theorised that history has a purpose which is moving inexorably towards an end point through a dialectical process of thesis, antithesis and synthesis, which will resolve all contradictions. This process assumed a materialist direction in Marx so that contradictions between the classes would culminate in a victory for the working class. At this point, I want to extend the notion of dialectics by introducing the concept of trialectics which attempts to capture within itself the elements of a process for the pursuit of 'truth' and 'justice' within the criminal justice system.

The argument being advanced is that the probation service should have a distinctive role to play within the workings of the criminal justice system. It is not synonymous with the Crown Prosecution Service, although it is involved in taking offences seriously by evaluating *what* the offender has done within the framework provided by the Criminal Justice Act 2003. Furthermore, it is concerned with the nature and seriousness of offending behaviour and its impact upon victims and local communities. Notwithstanding points of overlap and areas of common concern, it is not the role of probation to prosecute cases in court, which has been the domain of the Crown Prosecution Service since the 1980s. Nor does probation take the side of the client in direct opposition to the claims of the prosecution: it is not an extension of the defence role even though, as with the prosecution, there are points of overlap. Nevertheless, probation is not in the business of excusing, condoning or justifying the behaviour of those who offend. Rather, probation seeks to analyse, appreciate and understand those complex factors associated with the offending behaviour, which it proceeds to explain to the court. To achieve this, it draws attention to the significant variables which can be said to frame the person's offending and in this sense addresses the *why* question.

Therefore the concept of trialectics, as opposed to dialectics, captures a three-way process within court which is replete with contradictions (differences of perspective, emphasis, and ideology) requiring resolution between a) the prosecution/CPS case on behalf of the Crown; b) the defence solicitor who must defend the best interests of his or her client by proffering relevant mitigation; c) the contribution of the probation service. Within the operational dynamics of the criminal justice system, the probation service fulfils its central role through the provision of relevant information in the form of court reports. This is why the debate surrounding whether the report should be in the form of an FDR or full SDR/PSR assumes a high degree of importance, particularly if the end point of this trialectical process is to enable sentencers (magistrates and judges) to deliver both criminal and social justice by weighing the relevance of pertinent information of a personal and social nature, against the seriousness of the offence. It is at this point that one can be reminded of Benn and Peters when they said that 'To do justice is to treat men unequally only according to the degree of their relevant inequalities' (1959 p173).

Notwithstanding the process of modernisation and cultural change which has steered the criminal justice system in the direction of punishment (Cabinet Office 2006), it could be the case that the effective functioning of this trialectical process will, on occasion, challenge the drift towards punitiveness. But this will only occur if the probation service is allowed to make its distinctive contribution consistent with those principles and values associated with the probation ideal. Doing the right thing, delivering just outcomes within the court setting, does not mean unthinkingly adhering to the equation that justice = punishment; that it is inevitable that more people will be committed to prison by 2012; that the benefit sanction is a positive development which should be extended to all areas; that an onerous requirement is always the correct response in enforcement proceedings rather than a verbal warning. Consequently this process can be presented diagrammatically as follows:

Figure 6.1 Trialectics

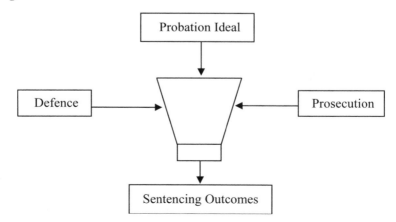

The notion of trialectics is captured well by the following research respondents. One solicitor, when commenting upon the main purpose of probation, said

> 'I suppose it is to give an independent view to the court of the defendant, the analysis of the offence, analysis of seriousness, analysis as to the likelihood of re-offending, likelihood of danger of physical harm to the public, himself or anyone else, and to offer a recommendation to the court…So I suppose it's an independent view, not one-sided with the prosecution, not one-sided with the defence; it's an independent view.'

Another respondent commented

> 'I think I see the probation service occupying the middle ground, so to speak, between understandably biased defence solicitors who are keen to achieve a good result for their client come what may, and the prosecution service who obviously are motivated to the opposite direction…'

Finally, and within the context of the provision of court reports, the task facing probation is

> 'To provide the magistrates or district judges with information upon the offender from an independent source. It's not just the Crown's version of events; it's not just the defence's version of events. It's information derived, I would hope, from a rigorous examination of the client and their circumstances and the circumstances surrounding the case that's provided to the bench in such a way that permits them to make a disposal commensurate with the seriousness of the offence. But in my opinion (the report) always has in mind the process of reform and rehabilitation and management, hopefully in the community, rather than prison.'

If the probation service could be enabled to be true to its distinctive essence, formulated in terms of the probation ideal explored earlier, then even within the current political climate it could make a difference to sentencing outcomes. Even within a sentencing system replete with philosophical contradictions (Taylor et al 2004 p174 on purposes of sentencing), penological confusion (Garland 2001), and the world weary periodic crises brought about by prison overcrowding, this is a propitious time to look again at the criminal justice system and what it intends to achieve, including the place of probation within it. Of course one of the tragic features of the modern criminal justice system is that it is often not the solution to the complex human problems with which it is presented on a daily basis. This is largely because such problems have their genesis deep within childhood experiences culminating in life-long psychosocial difficulties, complex family dynamics, the unequal nature of capitalist societies and multi-layered deprivations: and because sensationalist media reporting of offending behaviour results in politicians responding with alacrity without thinking through the longer-term consequences. Therefore, a criminal justice response is arguably not always the most effective. Nevertheless, the system continues to punish in the community and prison, not necessarily because it is the right or most logical thing to do, nor because it is effective or the most obvious solution. Rather, since the early 1980s and again since 1993, penal policy has been corralled into a more punitive cul-de-sac from which policy makers are unable to extricate themselves for fear of a loss of electoral face.

Even within the most unpropitious circumstances, it can be argued that promotion of the probation ideal has the capacity to make a difference, by persuasion and argument, in an anti-punitive and more humane direction. However, the organisation requires more independence than it has been allowed, particularly since it was nationalised in 2001, to move in this direction. For example, it should be relieved of the burden to achieve targets for fear of penal sanctions. It should also be relieved of excessive central control. Chief officers, reinstated as chief probation officers who are defenders of the probation ideal, should once again have the responsibility to lead local services rather than being hostages to the prevailing political mood. This will mean re-creating managerial structures which facilitate a professional probation service, rather than bureaucratic and computer driven structures, which prevent members of staff from doing the job of working with people who offend within the context of social work relationships. There must be a role for the political centre to be involved in probation work, as there has been since 1907, but the centre must re-learn how to listen to the voices of expertise which exist within local area services. In other words, this is a bid for an intelligent and more democratic two way process, rather than the top-heavy and top-down process which has been in vogue since the 1980s.

If it is possible to make adjustments along the lines suggested; if the probation service is not only allowed but also enabled to be a professional service rather than a bureaucratic system; if this trialectical process can be encouraged to function with a view to promoting criminal and social justice based upon the provision of all relevant information on individual offenders; then the courts will retain the power to resort to the ultimate sanction of custody. However, the important difference would be that such decisions would be made on the basis of each organisation's, distinctive contribution to the process of sentencing, including probation. Unfortunately, the last few years of modernisation and cultural change have diluted probation's distinctive contribution by the attenuation of the probation ideal. This is because probation has been reconstructed according to a political image, rather than being encouraged to remain true to its essence.

Final comments and recommendations

This book challenges the prevailing zeitgeist within the probation service, which has now reached its centenary year. As I said in the Introduction, it cuts across the grain and erects defences against the erosion of the probation ideal. It contends with a number of modernising trends which have colonised organisations throughout the public sector. This is why Chapter 2 presents a critique of targets and raises concerns about the language and meaning of risk. The argument is advanced, in Chapter 3, that attention should be given to a number of elements conducive to the re-creation of a framework of understanding for professional practice. Such a framework is required within an organisation that works with people because there are repertoires of behaviour requiring interpretation and explanation that are beyond the power to punish. However, at present, more factors militate against this framework than support its merits.

Chapter 4 questions the prevailing fashion for numbers and measuring things, particularly within people-orientated organisations. One can no more reduce philosophical debates surrounding ontology and epistemology to a scientific, positivist paradigm, than one can reduce the essence of probation work to what can be quantifiably measured. To do so is to distort and therefore misrepresent on the grounds that much of significance is omitted. Hence the heuristic device of *otherness* for flushing out qualitative and ineffable features which creates the space for discussions centred upon personalism, ethics and values. In Chapter 5, the book includes the first instalment of empirical research findings which provide some insight into, and challenge those political processes responsible for, modernisation and cultural change. Finally, Chapter 6 not only challenges but endeavours to maintain an alternative vision, a different way of thinking about and carrying out probation work.[2]

In this centenary year of 2007, those associated with the probation service should be doing more than marking the last 100 years; there should be celebration too. However, such celebrations are muted because of the implications of modernisation articulated in this book. Nevertheless, if I am permitted to make just one recommendation, then it is to call for the setting up of a departmental committee, the first since 1962, which would enquire into all aspects of probation work and should be initiated by the new Ministry of Justice in its first year of operation. This would be one way to pursue the legitimate concerns of both political and practice-based agendas, and I think it would be supported by all those concerned about probation work in the criminal justice system as it enters the next 100 years.

NOTES

[1]   Personalism: Within probation work, understood as a people-based social work profession, the doctrine of personalism places the unique individual and personal relationships at the centre of theory and practice. The concept has a long religious and philosophical pedigree throughout western history since the Greek period. Within what can be described as a more scientific, technological, computerised, bureaucratic and therefore impersonal situation for human beings, personalism, with its focus on personal/ human categories, constitutes an important corrective (Mounier 1952). Personalism conveys the value that it is the individual human being who has innate meaning. Accordingly, the human person is worthy of respect, should be appreciated and understood, and is not an object or '*it*' to be managed. It challenges, for example, the view that probation clients can be allocated to one of several categories of risk, determined by numbers, premised upon a computerised risk scale. Personalism complements the notion of the probation officer exercising therapeutic imagination rather than operating as a bureaucratic technician. For personalists, the fast delivery report constitutes a particular problem if it reduces the individual to a tick box format; that policies and targets take priority over assessing and understanding the needs of different individuals is a problem for personalists. For Kant and William Temple the individual is a rational being who should be treated as an end, not a means to an end. Within the probation service there is an identifiable personalist bibliography which can be cited as follows: Biestek (1961), Hugman (1977), Millard (1979), Bailey (1980), Stelman (1980), Raynor (1985), McWilliams (1987). This book supports this tradition by drawing attention to social work relationships enshrined within the probation ideal. It is difficult to be precise about how many probation staff, from practitioners to managers, operate within a personalist philosophy during the centenary year.

[2]   Theoretical Perspectives: An additional note is required on three theoretical perspectives at the conclusion of this book. First, the probation ideal suggests that probation work should operate from the starting point of the person as unique individual. Nevertheless, Michel Foucault reveals it is illusory to think of the person-individual-subject as the sole source of meaning. In other words 'Far from being the source of meaning, the subject is in fact a secondary effect or by-product of discursive formations' (McNay 1994 p5). Adapting this approach it can be argued that the latest system of thought within probation/penal policy (episteme, block of knowledge) made up of neo-classicism, NPM, risk and punishment, etc…, and flowing from the new politics after 1979, constructs the person according to a political image. In other words, and to adapt the Kantian perspective, the political requirement for power and control over offenders/the poor, in

addition to complementary organisational structures, does not conform to or flow from a desire to understand the person as subject; rather the person conforms to and is constructed by political and organisational demands. It is therefore difficult for probation and other criminal justice staff to think, operate and make decisions outside of this system of thought, the current block of knowledge.

Secondly, political economy. The probation service and wider criminal justice system usually deal with the recalcitrant poor rather than the well-to-do. This book does not operate with the view that crime is primarily a consequence of individual pathology or dysfunction. Of course individuals have their problems as probation officers know only too well, and it is readily acknowledged that individuals can behave inappropriately and irresponsibly. However, the probation officer must situate the behaviours of individuals within wider social contexts, socio-economic arrangements, differential opportunities, a capitalist mode of production with its markets, inequalities, disadvantages, producing winners and losers. In other words, theoretically insightful probation practice should locate and explain offending behaviour within the widest possible parameters of understanding, which means going beyond individual accounts. Some questions to pose are: What is it like to be this person from this background? What personal and social factors are relevant when explaining offending behaviour? To what extent is the offender a victim of circumstances beyond his/her control?

Thirdly, the text has made a number of references to Weber and bureaucratisation in conjunction with managerialism, computerisation and NPM. Bureaucratic developments have been referred to somewhat pejoratively in the sense that probation has been transformed from a professional organisation which encouraged autonomy, discretion, the responsibility to make judgements and arrive at decisions about people and their needs, to a more bureaucratic form replete with national standards facilitating greater standardisation, routinised behaviours and application of rules. The political centre has fashioned a probation organisation of technicians, auditors, target chasers, who have been put in the position of operating systems rather than spending time working with people/clients within the context of relationships. Probation is being culturally transformed into an impersonal machine for processing people as efficiently as possible, which arguably exercises as much control over its staff as offenders. Bureaucracy may well be the most efficient means by which capitalist societies are organised, but it has its downside: oppression, despair, rigidity, dehumanising tendencies. In fact it can create a mentality and culture that reduces staff to cogs in an impersonal machine – an iron cage of power, control, regulation and technical efficiency.

Therefore, the phenomenon of modernisation and cultural change in probation and criminal justice can be a) plotted and described over the last two decades; and b) also analysed by locating cultural transformations against the background of bodies of social theory which include Foucault, political economy and bureaucracy. Arguably, no one theoretical perspective has primacy: rather a combination of these three have explanatory efficacy.

REFERENCES

Abrams, P. (1968) *The Origins of British Sociology 1834–1914*, The University of Chicago Press, Chicago and London.

Armstrong, K. (1993) *A History of God: From Abraham to the Present: the 4000 Year Quest for God,* Heinemann, London.

Armstrong, K. (2005) *A Short History of Myth*, Canongate, Edinburgh, New York, Melbourne.

Audit Commission (2003) *Targets in the Public Sector*, Public Sector Briefing.

Ayer, A.J. (2000) *Hume: A Very Short Introduction*, Oxford University Press, Oxford and New York.

Bailey, R. (1980) 'Social Workers: Pawns, Police or Agitators?' in: M. Brake and R. Bailey (eds.) *Radical Social Work and Practice*, Edward Arnold, London.

Baldwin, J. (2000) 'Research on the Criminal Courts' in: R.D. King and E. Wincup (eds.) *Doing Research on Crime and Justice*, Oxford University Press, Oxford and New York.

Baldwin, J. and McConville, M. (1977) 'Plea Bargaining and Plea Negotiation in England', *Law and Society Review*, 13, 287–307.

Barnes, J. (2005) *Arthur and George*, Jonathan Cape, London.

Bean, P. (1981) *Punishment: A Philosophical and Criminological Enquiry*, Martin Robertson, Oxford.

Beck, U. (1992) *Risk Society: Towards a New Modernity*, Sage Publications Ltd.

Becker, H. (1963) *Outsiders: Studies in the Sociology of Deviance*, New York Free Press.

Bellamy, R. (1995 edn) *Beccaria: On Crimes and Punishments and Other Writings*, Cambridge University Press, Cambridge and New York.

Bendix, R. (1960) *Max Weber: An Intellectual Portrait*, Heinemann, London, Melbourne and Toronto.

Benn, S.I. and Peters, R.S. (1959) *Social Principles and the Democratic State*, George Allen and Unwin, London.

Bennett, A. (2005) *Untold Stories*, Faber and Faber Ltd., London.

Biestek, F.P. (1961) *The Casework Relationship*, George Allen and Unwin, London.

Boateng, P. (1999) Speech to Chief Probation Officers and Probation Committees, HMSO, London.

Bonger, W. (1916; re-issued 1969) *Criminality and Economic Conditions*, Indiana University Press, Bloomington, IN.

Bottoms, A. and Stelman, A. (1988) *Social Inquiry Reports: A Framework for Practice Development*, Community Care Practice Handbooks, Wildwood House, Aldershot.

Bottoms, A.E. and McWilliams, W. (1979) 'A Non-treatment Paradigm for Probation Practice', *BJSW*, 9, 2.

Bottoms, A.E. and McWilliams, W. (1986) 'Social Enquiry Reports Twenty-Five Years After The Streatfield Report' in: P. Bean and D. Whynes (eds.) *Barbara Wootton Social Science and Public Policy: Essays In Her Honour.* Tavistock Publications, London and New York.

Bottoms, A.E. and Wiles, P. (2002) 'Environmental Criminology' in: M. Maguire, R. Morgan and R. Reiner (eds. 3rd edn) *The Oxford Handbook of Criminology*, Oxford University Press, Oxford and New York.

Bowlby, J. (1971) *Attachment and Loss Volume 1: Attachment*, Penguin Books, London.

Bowlby, J. (1975) *Attachment and Loss Volume 2: Separation: Anxiety and Anger*, Penguin Books, London.

Box, S. (1981 2nd edn) *Deviance, Reality and Society*, Holt, Rinehart and Winston, London and New York.

Brake, M., and Hale, C. (1992) *Public Order and Private Lives: The Politics of Law and Order,* Routledge, New York and London.

Brown, S. (1991) *Magistrates at Work,* Milton Keynes, Open University Press, Buckinghamshire and Philadelphia.

Bruce, S. (1999) *Sociology: A Very Short Introduction*, Oxford University Press, Oxford and New York.

Bryant, C.G.A. (1985) *Positivism in Social Theory and Research*, Macmillan, Basingstoke, Hampshire.

Buber, M. (1970) *I and Thou* (translated by W Kaufmann) T. and T. Clark, Edinburgh.

Cabinet Office (1999) *Modernising Government,* presented to Parliament by the Prime Minister and the Minister for the Cabinet Office, The Stationery Office.

Cabinet Office (November 2006) *Prime Minister's Strategy Unit – Policy Review. Crime, Justice and Cohesion.*

Cailliet, E. (1944) *The Clue to Pascal*, SCM Press Ltd., London

Carnell, E.J. (1965) *The Burden of Soren Kierkegaard*, The Paternoster Press, Cambridge and New York.

Carson, W.G. (1974) 'The Sociology of Crime and the Emergence of Criminal Laws' in: P. Rock and M. McIntosh (eds.) *Deviance and Social Control*, Tavistock Publications, London.

Carter, P. (2003) *Managing Offenders, Reducing Crime. A New Approach,* Strategy Unit.

Cavadino, M., Crow, I. and Dignan, J. (1999) *Criminal Justice 2000: Strategies for a New Century,* Waterside Press, Winchester.

Cavadino, M. and Dignan, J. (2002 3rd edn) *The Penal System: An Introduction*, Sage Publications, London, Thousand Oaks and New Delhi.

Cherry, S. and Cheston, L. (2006) 'Towards a Model Regime for Approved Premises', *Probation Journal*, 53, 3, pp248–264.

Chui, W.H. and Nellis, M. (eds. 2003) *Moving Probation Forward: Evidence, Arguments and Practice,* Pearson Longman, London and New York.

Clarke, R.V. and Felson, M. (1993) 'Introduction: Criminology, Routine Activity, and Rational Choice' in: Clarke and Felson (eds.) *Routine Activity and Rational Choice: Advancements in Criminological Theory* (Volume 5 pp1-14) Transaction Publishing, New Brunswick, NJ.

Cloward, R. and Ohlin, L. (1960) *Delinquency and Opportunity*, Free Press, New York.

Cohen, A. (1955) *Delinquent Boys: The Culture of the Gang*, Free Press, New York.

Cohen, S. (1973) *Folk Devils and Moral Panics*, Paladin, St Albans, Hertfordshire.

Copleston, F. (2003 paperback edn; first published 1946) *A History of Philosophy, Volume 1, Greece and Rome*, Continuum, London and New York.

Copleston, F. (2003 paperback edn; first published 1950) *A History of Philosophy, Volume 2, Mediaeval Philosophy,* Continuum, London and New York.

Copleston, F. (2003 paperback edn; first published 1953) *A History of Philosophy, Volume 3, Late Mediaeval and Renaissance Philosophy,* Continuum, London and New York.

202 Modernising Probation and Criminal Justice

Copleston, F. (2003 paperback edn; first published 1958) *A History of Philosophy, Volume 4, The Rationalists: Descartes to Leibniz. Greece and Rome*, Continuum, London and New York.

Copleston, F. (2003 paperback edn; first published 1959) *A History of Philosophy, Volume 5, British Philosophy: Hobbes to Hume,* Continuum, London and New York.

Copleston, F. (2003 paperback edn; first published 1960) *A History of Philosophy, Volume 6, The Enlightenment: Voltaire to Kant*, Continuum, London and New York.

Copleston, F. (2003 paperback edn; first published 1963) *A History of Philosophy, Volume 7, 18th and 19th century German Philosophy,* Continuum, London and New York.

Copleston, F. (2003 paperback edn; first published 1966) *A History of Philosophy, Volume 8, Utilitarianism to Early Analytic Philosophy,* Continuum, London and New York.

Copleston, F. (2003 paperback edn; first published 1975) *A History of Philosophy, Volume 9, 19th and 20th French Philosophy,* Continuum, London and New York.

Copleston, F. (2003 paperback edn; first published 1986) *A History of Philosophy, Volume 10, Russian Philosophy,* Continuum, London and New York.

Copleston, F. (2003 paperback edn; first published 1956) *A History of Philosophy, Volume 11, Logical Positivism and Existentialism,* Continuum, London and New York.

Cullen, F.T. and Gilbert, K.E. (1982) *Reaffirming Rehabilitation. Criminal Justice Studies,* Anderson Publishing Co., Cincinnati, Ohio.

Cullen, M.J. (1975) *The Statistical Movement in Early Victorian Britain: The Foundations of Empirical Research,* The Harvester Press Ltd., Barnes and Noble Books, New York.

Davies, M. (1985) *The Essential Social Worker: A Guide to Positive Practice* (2nd edn), Gower, Aldershot

Davies, M., Croall, H. and Tyrer, J. (2005) *Criminal Justice: An Introduction to the Criminal Justice System in England and Wales*, Pearson-Longman, Harlow Essex.

Dawkins, R. (2006) *The God Delusion*, Bantam Press, London and Sydney.

Downes, D. (1966) *The Delinquent Solution: A Study in Sub-cultural Theory*, Routledge and Kegan Paul, London.

Downes, D. and Morgan, R. (1997 2nd edn) 'Dumping the 'Hostages to Fortune'? The Politics of Law and Order in Post-War Britain' in: M. Maguire, R. Morgan and R. Reiner (eds.) *The Oxford Handbook of Criminology*, Oxford University Press, Oxford and New York.

Downes, D. and Rock, P. (1988 2nd edn) *Understanding Deviance: A Guide to the Sociology of Crime and Rule Breaking*, Clarendon Press, Oxford.

Easton, S. and Piper, C. (2005) *Sentencing and Punishment: The Quest for Justice*, Oxford University Press, Oxford and New York.

Eysenck, H.J. (1970) *Crime and Personality*, London, Granada.

Farmer, M.E. (1967) 'The Positivist Movement and the Development of English Sociology', *The Sociological Review*, 15, pp5–20.

Feeley, M. and Simon, J. (1994) 'Actuarial Justice: The Emerging New Criminal Law' in: D. Nelken (ed.) *The Future of Criminology*, Sage, London

Field, G.C. (1969 2nd edn) *The Philosophy of Plato*, Oxford University Press, Oxford, London and New York.

Foucault, M. (1977) *Discipline and Punish: The Birth of the Prison*, Penguin Books, England and New York.

Freeman, C. (1999) *The Greek Achievement: The Foundation of the Western World*, Allen Lane, The Penguin Press, London and New York.

Garland, D. (1985) *Punishment and Welfare: A History of Penal Strategies,* Gower, Aldershot and USA.

Garland, D. (1990) *Punishment and Modern Society: A Study in Social Theory*, Oxford University Press, Oxford and New York.

Garland, D. (1997) 'Of Crimes and Criminals' in: M. Maguire, R. Morgan and R. Reiner (eds. 2nd edn) *The Oxford Handbook of Criminology*, Oxford University Press, Oxford and New York.

Garland, D. (2001) *The Culture of Control: Crime and Social Order in Contemporary Society,* Oxford University Press, Oxford and New York.

Garland, D. (2004) 'Beyond the Culture of Control', *Critical Review of International Social and Political Philosophy,* Volume 17, 2, Summer 2004, pp160–189.

Garland, D. and Sparks, R. (2000) 'Criminology, Social Theory, and the Challenge of Our Times' in: D. Garland and R. Sparks (eds.) *Criminology and Social Theory,* Oxford University Press, Oxford and New York.

Gerth, H.H. and Mills, C.W. (1948 edn) *From Max Weber*, Routledge and Kegan Paul, London.

Giddens, A. (1971) *Capitalism and Modern Social Theory: An Analysis of the Writings of Marx, Durkheim and Max Weber*, Cambridge University Press.

Giddens, A. (1974) *Positivism and Sociology*, Heinemann, London.

Giddens, A. (1989) *Sociology*, Polity Press, Cambridge.

Giddens, A. (1991) *Modernity and Self Identity: Self and Society in the Late Modern Age*, Stanford University Press.

Glover, E.R. (1956 revised 2nd edn) *Probation and Re-Education*, Routledge and Kegan Paul Ltd., London.

Glueck, S. and Glueck, E. (1950) *Unravelling Juvenile Delinquency*, Oxford University Press, Oxford and New York.

Goring, C. (1913) *The English Convict*, HMSO, London.

Graves, R. (1985) *Greek Myths* (illustrated edition), BCA London, New York, Sydney and Toronto.

Grayling, A.C. (2005) *Descartes: The Life of Rene Descartes and Its Place in his Times,* Free Press, London.

Grimsey, E.J. (1987) *Efficiency Scrutiny of HM Probation Inspectorate*, Home Office.

Guy, J. (1996) *The Victorian Social-Problem Novel: The Market, the Individual and Communal Life*, Macmillan, Basingstoke, Hampshire and London.

Halcrow, M. (1989) *Keith Joseph: A Single Mind*, MacMillan, London.

Hall, S., Critcher, C., Jefferson, T., Clarke, J. and Roberts, B. (1978) *Policing the Crisis: Mugging, the State and Law and Order,* Macmillan, London.

Healey, D. (1992) *My Secret Planet*, Michael Joseph, London.

Healy, W. and Bronner, A. (1936) *New Light on Delinquency and its Treatment*, New Yale University Press, New Haven, Connecticut.

Hedderman, C. (2003) 'Enforcing Supervision and Encouraging Compliance' in: W.H. Chui and M. Nellis (eds.) *Moving Probation Forward: Evidence, Arguments and Practice,* Pearson-Longman, Harlow, Essex.

Heidensohn, F. (1985) *Women and Crime*, Macmillan, Basingstoke, Hampshire and London.

Heidensohn, F. (2002) 'Gender and Crime' in: M. Maguire, R. Morgan and R. Reiner (eds 3rd edn) *The Oxford Handbook of Criminology*, Oxford University Press, Oxford and New York.

Henry, S. and Einstadter, W. (1998) *The Criminology Theory Reader*, New York University Press, New York and London.

Hick, J. (1993) *The Metaphor of God Incarnate*, SCM Press Ltd., London.

Hirschi, T. (1969) *Causes of Delinquency*, University of California Press, Berkeley, Los Angeles, and London.

Hollis, F. (1964 second edn) *Casework: A Psychosocial Therapy*, Random House, New York.

Home Office (1909) *Report of the Departmental Committee on the Probation of Offenders Act 1907*, Cmnd. 5001, HMSO.

Home Office (1922) *Report of the Departmental Committee on the Training, Appointment and Payment of Probation Officers*, Cmnd. 1601, HMSO.

Home Office (1936) *Report of the Departmental Committee on the Social Services in Courts of Summary Jurisdiction*, Cmnd. 5122, HMSO.

Home Office (1938) *The Probation Service – Its Objects and its Organisation*, HMIP.

Home Office (1962) *Report of the Departmental Committee on the Probation Service (Morison Committee)*, Cmnd. 1650, HMSO.

Home Office (1984) *Probation Service in England and Wales. Statement of National Objectives and Priorities*.

Home Office (2006) *Rebalancing the Criminal Justice System in Favour of the Law Abiding Majority: Cutting Crime, Reducing Re-offending and Protecting the Public*.

Home Office and Lord Chancellor's Office (1961) *Report of the Inter-departmental Committee on the Business of the Criminal Courts (Streatfield Report)*, Cmnd. 1289, HMSO, London.

Home Office Research Study 144 (1995) *Measuring the Satisfaction of Courts with the Probation Service*.

Hood, C. (1991) 'A Public Management For All Seasons', *Public Administration*, 69, Spring 1991, 3–19.

Hooton, E.A. (1939) *Crime and the Man*, Harvard University Press, Cambridge, MA.

Hopkins Burke, R. (2005 2nd edn) *An Introduction To Criminological Theory*, Willan Publishing, Devon.

Horn, D.G. (2003) *The Criminal Body: Lombroso and the Anatomy of Deviance*, Routledge, New York and London.

Hough, M., Allen, R. and Padel, U. (2006) *Reshaping Probation and Prisons: The New Offender Management Framework*, The Policy Press, Bristol.

House of Commons Official Report (2007) *Parliamentary Debates* (Hansard), Wednesday 28 February 2007, Volume 457, Number 51.

Hudson, B. (2003a) *Justice and the Risk Society: Challenging and Re-affirming Justice in Late Modernity*, Sage, London, Thousand Oaks, New Delhi.

Hudson, B. (2003b) *Understanding Justice: An Introduction to Ideas, Perspectives and Controversies in Modern Penal Theory,* Open University Press, Buckinghamshire and Philadelphia.

Hugman, B. (1977) *Act Natural*, Bedford Square Press, London.

Jarvis, F.V. (1974) *Probation Officers' Manual*, Butterworths, London.

Jenkins, S. (1995) *Accountable To None: The Tory Nationalisation of Britain,* Hamish Hamilton, London.

Jenkins, S. (2006a) 'Set a Silly Target and You'll Get a Really Crazy Public Service', *Sunday Times*, 24th September 2006.

Jenkins, S. (2006b) *Thatcher and Sons: a Revolution in Three Acts*, Penguin, London and New York.

Kelly, J.N.D. (1958 4th edn) *Early Christian Doctrines*, Adams and Charles Black, London.

Kemshall, H. (2003) *Understanding Risk in Criminal Justice*, Open University Press, Buckinghamshire and Philadelphia.

Kennedy, H. (2005) *Just Law: The Changing Face of Justice – and Why it Matters to Us All,* Vintage, London.

Kuehn, M. (2001) *Kant: A Biography*, Cambridge University Press, Cambridge and New York.

Kumar, K. (1995) *From Post-Industrial to Post-Modern Society: New Theories of the Contemporary World*, Basil Blackwell, Oxford.

Kung, H. (1976) *On Being a Christian*, William Collins, Sons & Co. Ltd., Glasgow.

Kung, H. (1992) *Mozart: Traces of Transcendence*, SCM Press Ltd., London.

Le Mesurier, L. (1935) *A Handbook of Probation and Social Work of the Courts*, NAPO, London.

Lea, J. and Young, J. (1984) *What Is To Be Done About Law and Order? Crisis in the Eighties,* Penguin Books Ltd., London.

Lilly, J.R., Cullen, F.T. and Ball, R.A. (2002 3rd edn) *Criminological Theory: Context and Consequences*, Sage Publications, Thousand Oaks, London and New Delhi.

Lishman, J. (1994) *Communication in Social Work*, Macmillan, Basingstoke.

Lloyd, C. (1986) *Response to SNOP*, University of Cambridge, Institute of Criminology.

Lowson, D. (1975) 'The Ethos of Probation' in: J.B. Mays (ed.) *The Social Treatment of Young Offenders: A Reader,* Longman, London and New York.

MacRae, D.G. (1974) *Weber*, Fontana Press, London.

Magee, B. (1978) *Men of Ideas*, The Viking Press, New York.

Magee, B. (1998) *The Story of Philosophy*, Dorling Kindersley Ltd., London.

Mair, G., Burke, L. and Taylor, S. (2006) 'The Worst Tax Form You've Ever Seen? Probation Officers' Views about OASys', *Probation Journal*, 53, 1, 7–24.

Mannheim, H. (1972 ed.) *Pioneers in Criminology* (2nd edn enlarged), Patterson Smith, Montclair, New Jersey.

Matza, D. (1964) *Delinquency and Drift*, John Wiley and Sons Inc., New York, London and Sydney.

Matza, D. (1969) *Becoming Deviant*, Prentice Hall, Englewood Cliffs, NJ.

McLaughlin, E., Muncie, J. and Hughes, G. (2001) 'The Permanent Revolution: New Labour, New Public Management and the Modernisation of Criminal Justice', *Criminal Justice*, Sage Publications, 1(3), 301–318.

McNay, L. (1994) *Foucault: A Critical Introduction*, Polity Press, Cambridge and Malden USA.

McNeill, F. (2003) 'Desistance-focused Probation Practice' in: W.H. Chui and M. Nellis (eds.) *Moving Probation Forward: Evidence, Arguments and Practice*, Pearson-Longman, Harlow, Essex.

McWilliams, W. (1983) 'The Mission to the English Police Courts 1876 – 1936', *Howard Journal of Criminal Justice*, 22, 129–47.

McWilliams, W. (1985) 'The Mission Transformed: Professionalisation of Probation Between the Wars', *Howard Journal of Criminal Justice*, 24, 257–74.

McWilliams, W. (1986) 'The English Probation System and the Diagnostic Ideal', *Howard Journal of Criminal Justice*, 25, 241–60.

McWilliams, W. (1987) 'Probation, Pragmatism and Policy', *Howard Journal of Criminal Justice,* 26, 97–121.

Millard, D. (1979) 'Broader Approaches to Probation Practice' in: J.F.S. King (ed.) *Pressures and Change in the Probation Service* (Cropwood Conference Series No. 11), Institute of Criminology, University of Cambridge.

Monger, M. (1964) *Casework in Probation*, Butterworths, London.

Morgan, R. (2002 3rd edn) 'Imprisonment: A Brief History, the Contemporary Scene, and Likely Prospects', in: M. Maguire, R. Morgan and R. Reiner (eds.) *The Oxford Handbook of Criminology,* Oxford University Press, Oxford and New York.

Morrison, W. (1995) *Theoretical Criminology: From Modernity to Post-modernism*, Cavendish Publishing Limited, London.

Mounier, E. (1952) *Personalism*, Routledge and Kegan Paul Ltd., London.

Mythen, G. (2004) *Ulrich Beck: A Critical Introduction to the Risk Society*, Pluto Press, London, Sterling and Virginia.

Nellis, M. and Gelsthorpe, L. (2003) 'Human Rights and the Probation Values Debate' in: W.H. Chui and M. Nellis (eds.) *Moving Probation Forward: Evidence, Arguments and Practice,* Pearson-Longman, Harlow, Essex.

Noaks, L. and Wincup, E. (2004) *Criminological Research: Understanding Qualitative Methods*, Sage Publications, London, Thousand Oaks, New Delhi.

O'Neill, O. (2002) *A Question of Trust*, Cambridge University Press, Cambridge and New York.

Oldfield, M. (2002) *From Welfare to Risk: Discourse, Power and Politics in the Probation Service*, Issues in Community and Criminal Justice, Monograph 1, NAPO.

Otto, R. (1958) *The Idea of the Holy*, Oxford University Press, London, Oxford and New York.

Pamuk, O. (2005) *Istanbul: Memories of a City*, translated by Maureen Freely, Faber and Faber, London.

Parker, H. (1975 paperback edn) *View From The Boys*, David and Charles Ltd., Newton Abbot, Devon.

Pascal, B. (1966) *Pensees*, Penguin Books, London and New York.

Pond, R. (1999) *Introduction to Criminology*, Waterside Press, Winchester.

Porter, R. (2001) *Enlightenment: Britain and the Creation of the Modern World*, Penguin Books, London and New York.

Power, M. (1997) *The Audit Society: Rituals of Verification*, Oxford University Press, Oxford and New York.

Radzinowicz, L. (1966) *Ideology and Crime: A Study of Crime in its Social and Historical Context*, Heinemann, London.

Radzinowicz, L. (1999) *Adventures in Criminology*, Routledge, London and New York.

Raine, J.W., and Willson, M.J. (1997) 'Beyond Managerialism in Criminal Justice', *The Howard Journal*, Volume 36, 1, Blackwell Publishers, London.

Raynor, P. (1985) *Social Work, Justice and Control*, Basil Blackwell, Oxford.

Raynor, P. (2002 3rd edn) 'Community Penalties: Probation, Punishment, and 'What Works'' in: M. Maguire, R. Morgan and R. Reiner (eds.) *The Oxford Handbook of Criminology,* Oxford University Press, Oxford and New York.

Reid, J. (2006) 'Check Against Delivery', Speech by the Home Secretary on Offender Management, *HMP Wormwood Scrubs*, 7th November 2006.

Ritzer, G. and Goodman, D.J. (1997 4th edn) *Classical Sociological Theory*, McGraw Hill, London, Boston and New York.

Rose, N. (1999) *Powers of Freedom: Reframing Political Thought*, Cambridge University Press, Cambridge and New York.

Roshier, B. (1989) *Controlling Crime,* Open University, Milton Keynes.

Russell, B. (1967) *The Problems of Philosophy*, Oxford University Press, Oxford, London and New York.

Russell, B. (1996 edn) *History of Western Philosophy*, Routledge, London and New York.

Rutter, M. and Giller, H. (1983) *Juvenile Delinquency: Trends and Perspectives*, Penguin Books, London and New York.

Ryan, M. (2003) *Penal Policy and Political Culture in England and Wales. Four Essays on Policy and Process,* Waterside Press, Winchester.

Sabine, G. (1951 3rd edn) *A History of Political Theory*, George G. Harrap & Co. Ltd, London, Toronto, Wellington and Sydney.

Safranski, R. (2003) *Nietzsche: A Philosophical Biography*, Granta Books, London.

Sartre, J.P. (1973) *Existentialism and Humanism*, translation and introduction by Philip Mairet, Eyre Methuen Ltd., London.

Schon, D. (1987) *Educating the Reflective Practitioner,* Jossey-Bass, San Francisco.

Scruton, R. (2001) *Kant: A Very Short Introduction*, Oxford University Press, Oxford and New York.

Seldon, A. (2004) *Blair*, Free Press, London.

Shapland, J. (1981) *Between Conviction and Sentence: The Process of Mitigation*, Routledge and Kegan Paul, London.

Sheldon, W.H. (1949) *Varieties of Delinquent Youths: An Introduction to Constitutional Psychiatry*, Harper, New York.

Sinclair, I. (1971) *Hostels for Probationers: A Study of the Aims, Working and Variations in Effectiveness of Male Probation Hostels with Special Reference to the Influence of Environment on Delinquency*, Home Office Research Study No. 6, HMSO, London.

Smith, David (2004) 'The Uses and Abuses of Positivism' in: G. Mair (ed.) *What Matters in Probation,* Willan Publishing, Devon.

Smith, David (2006) 'Making Sense of Psychoanalysis in Criminological Theory and Probation Practice', *Probation Journal*, 53, 4, 361-376.

Smith, Dennis (1988) *The Chicago School: A Liberal Critique of Capitalism*, Macmillan, Basingstoke, Hampshire.

Sobel, D. (2000) *Galileo's Daughter: A Drama of Science, Faith and Love,* Fourth Estate, London.

Sorell, T. (2000) *Descartes: A Very Short Introduction*, Oxford University Press, Oxford and New York.

Stanley, S.J. and Murphy, B. (1984) *Inner London Probation Service: Survey of Social Enquiry Reports,* Inner London Probation Service.

Statham, R.S. and Whitehead, P. (eds. 1992) *Managing the Probation Service: Issues for the 1990s,* Longman, Harlow, Essex.

Stelman, A. (1980) 'Social Work Relationships: An Exploration', *Probation Journal*, 27, 85–94.

Stewart, J. and Walsh, K. (1992) 'Change in the Management of Public Services', *Public Administration*, 70, Winter 1992, 499–518.

Stewart, J., Smith, D., Stewart, G. with Fullwood, C. (1994) *Understanding Offending Behaviour*, Longman, Harlow, Essex.

Stone, L. (1987) *The Past and the Present Revisited*, Routledge, London.

Storr, A. (1992) *Music and the Mind*, Harper Collins, London.

Tarnas, R. (1991) *The Passion of The Western Mind: Understanding the Ideas that have Shaped our World View*, Pimlico, London.

Taylor, I., Walton, P. and Young, J. (1973) *The New Criminology: for a Social Theory of Deviance,* Routledge and Kegan Paul, London, Boston and Henley.

Taylor, R., Wasik, M. and Leng, R. (2004) *Blackstone's Guide To The Criminal Justice Act 2003,* Oxford University Press, Oxford and New York.

Thatcher, M. (1995) *The Path to Power*, HarperCollins, London.

Tonry, M. (2004) *Punishment and Politics: Evidence and Emulation in the Making of English Crime Control Policy*, Willan Publishing, Devon.

Traux, C.B., and Carkhuff, R.R. (1967) *Towards Effective Counselling and Psychotherapy*, Aldine, Chicago.

Uglow, J. (1987) *George Eliot,* Virago/Pantheon Pioneers, New York and London.

Urmson, J.O. and Ree, J. (1991 paperback edn) *The Concise Encyclopaedia of Western Philosophy and Philosophers,* Routledge, London and New York.

Urwick, E.J. (1910) 'Juvenile Delinquents', *The Sociological Review*, Volume 3, Number 1.

Valier, C. (2002) *Theories of Crime and Punishment*, Longman, Harlow and New York.

Walker, M. and Beaumont, B. (1981) *Probation Work: Critical Theory and Socialist Practice,* Blackwell, Oxford.

Walklate, S. (2003 2nd edn) *Understanding Criminology: Current Theoretical Debates,* Open University Press, Buckingham and Philadelphia.

West, D.J. (1982) *Delinquency: Its Roots, Careers and Prospects*, Heinemann, London.

Weston, W.R. (1987 4th edn) *Jarvis's Probation Officers' Manual*, Butterworths, London.

Weston, W.R. (2006) *Critique of P. Whitehead and R. Statham (2006) The History of Probation: Politics, Power and Cultural Change 1876-2005*, unpublished.

White, R. and Haines, F. (2004 3rd edn) *Crime and Criminology: An Introduction*, Oxford University Press.

Whitehead, P. (1990) *Community Supervision for Offenders: A New Model of Probation*, Avebury, Aldershot, Brookfield USA.

Whitehead, P. (1992) 'Management Information Systems in Probation' in: R.S Statham and P. Whitehead (eds. 1992) *Managing the Probation Service: Issues for the 1990s,* Longman, Harlow, Essex.

Whitehead, P. and Statham, R. (2006) *The History of Probation: Politics, Power and Cultural Change 1876-2005,* Shaw & Sons, Crayford, Kent.

Whitehead, P. and Thompson, J. (2004) *Knowledge and the Probation Service: Raising Standards for Trainees, Assessors and Practitioners*, John Wiley and Sons Ltd., Chichester.

Whitehead, P., Saiger, L., Holden, J. and Brittain, T. (2003) *A Quality Standard For Domestic Violence,* National Probation Service, Teesside.

Wilson, A.N. (1991 edn) *C.S. Lewis: A Biography*, Flamingo, Harper Collins Publishers, London.

Wilson, E.O. (1975) *Sociobiology*, Knopf, New York.

Wilson, J.Q. and Herrnstein, R.J. (1985) *Crime and Human Nature*, Simon and Schuster, New York.

Young, A.F. and Ashton, E.T. (1956) *British Social Work in the Nineteenth Century*, Routledge and Kegan Paul, London.

Young, J. (1997) 'Left Realist Criminology: Radical in it Analysis, Realist in its Policy' in: M. Maguire, R. Morgan and R. Reiner (eds. 2nd edn) *The Oxford Handbook of Criminology*, Oxford University Press, Oxford and New York.

Young, J. (1999) *The Exclusive Society: Social Exclusion, Crime and Difference in Late Modernity*, Sage Publications, London, Thousand Oaks, New Delhi.

INDEX